THE ULTIMATE LIFE COACHING HANDBOOK

# THE ULTIMATE LIFE COACHING HANDBOOK

A COMPREHENSIVE GUIDE TO THE METHODOLOGY, PRINCIPLES, AND PRACTICE OF LIFE COACHING

KAIN RAMSAY

**Achology Publications**

COPYRIGHT © 2023 KAIN RAMSAY
*All rights reserved.*

THE ULTIMATE LIFE COACHING HANDBOOK
*A Comprehensive Guide to the Methodology, Principles, and Practice of Life Coaching*

FIRST EDITION

ISBN    978-1-5445-4481-6   *Hardcover*
           978-1-5445-4480-9   *Paperback*
           978-1-5445-4479-3   *Ebook*

# FOREWORD FROM THE AUTHOR

Contrary to popular belief, a Life Coach is not a people-fixer, just a facilitator of change and personal growth. With that said, I have witnessed extraordinary transformations happen in people's thinking, productivity, and efficiency upon grasping just a handful of wise personal growth principles. It is the role of a Life Coach to provide people with the accountability and support they need to achieve goals and make positive lifestyle changes. It is up to each person to choose the path they will take and commit to the process of making these changes happen.

In over a decade of teaching Life Coaching, among other applied psychology disciplines, I have guided over 650,000 people in their journey of personal growth and ongoing professional development by demonstrating how sensible ideas and life principles can be practically applied within the context of people's everyday lives, careers, relationships, and decision-making. I know without a doubt that the principles shared throughout this handbook will help you to improve aspects of your own life as you grow in the necessary insights that will subsequently equip you to also help other people transform theirs.

Life is a one-time opportunity. While you cannot control the circumstances of your life, you can learn how to respond to life's circumstances wisely. The choices we make are ultimately our responsibility, and so are the consequences that we walk in. There are no magic pills, deep breathing exercises, special diets, or energy healing gurus that come with solutions for life's problems. Problems remain problems until they have owners, and it's taking responsibility for solving problems that allows people to live empowered lives. Throughout this handbook, I will share many of the valuable lessons and principles that have equipped me to facilitate growth in my own life, and also the experiential insights I have gained after many years of coaching people in their lives, businesses, careers, finances, and relationships. The key to progressing in life is deciding who you will become and taking responsibility for becoming that person. The more responsibility you take for managing yourself and directing your future, the more productive and sustainable your life will become.

Most people read in order to build on what they already know. While some people only read to reinforce their current opinions, others approach texts of this nature with an open mind to think about how it fits in with their current outlook, whether to accept it and if they will use it or not. Reading for information is different from reading for insight. When you read for insight, you create space in your mind to consider how the ideas you read are relevant to your life. Those who read for insight put their biases aside and prepare to be impacted by what they read. The ideas in this handbook may take time to master, but if you seek to understand them and apply them to your life, you will increase your Life Coaching skills and soon become ready to provide a far richer Life Coaching experience for your coachees. Use this handbook as a point of future reference, and revisit it often. Every time that you do, you will uncover new insights and nuggets of understanding that will prepare you to connect meaningfully with other people. In time, you will become a conduit for positive change in your own life and also the lives of others.

In summary, this handbook takes a deep dive into human behavior, self-awareness, people skills, Life Coaching, and goal setting. It provides a systematic framework that is accompanied by questions and exercises to help improve your comprehension. Whether you wish to make positive improvements in your own life or help other people make improvements in theirs, this handbook will equip you with the knowledge, insights, and building blocks that you need for Life

Coaching yourself and for pioneering a respectable, results-orientated Life Coaching practice.

# PREFACE

Life Coaching has historically been a mysterious industry with many myths surrounding it. Some people assume that Life Coaches are just unqualified therapists or counselors, leeching off the vulnerable and spreading hyped-up pseudo-science. Others think Life Coaches are personified happy pills who exist to boost people's egos and confidence when they're feeling unfulfilled or sad—kind of like having an on-demand agony aunt or uncle. And many think Life Coaching is some new-age mumbo-jumbo or the shilling of common sense to unsuspecting recipients.

But Life Coaching is none of those things, and there is much more to it than what many practicing Life Coaches even give it credit for. As with all industries, there are experts, there are salespeople (who call themselves experts), and there are non-experts who mask their lack of knowledge or incompetence behind a facade of certified "professionalism." The purpose of this Life Coaching handbook is to serve you with the practical knowledge and understanding that you need to become the caliber of Life Coach that people will actually take seriously.

Life Coaching is more than just a series of techniques or communication skills. It's a methodical process through which people can be empowered to define, quantify, and exceed meaningful long-term goals that they set for themselves, personally or professionally. Life Coaching is the process of equipping people to evaluate themselves objectively and beyond self-sabotaging thinking or behavioral habits that undermine their ability to achieve goals. It involves getting under people's skin to learn the value they have to offer and identify what's holding them back.

Life Coach isn't a term that standardizes all those who call themselves a Life Coach. Some people call themselves a Life Coach after reading one book on the subject, while others study psychology, philosophy, and personal growth concepts—they develop their understanding of human behavior for years before attempting to coach others. I came across a man who called himself a "Life Coach," but all he really wanted to do was advance his network marketing business. The term "Life Coach" is often abused by people with ill intentions. Unfortunately, not everyone out there who calls themselves a Life Coach can actually help other people to improve their lives.

Throughout this handbook, there is a themed emphasis on you. You are the central focus of this handbook for a reason: your self-awareness, integrity, character, honesty, consistency, and social intelligence will play a central role in your effectiveness as a Life Coach. Life Coaching isn't something that you do; it's something that flows out of who you are. An aptitude to help people set sensible future goals and make wise decisions is at the heart of every healthy Life Coaching relationship. And integrity is crucial to this. You cannot congruently coach people through the process of generating positive life, career, or relationship outcomes that you haven't first generated for yourself.

This book contains over a decade's worth of insight that I've drawn from coaching thousands of people, individually and in groups. I do not claim to be the best Life Coach in the world, nor am I the wisest man. This handbook was created to provide you with a different approach to Life Coaching than what is available in most texts of this nature. I wrote this book with the intention of making it as accessible and relatable as possible. Whether you are reading it for your own benefit or to coach others, I address each chapter to "you," the Life Coach, and to the people you might someday coach as "coachees." Other times I will include us both as "we."

The ideas contained in this handbook are simple, applicable to any coach in any field, and to everyone who wants to improve their life. You might aspire to become a Life Coach or just use the teachings herein in your current vocation (e.g., as a parent, social influencer, entrepreneur, teacher, manager, or sports coach). The intention of this book is twofold: (1) to translate age-old life principles and psychological wisdom into an understandable framework of bite-sized ideas that you, the reader, can relate to and confidently share with others. (2) Present Life Coaching as a logical methodology that anyone can use to help people set goals and become a valuable skilled helper within their family, community, business, or social group.

When you grasp something, you have it in your hands and know what it feels like. You can read about COVID-19 or the common cold, but you cannot truly comprehend them until you catch them. This Life Coaching handbook will help you to comprehend the central principles of Life Coaching and the attitudes you must embody before you can earn your coachee's trust, and ability to influence their decision-making. Your coachee's willingness to be open and honest with you depends solely on your readiness to demonstrate integrity, wisdom, empathy, and realness through your personality, your communication, and also your non-verbal presence.

The life areas people struggle with most are those in which they haven't been educated. Sadly, school rarely teaches people how to design a fulfilling life, become self-aware, build healthy relationships, identify their strengths, contribute to society, or live with intentional purpose. Take the story of a stranger who arrived at a village on a horse. He made a scene and created a poor first impression on the villagers by galloping through the market square chaotically, weaving around people and through stalls at high speed. Villagers quickly dispersed from the scene to avoid being trampled by the horse. The stranger's utter disregard for others' safety enraged a village elder, who stormed into the market square and yelled at the stranger, "Where are you going in such a hurry?" The horse continued, undeterred, whilst the stranger, desperately clinging to the horse's reins, nervously exclaimed, "I have no idea! Perhaps you should ask the horse."

Much like the horse, many people navigate their way through life rushing aimlessly, busy and unaware of where they're going and what their end destination is. The faulty logic behind the majority of people's "busyness" is that if they continue to work quickly and diligently, they will reach a "good" end destination. Some people never set their focus on a clear end direction or purpose and believe that their path is set by external factors beyond their control. Other people waste the best years of their life viewing the purpose of life as nothing more than enjoying the ride itself—which is why many people end up feeling so disenfranchised and dissatisfied. People live life in different ways because life comes with no rulebook or prescribed way of "doing life" in a purposeful, satisfying, or rewarding way. This leaves most people to guesswork.

Most people want to improve their lives, but not all people are ready to. Some people resist driving change in their lives by making excuses such as "I don't know how to change" or "I tried to change, but it didn't work." "Trying" is nothing more than wanting credit for something that you never intended to do (as highlighted by Master Yoda in Star Wars: "Do, or do not. There is no try"). In truth, many people only commit to making positive lifestyle improvements once they've hit "rock bottom" hard enough—and once their desire to change is greater than their desire to remain exactly the same as they currently are. Most often, people turn to a Life Coach after they've decided to take control of their lives and improve it in some positive way.

- People need to decide upon a direction for their life.
- People need to choose a meaningful vocation or career.
- People need to set meaningful objectives for their future.
- People need to know who they are and who they can become.

Life Coaching is about encouraging people to live their best lives. With the help of a good coach, people can turn their needs into a compelling vision with clearly defined goals and action steps to be taken. A Life Coach is not responsible for answering people's questions or suggesting how life might be lived meaningfully. Rather, the purpose of Life Coaching should always be to help people ask the right questions, find their own answers and make wise decisions that align with their goals or priorities. The best possible outcome of a healthy Life Coaching relationship is a "coachee" who is wiser, more mature, responsible, stronger, more decisive, and consistent than they were before coaching first commenced. You will help people to mature in their decision-making to the same degree that you are mature in yours.

There are two basic choices: to accept life's circumstances as they are or take responsibility for changing them. Life Coaching must always center around achieving goals and never be about boosting people's self-esteem or helping them to find happiness. Rather, it involves holding people accountable for creating their desired life outcomes for themselves. People become empowered by taking responsibility for the role that their attitude and actions have played in creating their current outcomes. Thus, effective Life Coaching is reflective, in that it holds up a mirror and exposes the role people often play in sabotaging themselves.

I have included many examples of good practice, and have drawn on real examples from my own experience of coaching people in different contexts, including education, group work, and general 1-1 practice. Any details which could possibly identify individual coachees have been omitted. My method of writing is creative in the sense that it involves selecting common Life Coaching issues and placing them in a slightly altered context or background. In addition, my coachees' names are changed to always ensure confidentiality.

Throughout this handbook, you will learn how to help people decide on a clear and meaningful long-term agenda and hold people to account for their action-taking with a hand of assistance and an empathic set of ears. You'll deepen your self-awareness, understand what motivates all human behavior, and how to help people set goals that allow them to bring balance and inner peace into their lives. You'll be offered a strategy for helping people to stay on track with their goals without needlessly allowing self-doubt to become an obstacle. Without getting hands-on experience, knowledge is useless. For this reason, each chapter of the handbook concludes with a "Principles into Practice" exercise to help you apply your learning. The questions create an opportunity for you to reflect on the ideas and lessons presented in the book, as well as how they may be effectively integrated into your own life and those of your future coachees.

A competent Life Coach will ask questions that encourage people to think about their beliefs, worldviews, and find solutions to problems that they may not have yet identified. Coaching is the process of unlocking a person's readiness to take responsibility for creating their ideal future outcomes, scaling up their performance, and facilitating their own learning. Most people don't need to be taught, managed, or counseled—they just need to be unleashed. As this is where you can fill a gap in people's lives, including business people, entrepreneurs, parents, students, those in a career change, or looking for a more purpose-driven way of living life. But all of this requires a standard of competency and integrity from those who practice.

Which is why I wrote this book: to ensure that more people can receive the highest quality of Life Coaching. Because today, the quality of countless people's lives depends on it.

# CONTENTS

**SECTION ONE: FOUNDATIONAL LIFE COACHING PRINCIPLES**

How you view human potential will directly influence the value that people receive from you within a Life Coaching relationship. This opening section of the handbook introduces some foundational relationship-building principles, an overview of the Life Coaching process, and some of the personal qualities that you will need to function effectively as a Life Coach.

- The Purpose of Life Coaching—Page 23
- A Vision for Your Life Coaching Practice—Page 27
- The Prerequisites of Impactful Coaching—Page 31
- Winning People's Hearts and Minds—Page 37
- Overview of the Life Coaching Process—Page 49
- The Bedrock of Effective Life Coaching—Page 55
- A Standard for Effective Life Coaching—Page 59
- Principles for Positively Influencing People—Page 65
- Seek First Understanding before All Things—Page 69
- Section One Summary—Page 73

**SECTION TWO: THE FUNDAMENTALS OF SELF AWARENESS**

Self-awareness means being aware of your mind, character, and values. This section of the handbook will explore the thoughts, emotions, and habits that undermine people's capacity to grow, pursuing meaningful goals and generating the outcomes they want. By helping a person become self-aware, you will tap into their potential to change and shape their future.

- What is the Meaning of Life?—Page 77
- Human Meaning Making Machines—Page 81
- The Power of Being Relatable—Page 85
- Coaching for Cultivating Awareness—Page 89
- EQ: A Key Predictor of Success in Life—Page 95
- Seven Levels of Human Consciousness—Page 101
- The Human Being Identity Crisis—Page 107
- Psychoanalytical Identity Coaching—Page 113
- Looking for the Answers Within—Page 117
- Section Two Summary—Page 121

**SECTION THREE: UNPACKING THE HUMAN EXPERIENCE**

As people grow aware of themselves and how they interpret the world, they become more socially conscious. To sustain healthy relationships, people must know how their perception molds how they interact with themselves, others, and the world. This section presents decision-making as a central function within every effective Life Coaching relationship.

- Acknowledging the Human Experience—Page 125
- Making Sense of the Human Experience—Page 129
- How People See and Interpret Life—Page 135
- Personal Beliefs and World Views—Page 141
- Paradigm Shifts and the Kuhn Cycle—Page 149
- Locus of Internal and External Control—Page 153
- Navigating through Changes and Transitions—Page 159
- Life Coaching Breakthrough Sessions—Page 165
- Theory Determines What You Can See—Page 171
- Quantifying the Life Coaching Alliance—Page 175
- The Foundations of Facilitating Change—Page 179

- The Principle of Counting Opportunity Costs—Page 183
- Factors That Influence Decision-Making—Page 189
- Section Three Summary—Page 197

## SECTION FOUR: THE MOTIVATIONS FOR HUMAN BEHAVIOR

All human beings are naturally motivated by what they value the most in life. By understanding those core values, people will become equipped to find a greater sense of direction and purpose for their lives. They will be driven by their passions rather than their fears and insecurities, and they will be free to express their true selves fully. In this section, you will learn about the values and priorities that motivate all human behavior.

- Values: The Driving Force of Behavior—Page 201
- The Freedom vs. Security Conundrum—Page 207
- A Stoic Remedy for Times of Difficulty—Page 213
- A Theory about How Life Works—Page 219
- Human Values: The Law of Consistency—Page 229
- The Connectedness of Human Values—Page 233
- Responsibility First, Freedom Second—Page 245
- Section Four Summary—Page 251

## SECTION FIVE: COMMUNICATION SKILLS AND PRINCIPLES

Communication is about connecting well with people. Developing communication skills and practicing the communication principles throughout this section will equip you to listen to and understand the people who you work with as a Life Coach. You will also learn a powerful, outcome-oriented coaching framework that you can put into practice right away.

- On Becoming an Articulate Communicator—Page 255
- The Heart of Wholesome Communication—Page 259
- Curiosity: The Enabler of Healthy Discussion—Page 263
- The Person-Centered Coaching Approach—Page 267

- The Seven Stage Communication Cycle—Page 273
- Core Coaching Communication Skills—Page 279
- The Roadblocks to Healthy Communicating—Page 297
- Three Levels of Relating to People—Page 307
- The Four Phases of the Life Coaching Relationship—Page 313
- Section Five Summary—Page 321

**SECTION SIX: COACHING SKILLS AND GOAL SETTING**

Goal setting is central to the Life Coaching process, but, by now you will have learned that it's not a lack of goal clarity that foils people's best-laid plans—a person's mindset will ultimately determine how productive or ineffective they are. In this section, you will learn about the different categories of goals, and how they all inform the Life Coaching relationship.

- Quantifying Present and Desired States—Page 325
- An Existential Approach to Life Coaching—Page 329
- Uncovering Deficits, Passions and Purpose—Page 335
- Purpose First, Vision Second, Goals Third—Page 341
- Five Questions for Visionary Goal Setting—Page 345
- Categories and Approaches to Goal Setting—Page 349
- The S.M.A.R.T. Goal Setting Framework—Page 355
- The Eight Areas for Life Coaching Focus—Page 361
- The Four Seasons of Human Progression—Page 369
- Overview of the Goal-Setting Process—Page 377
- How to Create an Effective Action Plan—Page 383
- The Eisenhower Decision-Making Matrix—Page 391
- The "Two List" Time Management Strategy—Page 397
- A Top Ten of Problem-Solving Questions—Page 401
- Preparing to Leave a Coaching Legacy—Page 405
- The Operation Pete: Coaching Initiative—Page 409
- Summary and Conclusion—Page 419

SECTION ONE

# FOUNDATIONAL LIFE COACHING PRINCIPLES

Your belief in human potential determines the value you'll bring to your coaching relationships. Throughout this section of the handbook, you'll learn the foundational principles of building strong relationships, gain insight into the Life Coaching process, and discover the essential personal qualities required to be an effective Life Coach. Let's tap into the unlimited potential of the human spirit with Life Coaching.

# THE PURPOSE OF LIFE COACHING

*"Why do people need Life Coaches? Why not just ask friends or family for advice and support? It's just a shoddy, amateur form of therapy. They're not even qualified professionals—they're just money-grabbing scam artists."*

—VOICE OF POPULAR OPINION

Many people throughout the world still view Life Coaching as a mysterious and potentially pointless profession. Why would people pay someone to help them decide what's important to them and figure things out—isn't that what living life is all about? Whilst you can get support from friends and family, Life Coaches offer an elevated kind of help. Whether they're a sports, leadership, team, life, or career coach, coaches unlock people's potential to maximize their performance by helping them learn rather than teaching or telling them. Whilst your mother may advise you on how to raise a child, or your friend may tell you how to become more financially stable, coaches help people learn to set and achieve goals in a proactive way that is conducive to their ongoing personal growth and development.

Life Coaches don't instruct people on what and how to do things; they seek out ways to understand the coachee they're working with and help them design a congruent path to success that aligns with their needs, circumstances, and strengths. Over the past few decades,

Life Coaching has become a popular methodology that many people use for fast-tracking their learning, personal growth, and ongoing development. However, people who work with a Life Coach aren't guaranteed results. Results come solely from within when people recognize their self-worth and start believing in their ability to facilitate positive changes in their own lives.

Though there are many coaching models, this handbook will emphasize the Life Coach's role as a facilitator of learning instead of an expert at life in general. There is a vast difference between teaching people and assisting people in their process of learning and self-improvement. Essentially, coaching is about helping people to make wise decisions that align with their priorities and ultimately improve their day-to-day performance. This is important to note because there are no experts on life. So let us first define what Life Coaching isn't;

### LIFE COACHES DO NOT GIVE ADVICE.

Most people assume that Life Coaches offer "life advice" in the same way that many other forms of professionals do. For instance, if you hire a lawyer, you'll get legal advice. If you hire a financier, you'll get financial advice. But Life Coaches aren't advisors, nor should they ever be—they are simply facilitators of personal growth.

### LIFE COACHES DO NOT TEACH OR LECTURE.

We cannot learn about life in a classroom or by reading a book, and it is not the job of a Life Coach to teach someone how to live. If asked, Life Coaches may offer insight and make suggestions to a coachee, but the focus of Life Coaching is to help people learn from their own life experiences (and from their mistakes) rather than from yours.

### LIFE COACHES ARE NOT BUSINESS CONSULTANTS.

Business and career coaches are different from Life Coaches. While Life Coaches might indirectly help people improve their professional performance (such as gaining in confidence, setting boundaries or improving their work-life balance), the role of a Life Coach is to help people make the attitude adjustments and behavioral changes necessary for setting and pursuing meaningful goals that inspire them.

**LIFE COACHES ARE NOT THERAPISTS.**

Despite its many benefits, some therapists practice under the premise that people need healing from their pasts. This, within itself, undermines the human capacity to mature and learn from the past. A Life Coach's aim should never be to "fix" mentally ill people or to heal their problems. Instead, Life Coaches are disciplined in the sense that they focus only on the future, unless they are translating people's past experiences into "lessons learned" that can aid progression and productivity in any given goal-setting process.

**NOW, LET US DEFINE WHAT LIFE COACHING IS**

Let's clear up any confusion. Life Coaching is a future-focused process that helps people to quantify their priorities, build confidence, and achieve goals. It's not a quick fix or a band-aid solution, but a holistic approach that empowers people to thrive in all aspects of life.

Life Coaching is not too different from sports coaching. A sports coach will help an individual or group to identify specific objectives and create an actionable plan to achieve them. And the same may be said for Life Coaching. A Life Coach's objective is to help a person (or group) achieve a specific goal. They will analyze how far away the individual is from their target and then create a plan on how to close that gap. This might seem simplistic, but in essence, this is all that Life Coaching needs to be. And as with all areas of expertise, the more insight and knowledge you have about something, the better you'll be at its practical application.

**PRINCIPLES INTO PRACTICE QUESTIONS:**

1. What do you now understand Life Coaching to be, and how does it differ from what you previously understood it to be?

# A VISION FOR YOUR LIFE COACHING PRACTICE

*"You have to embark on your own personal journey to discover why you are alive, what gets you out of bed each day, and what you can uniquely add to the world."*

—STEPHEN COVEY

The reality of not having a meaningful vision for one's life is that without one, people suffer. They may not suffer financially or physically, but they'll suffer mentally and emotionally and will forever feel an ambiguous void burning away in their minds and the pits of their stomachs. They'll feel empty and stuck in a torturous time loop of cyclical unfulfilling relationships and dead-end jobs. When people come to a Life Coach, they're usually hungry for answers that they don't yet have questions for. They're unsure of what to do, what questions to ask, and are desperate for an objective opinion on what they're "missing" or "doing wrong." There's one thing you must never forget: even though other people want Life Coaches to take control of their lives and make decisions for them, that's not what we do. Life Coaches don't take control of people's lives or hand out blueprints for doing life "correctly—they are merely conduits through which positive changes can occur. But only when a coachee is ready to work.

If you give a man a fish, you feed him for a day. If you teach a man to fish, you feed him for a lifetime. Life Coaches aren't professional fishmongers. We aren't here to give short-lived ego boosts that leave people hungry for more. Instead, our role is to assist people as they take responsibility for maturing themselves, setting sensible goals, making tough decisions, and developing greater consistency throughout their different areas of life. Many aspiring Life Coaches fail because they become exceptional at giving people what they want, telling people what they want to hear, subsequently developing a codependent relationship with their coachees (i.e., they create dependencies on the fish they hand out—people keep coming back for more, and never get around to learning how to fish for themselves). Life Coaching isn't about being a professional pacifier that gives people what they can't already source for themselves; it's about teaching people to serve themselves and take responsibility for filling the voids in their lives appropriately. For this is how personal growth happens.

The mark of an effective Life Coach isn't a diary full of long-term coachees who are all dependent on receiving fish; it's the frequency by which their coachees outgrow them. Coachees must begin coaching with a specific end goal in mind, and we must ensure they fulfill this end by holding them accountable for taking the action steps necessary to produce the outcomes they want to see happen. Of course, not all people want to change, and even fewer people want to work hard. The majority of people just want change to happen to them, like an event that they don't need to get actively involved in. Changing requires investment and effort. Many adults, internally, still behave like children who comply with the demands of their emotions and engage in the endless pursuit of self-gratification under the illusion that short-lived appeasement is the path to long-term happiness. Addressing unfulfillment issues with online shopping or satiating jealousy by spreading gossip gets no one closer to where they want to be, although these things may spark some form of satisfaction for a short time. But happiness is an extremely poor substitute for fulfillment in life. Happiness is like ice cream; it melts away quickly when the pressures of life get heated.

As a Life Coach, people will come to you in their worst states. They may have lost a job, gotten a divorce, or gained so much weight that it's impacted their health; they're grieving or going through a midlife crisis. Sadly, most people wait for a traumatic or life-altering event to

[*Short lived appeasement ≠ Long-term fulfillment*]

occur before allowing themselves to seek expert support or guidance. It takes hitting rock bottom for some people to realize that they've been unknowingly sabotaging their long-term goals for months, years, or even decades. Some people spend years climbing a mountain, only to reach the top and realize that they've climbed the wrong one. Yet, despite how many people feel about themselves, nobody in this world needs "fixing." You can't fix anyone because no one is broken, and it's not your responsibility to make anyone feel better about themselves, either. However, it is your coaching responsibility to unearth a person's potential by facilitating their self-exploration and exploring with them how they might begin to take responsibility for quantifying what they want and deciding upon how they'll get it.

The purpose of Life Coaching is to help people find fulfillment in life by determining the skills and character traits they must develop to attain their goals. Once a person knows how to prioritize pursuing fulfillment instead of happiness, they tend to naturally pass those lessons on to the other people they know. The more effective you are at sharing wise life principles with your coachees, the wider your coaching impact will become without you even necessarily trying. Because that's what every integral Life Coach should aim for: coachee's who can share what they've learned from you with other people.

*fulfillment thru skill + traits that ↓ goal*

The proverb "If you give a man a fish, you feed him for today. If you teach a man to fish, you feed him for a lifetime" is often cited to make the case for educational interventions over direct aid. The logic is that by investing in someone's ability to fish, you enable them to not only meet their immediate needs but also to become self-sufficient and potentially even generate surplus. While this is certainly true, the proverb fails to mention the third and perhaps most impactful possibility: that each person you coach might go on to teach others how to fish (which is essentially what they've learned from you). When viewed in this light, it becomes clear that your Life Coaching can have an exponential impact, touching not just one life but many. Who'd have thought that your Life Coaching might play a part in ending world hunger? Well, it can. Society as a whole will benefit from the positive changes you help facilitate in a single person, and that's the ultimate Life Coaching impact you can make.

Metaphors are often used in coaching as a way to help clients understand principles that might be difficult to grasp otherwise. By relating a new concept to something that is already known, metaphors can make the unfamiliar more relatable and easier to understand. Throughout this handbook, you will see me use metaphors to emphasize important points that might not be clear otherwise. I believe that metaphors can be incredibly helpful in coaching, as they have the ability to make complex ideas more understandable and memorable. I hope that you will find these metaphors useful in your own journey of self-discovery and growth.

In order to become an influential and effective Life Coach, it is essential to understand and implement the principles set forth in this handbook. If you take the time to reflect upon these principles and answer the questions scattered throughout, you will develop a strong foundation on which you can build a sustainable coaching practice. Wisdom comes about by putting wise life principles into practice and applying what you learn from these pages. When you see "Principles into Practice Questions," take time to think about them deeply and answer them honestly. By doing so, this handbook will become an invaluable part of your personal growth and ongoing professional development journey as a Life Coach for years to come.

**PRINCIPLES INTO PRACTICE QUESTIONS:**

1. In your personal life, what would be the most inspiring impact you could make? Write down your vision and be as specific as you can be.
2. As a Life Coach, what might be the most inspiring social impact that you could make? Write down your vision and be as specific as you can be.

# THE PREREQUISITES OF IMPACTFUL COACHING

*"A life is not important except in the impact it has on other lives."*
—JACKIE ROBINSON

As you grow as a person and develop your Life Coaching competencies, the level of impact you can make will deepen. For example, if you are a newly certified Life Coach, you may have only a limited amount of coaching experience. As a result, your impact may be mostly limited to providing basic encouragement or motivation. However, as you gain more experience, you will be better equipped to help your coachees achieve more complex goals. In addition, you will also become more aware of the subtleties of human behavior, allowing you to fine-tune your coaching approach and deepen the value of your Life Coaching over time.

If asked what would make your life more satisfying, you might suggest materialistic improvements, such as making more money, acquiring a larger home, pursuing a new career, getting a faster car, or disciplining yourself into a healthier body. People tend to evaluate their contentment in life according to what they lack or would like more of. People who evaluate the quality of their life in terms of contentment, tend to focus more on what they don't have and less on what they do have that already gives them fulfillment, such as spending time with family and loved ones or expressing their creative flair. Inner peace walks hand in hand with fulfillment, and fulfillment only comes by knowing that one has meaningfully progressed in some way relationally, financially, professionally, or via the depth of impact one has made.

Most people want to feel like they're doing something in life that matters and that will leave the world in a slightly better condition. And one of the best ways to do that is by investing time in others. It doesn't matter whether you volunteer for a local charity, coach (or mentor), a young person, or simply offer a listening ear to a friend in need—by investing your time and wisdom in others, you can make a practical difference in their lives. And as your actions ripple outwards, you may find that you inspire them to do the same.

To build credibility as a Life Coach, you must live your life according to the principles you claim to hold important. People will learn more from HOW you are in their company than from WHAT you say to them. The more diligently you work to grow, progress, and achieve goals in your life, the more insights you will have to share with others who aren't at the stage of development that you are. If you want to be respected as a wise Life Coach, live your life by example and serve as a role model for those whom you coach. People will be drawn to you if they see that you live with integrity and work to a standard of excellence. Of course, this doesn't require you to be perfect. But it does mean you should live in a congruent way that reflects your values and character. When you do, you'll not only attract more coachees, but you'll also become more relatable and appealing to the other people you do life with.

People typically seek out a Life Coach to help them become more effective, fruitful, efficient, productive, and fulfilled. While it is important to have theoretical knowledge, skill, and experience, it is also important that you live your life in a way that people are naturally drawn to you. This means you should have a certain amount of appeal and charisma.

I've seen too many emotionally unintelligent, behaviorally chaotic, and financially broke individuals try to jump into the Life Coaching business without first having created for themselves a lifestyle that is in any way remotely attractive. And yet, they market themselves as Life Coaching "gurus" and try to deceive people into believing that they are experienced in what they do. This is fraud, plain and simple. There's an old saying that goes: you can only take someone as far as you've gone yourself. In other words, you cannot coach other people beyond a stage of maturity, responsibility, character, integrity, or professional success that you have not already reached for yourself. This simple truth is overlooked by many who would rather sell a bog-standard service than deliver excellent Life Coaching. Trustworthy Life Coaches are those who've already created a productive and fulfilling lifestyle for themselves and use this knowledge to guide other people in doing the same.

Back in 2016, I launched an online forum where new and aspiring coaches would come together to exchange notes with each other and practice their competencies. Within this group, I would often host live discussions or presentations. One day, in particular, I hosted a discussion on the topic of business coaching and suggested that the only business coaches who can be deemed trustworthy are those who have built a sustainably profitable business for themselves. Much to my surprise, I got scoffed at by hundreds, who disagreed with me, and regurgitated an excuse that is typically used by many incompetent coaches, stating that "no business experience is required to offer business coaching." I often wondered if the same ideology would apply to medical professionals. Would it be OK to come under the knife of a surgeon who had only ever read about human anatomy via a textbook? Most likely not. In the same way that you wouldn't trust a teenager with the keys to your car, it would be equally unwise for anyone to trust a "Life Coach" who has no experience in generating the results for themselves that they promise to be able to generate for other people. Period.

When I started my journey of studying personal growth, professional development, Life Coaching models, and applied psychology in general, I had no idea where it would take me. My main goal at the time was to grow in self-knowledge and become a vessel for the greater good. I was simply motivated by a desire to improve my life and well-being. As I committed to learning, self-reflection, and investing in myself, I began to notice subtle but profound changes in my mental state. These changes soon cascaded into other areas of my life, such as my relationships, finances, work performance, and health. As my understanding deepened, I felt a growing desire to share what I had learned with others. So, I launched my first Life Coaching practice (from my own living room). I started out investing what little knowledge and understanding I had with ex-military veterans, pro-bono. As time passed, I turned my hand toward delivering group coaching, mentoring, and eventually hosting larger training events for greater numbers of people. What I'm trying to explain here is that as I got my life in order and matured as a man, my vision for making a difference in other people's lives expanded. In 2013, I began providing online Life Coaching and personal growth training materials to a worldwide audience. Since then, I've trained 615,000+ people across the world in Life Coaching, personal growth, and other modern applied psychology-related topics.

My reason for telling you all of this is not to impress you with statistics but rather to emphasize the importance of getting your own life in order before you even think about attempting to coach or support anyone else. As the saying goes, you can't pour from an empty cup. If you've ever been on a flight, during the safety brief, the stewards will tell you to put your own mask on first before you attempt to help others in the event of an emergency. The reason for this advice is that low cabin pressure and oxygen levels will likely cause you to blackout and render you useless to all other people. So, if you prioritize yourself and put your own oxygen mask on first, then you will be best equipped to assist others. This principle is also true when coaching people. If you are not in a balanced place mentally or physically, you will be of little value to those who come to you for guidance. It is, therefore, essential that you learn to balance out your life before all other things. Only then will you be ready to provide other people with the caliber of coaching support they deserve.

**PRINCIPLES INTO PRACTICE QUESTIONS:**

1. If an objective third party was to evaluate your readiness to deliver high-caliber Life Coaching, what areas of your life might they recommend that you first work hard to "get in order?"

# WINNING PEOPLE'S HEARTS AND MINDS

*"Trust, honesty, humility, transparency, and accountability are the building blocks of a positive reputation. Trust is the foundation of any relationship."*

—MIKE PAUL

Between 1996 and 2005, I served with the Royal Engineers, British Army. During this time, I traveled the world and had the opportunity to experience many different cultures. One of these cultures was Iraq before, during, and after the Gulf War II. At the time, the allied forces (US and UK) were fighting an aggressive public relations campaign to win over the Iraqi people, who were less than trusting of our presence in their country. The campaign was called Operation Hearts and Minds after a similar operation during the Vietnam War.

At first, the Iraqi people were uncooperative with my unit as we worked to lay pipelines that would provide drinking water to the surrounding rural towns. However, as we continued serving them, they gradually grew less hostile and became more inviting. Some days, we would steal food, Gatorade, chocolate, and other items from the UN compound where we had established a base camp to hand out to the locals. As a result, we forged friendships with some of them. One morning, a young girl we gave rations to previously greeted us with a chunk of her head missing. She was an unfortunate casualty of the crossfire from an attack on our station the evening before. That day, we offered medical supplies to her father from the limited supplies we had access to, who, in turn, used it for the benefit of his daughter and three of his other family members. In return, these people who were initially closed-off to receiving us, welcomed us into their homes and gave us their trust.

In my experience, I have found that all human beings share the same fundamental needs, no matter how unique we are in terms of culture or background. Everyone requires clean water and food, a place to live, and clothes to wear. All parents hope for their children is that they can achieve success in life. People of all ages need a sense of security and the opportunity to thrive. No one wants to go to bed at night fearing that their home will be gone by morning. I learned early on that you can't assist someone until they trust you. As Royal Engineers, it was our duty to play a modest part in rebuilding Iraq after the initial airstrikes, but we had to earn the locals' confidence before we could make a substantial difference. I discovered that people who try to convince others may persuade them mentally, but only those who address people's needs win their hearts—and subsequently gain their trust.

Sustainable relationships are built on trust, and that includes your Life Coaching relationships. Some people who give you access to their time will be vulnerable, raw, unsure about their future, and scared about making major changes. It takes courage to approach a stranger and be vulnerable with them. As the stranger who's being approached, it is important to demonstrate that you are trustworthy and validate their courage. Through my years of delivering coaching services and building collaborative "helping" relationships, I've identified Eleven Attitudes that every influential Life Coach should possess. These attitudes aren't universal facts. They're just guidelines (or healthy attitudes to adopt) that can help a Life Coach build stronger connections with his or her coachees.

*11 Attitudes*

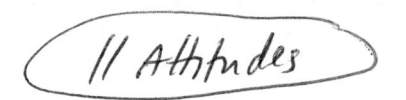

## ESSENTIAL ATTITUDES FOR EFFECTIVE LIFE COACHING

### ATTITUDE 1. THE MIND AND BODY ARE INTERCONNECTED

Some people view the human mind and body as two different entities, but as a Life Coach, it will be more useful to assume that the two are completely intersected and also that <u>the health of one will influence the health of the other</u>. ★ Let us also assume that the mind is different from the brain. Your body is a physical object that occupies space. It has certain dimensions and weight under Earth's gravitational conditions. On the other hand, your mind does not exist in any particular physical location. Nor does it have dimensions or weight.

Where the brain is physical, the human mind seems non-physical. Put simply, the health of our mindset can affect how healthy our bodies are, and how we act can impact our mental or emotional well-being. For example, if we are anxious about an upcoming event, our stress levels will skyrocket, affecting our digestion, heart rate, and sleep patterns. In contrast, if we are feeling joyful and content, those emotions will physically relax our muscles and boost our immune system. Therefore, it is evident that the relationship between mind and body is a complex one where each side constantly impacts the other for better or for worse. As a Life Coach, it is important to be aware of this dynamic so that you can always help your coachees to make balanced decisions that will have positive consequences on both their physical body and also the health of their mental composure.

### ATTITUDE 2. EVERY BEHAVIOR IS FUELLED BY POSITIVE INTENT

It's easy to assume the worst of others after someone cuts you off in traffic, pushes you in a crowd, or otherwise mistreats you. There's a lot of violence on the planet, and people do awful things. Human behavior is generally habitual, which means that most people live out their days without considering how their attitudes, habits, or behaviors affect others. The purpose of this assumption is not to spark a philosophical or moral debate, but rather, is just to state that your approval or judgment of another person's behavior is not appropriate within a Life Coaching relationship. You are not the moral police, and thus your opinion regarding a coachee's behavior outside of the coaching relationship is neither necessary nor welcome.

I know it's not easy. You have to be disciplined to walk away from an online debate when you see someone with a different opinion than yours. However, if you want to build trust-based coaching relationships (and maintain your own inner peace), it is essential that you practice assuming the best of people. In your relationships, you can either choose to assume the best or worst of people. assuming the best of others will help maintain trust and avoid developing a reputation for being judgmental. It is impossible to understand the reasons why people act or behave as they do, no matter how "textbook" you think their psychological profile may be. Assumptions are the termites of relationships, and the more you allow yourself to assume the worst of people, the less inclined people will be to be honest with you about what their priorities or intentions truly are.

Receiving honest answers to sincere questions will let you see what another person's intentions are. Sometimes, people make mistakes and behave out of character. Just as you wouldn't want someone to assume the worst of you, avoid assuming the worst about others. When you don't know a person's real intentions regarding a certain issue, the only way to form a profile of them is based on your judgments and opinions about what they said or did, which is unjust and undermines any trust you've established with them.

## ATTITUDE 3. ALL BEHAVIOR IS GEARED TOWARD SELF-PRESERVATION

It's often said that human beings are selfish by nature. But when you think about it, is that really true? After all, we are all social animals who rely on human connections for our very survival. So perhaps it would be more accurate to say that some people's primary motivation in life is preservation. That is, people act and behave in ways they believe will enable them to survive and thrive. Of course, what constitutes survival-enhancing behavior can vary greatly from one person to the next.

For some, it may mean hoarding resources and keeping others at arm's length. For others, it may mean being generous and forming close relationship bonds. But ultimately, everything that most human beings do can be traced back to this fundamental need to self-preserve. *survive* And once we understand that, it becomes a lot easier to empathize with even those who seem to be behaving in ways that are hurtful or counterproductive. After all, they're also just trying to preserve themselves and get ahead in life, just like the rest of us.

### ATTITUDE 4. MOST PEOPLE ACT OUT OF THEIR OWN INNER TURMOIL

Think about the times you've acted in a way you later grew to regret. Those times you behaved irrationally or selfishly. Whether you behaved in these ways decades ago or just last week, recalling some of our past actions can sting us with shame and embarrassment for an entire lifetime. However, do those past actions or behaviors accurately represent who you are today? No, of course they don't. The depth of human potential is too vast to reduce people to their past behaviors, beliefs, gender, personality, or skin color. What a person said last year or did in their twenties does not reflect who they are today or who they can become tomorrow.

One person's wrong is another person's right, and people's intentions are rarely ever understood or considered. Sometimes, hurt people hurt people. Are these justifications for destructive human behavior? Absolutely not, but they do explain it. What we see in people is only a thread of a deeply complicated, layered tapestry that we'll never fully access.

Most people act out of their own inner turmoil. Whether we're dealing with a pathological liar, an ex-convict, a pimp, a prostitute, or a serial killer, people's most malicious behaviors, habits, and attitudes do not diminish their worth as human beings. It's important to accept this while acknowledging that certain behaviors are not acceptable. By separating a person's *worst* actions from who they are, it becomes possible to accept people unconditionally, without compromising your standards or condoning destructive behavioral patterns.

One of the main principles of Life Coaching is to accept people for who they are, regardless of their actions or behaviors. Psychologist Carl Rogers introduced this concept, which is called "unconditional positive regard." Although it can be challenging to achieve, mastering this social skill is crucial if you want to form healthy and positive relationships as a Life Coach.

## ATTITUDE 5. FAILURE ISN'T WHAT MOST PEOPLE THINK IT IS

What's the difference between knowing your limitations and thinking like a failure? The product of your efforts. Failure thinking leads to failure. Recognizing limits leads to growth and exciting new possibilities. When identifying moments of failure, most people recall times they didn't succeed at something. However, this narrow and negative perception of failure prevents people from embracing it for what it is: the precursor to success. Failure is an integral part of any success story; it's part of Steven Spielberg's, Walt Disney's, Oprah Winfrey's, Fred Astaire's, and Hwang Dong-hyuk's stories. These people embraced failure as part of the creation process and just carried on. They didn't abandon their goals or lose faith when faced with challenges, setbacks, and obstacles and were thus rewarded for their perseverance.

The past doesn't determine your future, and the same is true for those whom you coach. After over a decade of rejection, Hwang Dong-hyuk's script, *Squid Game*, broke international and Netflix streaming records. The script, deemed "too dark" and "weird," was watched by 142 million households in its first month of release, giving Netflix a projected revenue of $900 million. Like J.K. Rowling and countless other writers before him, Hwang Dong-hyuk didn't see rejection as a failure, and he didn't allow rejection to influence how much he valued his work.

Failures aren't catastrophes, nor do they reflect a human being's worth, talent, or value. Instead, failures can be treated as helpful nudges that encourage humble self-reflection, reevaluation, adjustments, and reassessments wherever necessary. As you progress on your Life Coaching journey, you will work with people who've experienced soul-crushing professional and personal failures. When one of your coachee's confidence has been eroded by failure, help them reframe their experiences and, instead, explore the lessons that failure has provided them with. Failure should be something to strive for, not avoid.

## ATTITUDE 6. EVERYONE HAS A UNIQUE AND FASCINATING PERSPECTIVE

Imagine two people looking at the same landscape. One person sees the serene valley with a river running through it, while the other person sees the hungry alligator lurking in the river, waiting to pounce on its unsuspecting prey. Which person is seeing reality clearly? The answer, of course, is that both people are seeing reality—but just from different perspectives.

Our personal experiences, values, mental well-being, environments, and assumptions all influence our perspective (which is just how each of us see things). As a result, everyone has a different view of the world around them. And while one perspective may be more accurate than another, there is no such thing as a "correct" or "incorrect" perspective, there are just billions of different ones. Perspectives are filtered versions of reality. They help us make sense of the world, but they are rarely reality within itself. As a Life Coach, you can question perspectives to gain valuable insights into the reasons why people act and behave in the way that they do. You can ask people questions such as, "Tell me how you see things?" Or "How did things seem from your perspective?" Sometimes, if it would be useful to challenge a person's perspective, you might ask them, "And how do you know that your perspective is accurate?" Exploring people via their perspectives is a compassionate, empathetic, and enlightening conversational process that will allow your coachees to feel seen, heard, understood, and appreciated and to also become more flexible in their thinking.

## ATTITUDE 7. THERE ARE NO BAD PEOPLE, JUST DYSFUNCTIONAL BEHAVIORS

One of the most difficult concepts I teach is the idea that there are no inherently "bad" people. Often, individuals are quick to categorize those who have committed atrocious acts against humanity, such as Adolf Hitler, murderers, rapists, or child abusers. It is simply insufficient to label these individuals as "dysfunctional," as it demeans the severity of their actions.

This principle doesn't ask you to throw away your moral compass or support people who have committed horrendous crimes: it merely asks you to lay down your subjective opinions within a Life Coaching relationship. The same principle that defense lawyers live by is also true for coaches. Every person charged with a crime is given a fair trial under the justice system, which includes having a legal defense team to fight on their behalf. Does that make lawyers "bad" people who side with villainy? No, it's simply their professional responsibility to treat people as innocent until they are proven guilty. They have to overlook their personal feelings for what their client has done and build a defense that benefits the criminal. Labels such as "good" or "bad" are reductive and, technically, subjective. For every "bad" person you know, there is another person who loves them and doesn't see them the same way that you do. Labels like "good" and "bad" judgmentally categorize people, whereas professionals such as lawyers, achologists, and Life Coaches must maintain neutral, respectful, and non-judgmental relationships between themselves and those they're committed to serving.

I believe that a Life Coach's responsibility is to explore the psychological motivations behind people's behavior, which go much deeper than simple actions and surface-level desires. In other words, we should address people not as they are now but according to who they can grow to become. It is only through understanding people's motivations that we can hope to influence people to change for the better. Some organizations that profit from categorizing people might claim that humans are incapable of changing or improving their behavior. But in reality, everyone has the potential to mature and become someone better, regardless of their past. Just like you're doing right now.

## ATTITUDE 8. PEOPLE MAKE THE BEST DECISIONS THEY CAN IN THE MOMENT

We've all had moments when we look back at our past decisions and cringe. But we only shudder because we now know better, whereas, at that time, we made the best choices we could with the resources we had access to. Hindsight is 20-20. We can't undermine ourselves for not knowing something yesterday. All we can do is learn from mistakes and move forward, armed with the wisdom that comes from making unwise decisions.

We've all made choices that we later regretted. Whether it's an error in judgment or a catastrophic life-altering decision, we've all been there. But it's wise to remember that every decision we make is the best option we see at that time, based on our maturity, wisdom, and life experiences. Some people make decisions that seem extremely difficult to understand. But your responsibility as a Life Coach is not to project your judgment or logic onto people. Your understanding of life, being human, or the world cannot be projected onto those whose lives you have not lived. What you can do, however, is offer unassuming support and guidance as your coachees work through their own process of self-discovery and growth.

Human behavior isn't formulaic. Just because the forty-year-old you are coaching hasn't achieved the results you achieved at the age of thirty doesn't mean he has failed at life, because he hasn't. Retrospectively, some people make poor financial decisions, but they were still the best decisions they could make at the time, according to their circumstances, upbringing, environment, maturity, and wisdom. No one intentionally goes out of their own way to self-sabotage. Yet, it happens. Mistakes are a part of life that people can learn and grow from. Your Life Coaching can support this process.

## ATTITUDE 9. LIFE DOESN'T COME WITH DEADLINES—ONLY PEOPLE DO

In a world of incessant self-comparison, it's easy to assume that our lives should meet certain deadlines. People often expect to graduate by a certain age, secure a career by a certain age, start a family by a certain age, and so on. But the truth is—life doesn't come with deadlines. Only people do. Those who try to force their lives into boxes often end up feeling stressed, anxious, and "not good enough." People who structure their lives around deadlines often find themselves constricted in their thinking and followers of set paths. The hard truth is that life is always unpredictable and doesn't always unfold the way that we plan it.

In your coaching endeavors, you will inevitably encounter people who question their ability to grow and change. All people benefit from having someone with whom they can articulate their passions, identify their resources, provide context for goals, and plan what steps they need to take next in their journey. Your role is to help them identify innovative ways to progress in life at their own pace, not someone else's. It is good to respect people's unique journeys by understanding that each individual has different starting points, experiences, and circumstances. Keep this in mind as a coach so you can help your coachee discern what their "right" next steps are while providing them the support and encouragement they need.

## ATTITUDE 10. ALL THINGS ARE POSSIBLE WITH THE RIGHT ATTITUDE AND STRATEGY

Not even a century ago, if you told the general public that man would walk on the moon, they probably would have laughed at you. And if you said we could send cameras to Mars with telescopes that could view the formation of new galaxies, you'd have likely been locked up in a mental asylum! Human limitations are rapidly being debunked as technological and scientific advancements in recent decades have continually defied entrenched beliefs about humanity's limits, from space travel to contemporary medicine and lab-grown organs and meat.

Over the years, I've learned that there's truth in the saying that "everything is possible with the right strategy." Whether it's building a successful business, losing weight, or achieving any other goal, the key is to develop a plan and find the right strategy that will convert the goal into a reality. A major part of achieving goals is finding an effective strategy, which can be difficult and often where people "fail." Note that failing to find a successful strategy is different from simply not reaching a goal. If you're questioning if something is possible for one of your future coachees, ask them what strategy they need to put into place. More often than not, this will create a newfound coaching requirement.

## ATTITUDE 11. COACHING THAT DOESN'T ENABLE PERSONAL GROWTH ISN'T COACHING

Coaching isn't a technique to be rigidly applied in all situations. It is a way of leading and influencing people's decision-making. The underlying purpose of coaching is building up people's self-belief, regardless of the goal they want to pursue. When you coach, the effectiveness of what you do depends on your beliefs about human potential. A coach who doesn't believe people can become more than they currently are will be ill-equipped to help anyone. So, try to view people in terms of their potential and never their past performance.

People grow in self-belief when they make decisions or take actions that contribute to their personal growth and progression. For people to build self-belief, they must know that their success is largely due to their own hard work and efforts. They must also know that someone believes in them, which means being encouraged and supported to make tough choices and decisions. In essence, this is the very nature of Life Coaching.

Life Coaching isn't about making people happy. To coach people and positively influence them, we must adopt an optimistic view of human potential. Pretending to be optimistic about what people are capable of is insufficient because beliefs get conveyed in unavoidable ways. To draw the best out of people, we must assume that their best is yet to come. The potential for human growth is what fuels effective coaching. Sadly, the coaching industry can often be exploitative. Some self-proclaimed "coaches" have an overriding agenda to generate regular sessions fees from disempowered others who believe they need a "guru" to rely on. Your role as a coach is to inspire people to improve in every way possible. This includes instilling courage, inspiring decisiveness, and helping people become self-reliant. Also, part of your job is to ensure that people are taking the right measures so they can continuously develop and progress into wiser and more self-assured versions of themselves.

Before all things, remember that trust is the foundation of every successful Life Coaching relationship. You must first earn people's trust before they will be completely genuine with you. Their honesty and transparency are essential in order for you to effectively help them define what their priorities are and ultimately reach their goals. This can be a tough process that requires objectivity and that you embody these attitudes for effective Life Coaching.

**PRINCIPLES INTO PRACTICE QUESTIONS:**

1. Which of these attitudes stood out to you as being most notable, and why?
2. How have these attitudes influenced your perspective of what Life Coaching can be?
3. How might applying these attitudes affect how you interact with others as a Life Coach?

# OVERVIEW OF THE LIFE COACHING PROCESS

*(✱) support for future not just feel better about past*

*"The delicate balance of coaching someone is not creating them in your own image, but giving them the opportunity to define and create themselves."*

—STEVEN SPIELBERG

It is often said that people without goals are like ships adrift on the sea with no obvious destination. This analogy is particularly apt, as both journeys can be long, difficult, and full of perils if not properly planned for. In life, as on the sea, it is easy to get lost along the way if you don't have a goal in mind. This is where Life Coaching comes in. Life Coaching is a type of human interaction in which people are supported in planning for the future rather than just feeling better about their pasts. A Life Coaching relationship will vary depending on the two people who are participating in it, but essentially, it should always primarily involve one person assisting another in devising a strategic plan for progressing in all aspects of their lives as well as defining action steps that must be taken to turn goals into a tangible reality. In this way, Life Coaching can help prevent people from aimlessly drifting through life without ever reaching their full potential.

*plan ↓ steps*

Goal setting is central to the Life Coaching processes. It helps people to define what they want and create a step-by-step plan for how to get it. People want a fulfilling life; people want to use their

*[Margin notes: People want: - fulfilling life; - use strengths & talents; - build healthy rel'ships; - do work they enjoy; - make impact on world]*

strengths and talents; people want to build healthy, connected relationships; people want to do work that they enjoy and make a positive impact on the world. Without clear goals and a plan of action steps to be taken, it's all too easy to get caught up in the day-to-day grind and miss out on opportunities for growth and progression. A full section is dedicated to goal setting later on in this handbook, but for now, here's a high-level overview of the five basic steps that make up most Life Coaching processes.

### STEP 1: QUANTIFY A POSITIVELY FRAMED GOAL

Every coaching relationship begins with a goal and ends with an achievement. Life Coaches don't determine what people's goals or priorities are; they only help to quantify them. Only the coachee will know what goals are best suited for them at the stage of life they are in; it's then your role to guide them in deciding what their priorities are and hold them accountable until their objectives have been realized. In the following chapters, we will explore goal setting from a range of viewpoints. As a Life Coach, you must understand how to set goals with your clients that are realistic, achievable, and inspiring. We will later explore a simple methodology that can be used to help people establish goals that are "right" for them.

### STEP 2: ENSURE GOALS ARE TIMELY AND REALISTIC

As humans, we are constantly striving to better ourselves. Whether it is getting a promotion at work, losing a few pounds, or finally taking that dream vacation, we are always setting goals. Setting goals can help people change, improve, achieve satisfaction, and feel like they're moving in life with a purposeful sense of direction. Setting realistic goals requires a coachee to be honest about what their priorities are at the stage of life they are currently in. A coachee may want to be married with 2.4 children before the age of 35 but has come to you at age 33.5, newly single and distressed. The likelihood of this coachee achieving her goal within a twelve-month timeframe is, technically, possible, but it's certainly not within a Life Coach's power to conjure up the "right" person, or even come up with a realistic plan regarding where Mr. or Mrs. Right might be found.

Part of the Life Coaching process involves managing people's expectations by setting realistic (short-) and (long-term goals). This helps keep the individual's goals in perspective while also thinking about what short-term goals might be wise to set today that could help accomplish more meaningful long-term aspirations tomorrow. Just like learning to ride a bike, you'll get better at this over time as you spend more time coaching people.

## STEP 3: EXPLORE POTENTIAL OPTIONS AND SOLUTIONS

Coaches sometimes say they coach to the gap between what people want to achieve and what currently exists. Coaching is, at its heart, a conversation about the goals and priorities people have in life. People who enter the profession of coaching often assume that they are expected to know what's best for people. This isn't true.

The burning desire to make a difference that some well-intending Life Coaches have can get muddled with an unconscious inclination to impose their own beliefs, preferences, and ideals. Once a gap has been identified between what people aspire to achieve and what currently exists for them, that is the time to explore potential solutions for closing the gap.

## STEP 4: DECIDE ON THE BEST NEXT STEPS TO TAKE

Gaining absolute clarity in what the coachee specifically needs, wants, or hopes to achieve is pivotal to the coaching conversation moving forward. Which might go something like this; "Okay, so now that we're both clear on what you want, you know what your options are, so what are the first few steps that you need to take?" Once a coachee has identified what potential next steps they could take, it's then important for the coach and coachee to mutually agree upon the wisest next steps that they are actually willing to take. Defining clear action steps removes any confusion that might exist in light of them progressing toward their goals.

## STEP 5: HAVE A CLEAR VISION OF THE OUTCOME

Have you ever set a goal only to find yourself struggling to take the first step? We've all been there. Visualizing the end result is a powerful way to get unstuck and jump-start the goal-setting process. When we can see ourselves achieving a goal, it becomes much easier to take action toward it. However, before we can visualize an end result, we need to be clear about what we hope to achieve. Once we have a clear vision of our desired outcome, we can begin to create a mental pathway that will lead us there. For visualization to be successful in a Life Coaching relationship, a coachee must be clear about what they hope to achieve before being able to visualize the reality of having achieved it. The visualization process simply enables people to turn an abstract idea (or a nice idea) into a reality in their mind's eye.

Without a clear destination, it's hard for people to know where they're going or how to get there—kind of like trying to walk through a dark room at night. A coach's capacity to hear and feed back everything a coachee says is like shining light toward the end of their tunnel. Doing this will allow their goals to become more alive and spacious. Visualization will also allow a coachee to evaluate the distance they must travel to fulfill a goal, the barriers they may need to overcome en route, and even how willing they are to put in the hard work and the time investment required to achieve anything significant in life.

Goals that aren't vivid or compelling don't motivate people. Until a coachee has a compelling vision for the specific outcomes they want, finding the motivation to sustain the effort required to transform a goal into a real-world outcome will remain challenging.

These five steps of the Life Coaching process are just your starting point. There is much more to learn about human behavior, psychology, goal setting, and communicating to become a wise and influential Life Coach. However, if you work hard to familiarize yourself with these steps and build them into your daily disciplines, you will be well on your way to becoming a competent coach and positive role model for your future coachees.

**PRINCIPLES INTO PRACTICE QUESTIONS:**

1. What is your primary goal for wanting to become an effective Life Coach?
2. What do you envision as the greatest outcome you could achieve via working with people?

# THE BEDROCK OF EFFECTIVE LIFE COACHING

"We think we listen, but very rarely do we listen with real understanding, true empathy. Yet listening, of this very special kind, is one of the most potent forces for change that I know."

—CARL ROGERS

What forges a great relationship? Is it luck? Chemistry? Fate? Or is there something else at play? Communication is the DNA that forges all healthy human connections. People skills, communications, and integrity are the keys to all coaching, personal, and professional success.

In the context of Life Coaching, listening is extremely different from typical, everyday listening that you might participate in with your family or peer groups. Even when done well, everyday conversational listening tends to lack the substance, intentionality, and focus that a skilled Life Coach can inject into a discussion. A skilled Life Coach will always listen to people without any other agenda than to hear the heart and essence of what a coachee has to say.

Listening forms the bedrock of effective coaching and is central to every healthy human interaction. Making noise is easy for most people as they've been doing it since birth. Even hearing comes naturally to many, but listening requires self-discipline. Listening is different from hearing, as listening requires intentional effort, whereas hearing is passive. All good coaches listen more than they speak. This idea can sometimes come across as confusing for new coachees who expect the Life Coaching process to be similar to client-centered forms of therapy—where people with problems show up, sit down, get talked at, and wait patiently for their "inner healing" to somehow occur. Some people spend their money with a Life Coach, expecting the coach to transform their woes or make their goals happen.

While you may sometimes feel pressured to talk more as a Life Coach, the real value lies in how effective your listening skills become. Passively hearing people is easy, but actively listening to hear the true essence of what they are (and aren't) saying is what will equip you to detect people's thinking habits, worldviews, and self-oriented beliefs.

Healthy discussion between two people is known as dialogue. Dialogue occurs when two people are equally as interested in listening to and hearing each other. Most people don't dialogue; they just monologue at each other while desperately wanting to be listened to.

At this stage of your Life Coaching journey, your greatest opportunity for learning is to become an effective listener. Life Coaching isn't about listening out to identify people's hurts, problems, pathologies, past history, or woes—it's about listening to hear the opportunities, possibilities, goals, priorities, and aspirations that will inspire a person to make positive behavior or attitude changes. It's also about identifying, expanding, and leveraging on the ability people have to put a plan in motion that will increase the quality of experience they have across their broad spectrum of life areas (such as relationships, career, finances, routine responsibilities, support network, social contribution or personal growth). Coaches who listen out for solutions to people's problems limit the effectiveness of the coaching process by turning their coachee into a problem to be fixed with their desired end goal solution.

As previously mentioned, the purpose of Life Coaching is not to solve problems or make people happy. Those who do view this as the purpose of Life Coaching often end up distorting the Life Coaching process by imposing their own warped agenda onto people. Life Coaches who can learn to observe their own listening process and let go of any ego-centric need they have to "be the expert" and "have all the answers" tend to be those who earn the most recommendations for being agenda-less, authentic, and remarkably helpful.

Most people like to think of themselves as good listeners. Even many of those who claim to be trained professionals nod heads sagely as the people we communicate with unburden themselves before prattling on enthusiastically when it's their turn to speak. But is this listening? Of course not. True listening is a skill that must be cultivated, and it starts with a genuine intrigue to hear what another person has to say. This involves setting aside an agenda, being present in the moment, and resisting the urge to interrupt or give advice.

We learn much from listening to people carefully. Listening isn't an easy people skill to develop, but as previously mentioned, forms the bedrock of effective Life Coaching and is central to every healthy human interaction. Until you can listen, you cannot coach. Listening is the prerequisite to good coaching. When you listen, you create a space in which another person can feel heard, which is the key to unlocking the trust that will be required for a Life Coaching relationship to be taken beyond its first or second session.

Life Coaching is, above all other things, a dialogue between two people. All coaching relationships should begin through the five stages previously discussed to define a coachee's vision, hopes, and long-term ambitions. And as with all good discussions, coaching simply requires you to be interested enough in people to listen to them and sustain healthy dialogue.

As a topic, I've built these basic principles of listening into this handbook so early, as it's listening alone lays the foundation on which all strong relationships can be built and through which all exceptional Life Coaching is delivered.

**PRINCIPLES INTO PRACTICE QUESTIONS:**

1. How would you currently rate the quality of your listening skills?
2. How might the people closest to you rate the quality of your listening skills?

# A STANDARD FOR EFFECTIVE LIFE COACHING

*"Boundaries provide a standard for how our relationships must be. We don't set high relationship standards to keep people out, we do so to ensure that only the right people get in. This can save us much unnecessary hardship, and anyway, high standards are essential when building anything meaningful that thrives."*

—DR. HENRY CLOUD

For a Life Coaching relationship to work, there must be commitment on the part of the coachee to explore, change, learn, take risks, and persevere with their self-betterment. Even when difficult, a coachee must commit to investing time and energy and be willing to exit their comfort zone and enter uncertainty for the purpose of facilitating positive change. Without this level of devotion, coaching can become disempowered future gazing. Fortunately, most coachees are ready for hard work when they start a coaching process—but as with all things, this isn't a universal principle that can be banked on. Life Coaches, in turn, also need to be clear about how committed they will remain to certain types of coachees. It is a commitment to dig deep and listen intently that makes Life Coaching exciting and impactful. A coach who is committed to helping people reach their goals will always be ready to challenge, provoke, encourage, and sometimes insist that clients take charge of their learning. When a Life Coach brings 100 percent effort and expertise into a relationship, unless this is matched by the coachee, over time, the future longevity of a coaching relationship might be questionable.

Coaching sessions usually begin with small talk and checking in. The moment the discussion is directed toward the coachee's goals is the moment the coaching dialogue has begun. The coach employs open-ended questions that usually start with "What do you need/want?" to encourage the coachee to discuss their current priorities. The initial questions asked during a coaching session should center around a positive goal that the coachee is willing to put effort toward. Subsequent questions can then ask for more detailed information.

When you listen to and reflect back a coachee's response to the question, "What do you need/want?" the gap between what a coachee has and what they want to have will become evident. Once this gap has been identified, further questioning is needed to verify your understanding of what your coachee has said: "Am I understanding you fully?" "Am I hearing you clearly?" What else do you need?" "Is there anything else that I'm missing?"

Life Coaching is about helping people to gain clarity about what they want—it's NOT about creating a tranquil "talking space" for disempowered people to talk about their problems and all of the things they don't want. The importance of gaining this level of clarity is that, once clear, the Life Coaching conversation can progress and focus on devising the plans and strategies that will equip a coachee to take action steps, work hard, and start getting what they want. It's important to understand all of this because not all people who seek out a Life Coach have a specific objective in mind that they're prepared to work toward, nor do they have any intention of engaging in any form of effortful hard work at all. Some people see Life Coaching as a form of therapy where they can discuss their emotions and complaints.

Many years ago, a lady approached me, wanting a Life Coach. During our initial consultation, it became apparent that she wasn't interested in setting goals or carving a new path in life. She just wanted to complain about her former manager and blame him for sparking her latest bout of depression. After fifteen minutes of listening to her complain, I intervened and suggested that we focus on what goals she wanted to work toward due to being in an exciting new phase of life. To say that she emotionally erupted would be an understatement. The lady quickly became irate at me and started yelling that I was an unprofessional therapist. Through her anger, it was apparent she assumed my role was to listen to her complaint, console her and in some way improve the quality of emotions she was experiencing. After briefly attempting to negotiate with her, I ended the relationship, which the lady wanted to be a therapeutic one rather than a responsible coaching-oriented one.

Occasionally, you will be contacted by people who want you as their shoulder to cry on. Other times, you will come across people who want to improve their lives without having to change or grow in any way. However, the true value of Life Coaching is when a coachee takes full responsibility for managing themselves, taking charge of their circumstances and making the necessary changes to achieve their short, medium, and long-term goals.

The first coaching conversation you have with a person is your chance to explain what coaching is and what a coachee can expect from it. When doing this, you can explain what your coaching entails. Many people enter the coaching industry for self-serving reasons, such as inflating their ego or wanting to make money. But if you hope to grow a reputation that earns referrals and repeat business, you must be choosy about who you give your time to. Decide on the maturity of those you will coach to protect your time, reputation, and energy. Being picky isn't about making yourself exclusive; rather, it's about lowering the risk of your reputation being tainted by people who would label you as incompetent rather than taking personal responsibility for creating the solutions that will resolve their major life challenges.

Therefore, to make a well-informed decision about the suitability of the people you agree to coach, listen to how they respond to your initial question, "What do you need?" and then take time to consider what your honest answers might be to the following questions:

### 1. IS THE PERSON OPEN TO YOUR COACHING INPUT?

You can determine a potential coachee's intentions within the first fifteen to twenty minutes. If they seek support in developing themselves and making key life changes, it's a green light to proceed with your Life Coaching process. However, if they want you to magically solve all of their problems and boost their self-esteem in some way, it's a serious red flag warning. In these cases, refer these individuals to a talking therapist (or a magician) and move on.

### 2. ARE THEY RECEPTIVE TO WHAT THEY'RE LEARNING?

Life Coaching sessions can be transformative when a coach listens to their coachee, offers wise feedback, and asks questions that are relevant to a coachee's situation. The coachee may be open to the insights they receive within a coaching session, but these insights are empty if they do not take subsequent action. On my website's inquiry form, a user once asked me about the guaranteed results of my coaching. I replied by stating that, as a coach, I do not guarantee specific results; however, I can help people to identify the action steps they must take for themselves in order to generate the life outcomes that they are motivated to pursue. Life Coaches cannot deliver results; these are entirely dependent on each coachee.

### 3. ARE THEY APPRECIATIVE OF YOUR COACHING INPUT?

What you contribute to a coaching relationship goes beyond your expertise or abilities; it includes your personality, life experience, and integrity, all of which set you apart. If someone doesn't appreciate these characteristics, however, you might want to think about whether they are a suitable prospect for more of your time. Suggesting that you're not the "right" Life Coach for someone isn't to say you're not good or capable enough; it's simply about you being in control of the people you give your time to. Being appreciated isn't about getting your ego stroked; It's about asserting a boundary and showing what your personal, moral, and professional standards are. If you wouldn't work with a colleague who doesn't appreciate your qualities, then don't sell yourself short by prostituting yourself to anyone who is neither mature enough nor interested enough to benefit from your life experiences and wisdom.

As your conversation with a potential coachee progresses, if you perceive that the person is not coachable at this time, make a helpful referral to another coach that might be a better "fit" for them, or suggest books, training courses, or workshops that you know will be beneficial to them. At this stage of the handbook, please know that time is your most valuable resource, and being a Life Coach doesn't mean that you must say "yes" to all people. Sometimes, you might be presented with a coaching scenario that's outside of your competency zone, in which case, again, refer the person on before ending the conversation and moving on.

Some new Life Coaches feel ready to take on the world and tackle every challenge that comes their way, but it's wise to note that coaching wisdom cannot be found in a training course or even in a handbook like this. Developing coaching wisdom and knowing who to say "yes" or "no" to will become apparent over time—as you grow in experiential knowledge.

**PRINCIPLES INTO PRACTICE QUESTIONS:**

1. How does people's openness toward you affect how much time you want to give them?
2. How does people's receptiveness of you affect how much time you want to give them?
3. How does people's appreciation of you affect how much time you want to give them?
4. Which other factors might determine whether you accept a Life Coaching request or not?

# PRINCIPLES FOR POSITIVELY INFLUENCING PEOPLE

*"We can know a person by observing his behavior, understanding the reasons for his actions, and learning about his innermost intentions. If we do this, how can we not know him?"*

—CONFUCIUS

There are over 8.5 billion people on earth. Each person has unique ways of being, beliefs, values, and experiences, which constitute their value to the world. As much as many of us would like to consider ourselves experts in human psychology and behavior, the vastness of human experience and personality makes understanding people an interesting process.

After many years of studying and working with different people, Life Coaches can sometimes become overconfident in their reading of people and circumstances. Take, for example, the story of Maud, the woman who was appalled at the state of her neighbor's laundry, which she could see out her kitchen window. Every Tuesday, Maud's neighbor would put her laundry out on the washing line to dry, and Maud was always horrified at how filthy the freshly washed laundry was. Every time Maud bumped into her neighbor, she would make subtle hints at the state of her laundry by suggesting certain laundry cleaners or washing machine brands. Then one Tuesday, Maud looked out her kitchen window and saw, to her glee, the neighbor hanging up clean laundry. Proud of herself, Maud called in her husband to gloat at her excellent work. Her husband looked out the window and nodded, "Very good, dear. In fact, everything looks so much cleaner out there since I cleaned the kitchen window this morning. I couldn't believe how dirty it was."

What you think of as reality may not always be true. Your brain has filtered much of the data to make it easier to handle, giving your perceptions a false sense of reality. In other words, your perception of reality tells you more about who you are, your values, and what you believe in than it does about reality. Life Coaches must always be hyper-vigilant about how their perceptions may interfere with a coaching relationship, as unmanaged, closed-mindedness will destroy a coachee's trust in a coach.

Similarly, when you coach someone, keep in mind the woman in the story; many will come to you with a preconceived notion of reality, and those who believe their view is reality will be the most difficult to help change. I'm not saying that Life Coaching entails changing people's views on reality; rather, it should be focused on helping people experience their world with greater clarity, openness, receptiveness, and understanding.

Some of the principles below may appear as wise or outrageous, depending on your understanding of human behavior. Your reaction to these concepts will play a role in how positively or detrimentally impactful you are during your future Life Coaching conversations.

### EMOTIONS DO NOT EVER HAVE TO BE HARMFUL

Emotions serve as markers that point in the direction of our needs being or not being met. Emotions influence how many people perceive reality, and through perception, people act. We use feelings to anticipate what the world has in store for us. For example, if you walk into an alley late at night in a dark neighborhood, an emotion of fear or anxiety may strike you, prompting you to alter course and look for another route home. It's important to note here that in a situation like this, it's only fear that forces you to react, not any actual outcome.

Emotions are determined by how you perceive a given situation, what the psychologist Sigmund Freud referred to as the "reality principle." Thoughts determine how you feel. Those who live in the volatile space between emotions and action tend to succumb to unproductive habitual behaviors. However, those who learn to discipline themselves and focus on the thoughts that birth their emotions will see a different course that can always be taken. Emotions needn't be harmful, they just need to be understood.

**BIG PICTURES CAN'T BE SEEN THROUGH SMALL FRAMES**

Some people make the mistake of living in a narrow-minded echo chamber and shutting out all perspectives and opinions that differ from their own. People who refuse to challenge their perspective on things become closed off from reality, which prevents them from identifying innovative new ways to improve their circumstances. People who are curious think outside the box, get different opinions from those with other perspectives, and adapt their views to what will work best for them and the people they care about. This is a significantly different approach to life than that taken by others, such as the woman with the filthy window, who blindly believes that every notion that enters their head is an objective and universal truth.

Thus, coaching is about encouraging people to think about fulfilling meaningful, big-picture goals that reach beyond people serving only themselves. Those who pursue such objectives become more interested in the world around them as a consequence.

**SELF-DISCIPLINE REDUCES THE RISK OF REGRET**

Discipline is choosing between what you want now and what you want most. Being disciplined enough to do what is sensible, value-adding to other people, and wise, although difficult, paves the high road to a lifetime of personal satisfaction. Discipline is the bridge that spans the gap between setting goals and achieving them. The more disciplined people are in their mind, the easier and more rewarding life becomes for them.

Facing delay, rejection, or hardship is OK for disciplined people.

When it comes to making wise lifestyle choices, self-discipline is key. Those who are disciplined are less likely to regret the decisions they make. This is because they are more likely to act in accordance with their beliefs and values rather than let emotions dictate what they do.

Discipline is key to success in any area of life. When you have the discipline to stick to your goals and plans, you are less likely to make hasty decisions that you will later regret. The first step toward becoming disciplined is to set realistic goals. Once you have a goal in mind, break it down into smaller steps that you can take action on immediately. Follow through with your plan, and don't be discouraged if you sometimes fall off track. The important thing is that you get back on track as soon as possible and continue working toward your goal. The more disciplined you become, the easier it will be to stick to your goals and achieve success in life. Exactly the same will be true for your future coachees.

**PRINCIPLES INTO PRACTICE QUESTIONS:**

Consider times in the past when you saw that your perception wasn't in sync with reality.

1. What ideas do you have about human potential that you wouldn't change your mind about?
2. When was the last time that you changed your mind about something significant?
3. How important do you think it is for a Life Coach to manage their client's perceptions?

# SEEK FIRST UNDERSTANDING BEFORE ALL THINGS

*"The range of what we think and do is limited by what we fail to notice. And because we fail to notice that we fail to notice, there is little we can do to change; until we notice how failing to notice shapes our thoughts and deeds."*

—R. D. LAING

In this opening section of the handbook, my goal has not been to present you with a cohesive coaching procedure that you can robotically take people through as you go about building something that might resemble a Life Coaching practice. Instead, I have simply offered you a handful of ideas and guiding principles that, if you embody them, will equip you to relate well with people. Relating well to people, as you might guess, is a key prerequisite of coaching.

We have discussed the principle of listening, which rests among the most important communication skills you can develop. While the majority of people learn to read and write from a young age, the ability to listen—listening for the purpose of truly understanding another human being—is something many people receive very little guidance in mastering.

To be listened to is a striking human experience, partly because it happens so rarely for many people. Think about a time when another person was 100 percent totally with you—totally engaged in what you were saying, interested in every word, eager to empathize—you most likely felt valued and understood. People open up when they know they're being listened to and heard; they expand; they have more presence. They feel safer and more secure as well, and trust grows. This is why listening is so important within every Life Coaching relationship.

In his bestselling book, *The 7 Habits of Highly Effective People*, Stephen Covey offers a framework for personal effectiveness and presents his teachings through a series of seven habits, number five of which is: *"Seek first to understand and then to be understood."* According to Dr. Covey, the way we see the world is based entirely on our own perceptions. In order to change a given situation, we must change ourselves, and in order to change ourselves, we must be willing to constantly evaluate the accuracy of our perceptions.

People often listen with the goal of responding, not comprehending. In other words, while someone else is talking, one might be more concerned with voicing one's perspective than hearing the essence of what another person is saying. This creates a selective listening habit where we just focus on keywords instead of ballpark understanding and a gist of the conversation—which often leads to misinterpreting the speaker's meaning entirely.

As Covey explains, *"we sometimes listen only to prepare ourselves for what we want to say next. We filter everything we hear through our own past experiences, or our frame of reference. We're checking what we hear against our own "autobiography" and consequently, we decide prematurely what the other person means before he or she finishes communicating."* Does any of this sound remotely familiar?

Seeking to understand involves stepping into the shoes of the other person and asking for clarity in what their words mean, rather than making a judgment or assumptions. In other words, asking people questions before responding to what you think "might" have been said—this will allow you to tailor suitable and unbiased responses to people. Learning to listen is essential for effective Life Coaching, and Life Coaches who make developing their listening skills a priority will develop strong relationships that encourage commitment and trust.

## FIVE TIPS TO HELP YOU HEAR PEOPLE WITH CLARITY

Picture yourself climbing a mountain with a friend. Instead of climbing together, you both choose to climb on separate faces of the mountain. You take the north face, and your friend takes the south face. You keep in touch with each other through walkie-talkies.

Your side of the mountain is rocky and covered in ice, making it slippery underfoot, while your friend's terrain is greener full of foliage, and it is wet rather than icy. Climbing the same mountain as someone doesn't mean you both get the same experience. You may have had it easier and reached the top faster, or your friend may have had an incident that affected their climb. Perhaps the path chosen by your friend was treacherous, and they had to stop. Thus, your perspective of the mountain is influenced by your unique experience of it.

Imagine that you and your friend compare notes after completing your descent. You assume that the only experience that can be had of climbing the mountain is the one that you've had. This would mean that no one else in the world could possibly have an experience that differs from yours. Your friend then tells you about their unique experience, which you must disagree with because the narrative of their personal experience doesn't align with yours. Unfortunately, this "closed-minded" attitude towards difference is what many people carry into their relationships with other people.

It is wise to note that there is no right or wrong perspective to take towards life, just varying degrees of difference. Likewise, there is no right or wrong way to climb any mountain, live life, do relationships, build a business, raise children, or leave behind a life legacy; however, one must be mindful that nobody starts their journey of life on equal footing, and everyone spends their lifetime climbing amidst different climates and through various terrains.

Usually, coaching involves assisting people in overcoming their challenges, similar to climbing a mountain. To accomplish this, one must have strong communication skills. According to Sri Nisargadatta Maharaj, "If you want to understand another, listen with attention and an open heart." This is the basis for gaining clarity when listening to people—developing active listening skills that truly hear and understand another person's unique perspective.

Thus, effective communication is crucial for fostering positive coaching relationships. We will explore communication skills and important people principles later in the handbook, but for now, here are five tips to help you hear people with clarity and develop stronger, healthier Life Coaching relationships:

Tip 1. Maintain eye contact with people. Maintaining good eye contact indicates to other people that you are genuinely interested in who they are and what they are saying. It also helps to keep your focus on the conversation and not get distracted.

Tip 2. Listen actively, rather than passively. Active listening means that when someone is talking to you, you are paying attention to understand what they are saying—rather than just nodding along or providing superficial responses. We'll discuss this in more detail later on.

Tip 3. Remain objective. Listen to hear and never to respond. The moment you let your biases or opinions flood a conversation is the same moment that you'll prove to another person that you are not even remotely interested in understanding them or their perspective.

Tip 4: Be fully present. To demonstrate that you're paying attention, be fully present in the conversation. Avoid letting your mind wander while maintaining eye contact with the person you're talking to. Always take time to reflect on what has been said to you before responding.

Tip 5: Ask only relevant questions. When you need more information about someone's situation, ask questions that relate to previously discussed topics without judgment. People will open up and be honest with you to the degree that you are genuinely interested in them.

These five tips are a great starting point for learning how to listen with clarity and presence. But it is important to remember that effective communication is an ongoing process. As a Life Coach, you must continue to refine and hone your communication skills by actively listening to your clients and seeking to understand their unique perspectives. With this approach, you can not only reach common ground but also build robust relationships with those whom you serve.

# SECTION ONE SUMMARY

A Life Coach's main goal is to help people improve their overall quality of life rather than fix individual issues or help them meet performance goals. However, as a result of good coaching, these things will naturally fall into place. Life Coaching is just a conversational process that aids self-discovery, awareness, and choice. It is a way of empowering people to find their own answers and supporting them in making well-considered decisions. How you view human potential will affect how much value people receive from you within a Life Coaching relationship. Questions serve many purposes in Life Coaching. Questions can open a specific life area up for expansion, or they can probe and intensify a point of focus. Always make it your priority within a coaching relationship to understand whom you're working with and create the space that is necessary for that person to evolve into someone greater.

**IMPORTANT LESSONS TO REMEMBER:**
- To understand people, you must transcend your perceptions and biases and be willing to learn.
- Life Coaching is most effective when you develop trusting relationships with your clients.
- Life Coaches don't offer solutions. They assist people in defining their goals and priorities.

- Without a positive and clearly defined goal, there is no basis for a Life Coaching relationship
- Your influence as a Life Coach will largely depend on your ability to listen effectively.
- Perception and reality are not synonymous. Another person's reality is independent of you.
- Those who view perception and reality as one will struggle to make positive life changes.

**SECTION ONE NOTEWORTHY IDEAS**

Use this space to note down any ideas that have struck you as important throughout this section of the handbook. Also, write down any questions that might be beneficial for your future consideration and self-reflection.

SECTION TWO

# THE FUNDAMENTALS OF SELF-AWARENESS

Self-awareness means being aware of your mind, character, and what makes your life both meaningful and purpose-oriented. This section of the handbook will explore the ideas, emotions, and habits that undermine people's capacity to grow, pursue meaningful goals and generate purposeful outcomes. By helping a person become self-aware, you will tap into their potential to change and play a crucial role in helping to shape their future.

# WHAT IS THE MEANING OF LIFE?

*"Purpose, meaning, and goals are like a feedback loop. Our purpose helps us create goals, and our goals help us do what's meaningful to us. Over time, those things add up and become something greater: our sense of purpose—which is like having an in-body GPS, and the goals we set define the steps we must take to move forward in a direction that is right for us."*

—DR. SELWYN HUGHES

What is the meaning of life? What is the purpose of life? The questions of life's meaning and purpose have puzzled scientists, theologians, and philosophers for millennia. Everyone will have a different view regarding an answer to these questions, but in truth, opinions definitely won't cut it when it comes to taking our future and the meaningfulness of our lives seriously. Many theories of meaning have been proposed over the last few centuries, as humans struggled to arrive at a coherent understanding of what meaning is, how it is made, and how it can be found. However, no theory has been proposed that answers these two big questions.

Throughout history, and especially since the dawn of the internet, one of the most commonly searched questions people have asked is, "What is the meaning of life?" This might be a fair indication that the majority of humans are hungry for meaning, for a sense of purpose, and for the feeling that life is worth more than just the sum of its own parts.

Some people have a doom-and-gloom take on the meaning of life. Many cynics, existentialists, scientists, and disenchanted former spiritualists believe life has no meaning. They posit that the meaning of life is nothing more than an evolutionary drive to maintain species population and genetic lineage. While this outlook is legitimate, its Darwinistic stance overlooks psychology's role in sentient life, particularly human life. Whilst we can say plants and many animals might be primarily motivated by survivalist and procreative drives, there's a unique nuance to human existence that challenges this outlook.

They're technically correct; life has no meaning in itself. There's no universal meaning to be found in the stars or in studying ancient texts. There's no one alive who witnessed the big bang, monkey-to-man evolution, or Adam and Eve in the Garden of Eden. So it's best to accept that there is no set formula for finding purpose or meaning in life.

But don't be discouraged because there is another truth that you can share through your Life Coaching that has the potential to set some people free from their self-constructed prisons of meaninglessness, helplessness, and hopelessness (which obviously isn't all people).

In modern psychology, life meaning is generally no longer questioned; psychologists who understand Freudian, cognitive, and developmental psychology understand that meaning exists only as a concept and that people assign a unique meaning to their every experience.

People assign meaning to every life experience they have. Meaning is the psyche's fuel for inspiring motivation and driving action; therefore, the meaning of life is entirely personal, and future events cannot be interpreted for meaning. Rather, people can only find meaning in how they've interpreted their spectrum of life experiences.

Many people wait for meaning to come to them like a stroke of inspiration rather than seeing meaning as something they have already decided on. A person's view of whether life is meaningful or not is their own decision. Some people believe having a relationship, raising children, holding a certain job for a specific salary, or going to college will provide their life purpose. But meaning doesn't come from external factors; it always comes from within.

## WHAT IS THE DIFFERENCE BETWEEN LIFE MEANING AND LIFE PURPOSE?

First, let us define both of these terms. Understanding how they differ from each other can help us create alignment between what we do, why, and the impact that we want to have.

The emotional significance that we attach to people, experiences, and things is what we call "meaning." Meaning is the degree of importance that we ascribe to something. It's why we do what we do. Meaning doesn't exist on its own, it's something that we each create for ourselves and feel differently, and it's closely linked to motivation. In a coaching session, if someone said to you, "My life has no meaning." This isn't correct. It's just that some people never commit to pursuing anything in life that they view as being meaningful. It's a choice.

Purpose is the cumulative outcome of meaningful goals. Purpose is a long-term objective or guiding principle that is deemed meaningful. For example, your purpose is the impact you want to have in your relationships, throughout society, or on the world. You might decide that your purpose is giving people fish, teaching people to fish, or teaching people how to teach people how to fish. The relationship between your goals, meaning, and purpose is non-linear, which means that these three concepts simply reinforce one another.

If you want to find meaning in life, one way is to follow a meaningful purpose. For example, imagine you have a valuable life experience, like benefiting from a local food bank. You could use this experience to help you figure out a purpose for your future—like starting a new, bigger food bank. This way, you can help other people the same way someone once helped you. Does that make sense? Have you ever had an experience like this?

So as a Life Coach, how can you help people to find a sense of meaning and purpose in their lives? Whilst there's no universal formulation, there are a few principles worth considering.

The first principle is that experience matters. People look back on their past life experiences and adopt one of two attitudes: sorrow or optimism. The first (and most damaging) attitude is that of sorrow and self-pity. People who believe in the "hero myth" often spend their lives feeling sorry for themselves and waiting for someone to come along and miraculously fix everything. This way of thinking is not only irresponsible but completely ineffective. The second, more empowering attitude is optimism. An optimist can take something negative from their life, such as abuse or rejection, and use that pain to motivate themselves to support others who have had similar experiences.

The second principle is that rejection can be a positive. Rejection usually brings feelings of inadequacy to those who view it as a reflection of their self-worth. However, rejection can serve as a redirection toward more meaningful and purposeful ends. Rejection is rarely a lost opportunity and seldom happens to those who have not already committed to a serious life pursuit. Those who risk the most are usually those who are rejected the most. Rejection presents an opportunity to learn and redirect one's focus toward something more meaningful. Rejection strengthens inner resolve, integrity, and resilience, which are the key character attributes that allow people to achieve great things in life—which is, essentially, a reason why many people approach a Life Coach. Which is where you come in.

**PRINCIPLES INTO PRACTICE QUESTIONS:**

1. What are the factors or experiences that make your life meaningful today?
2. What purposes, goals, or pursuits would make your life even more meaningful?
3. Who is solely responsible for determining how meaningful your life is?
4. Who is solely responsible for determining how meaningful other people's lives are?

# HUMAN MEANING MAKING MACHINES

*"The meaning of life differs from person to person, from day to day, and hour to hour. What matters is not the meaning of life in general but rather the specific meaning of a person's life at any given moment."*

—VIKTOR FRANKL

Viktor Frankl was an Austrian neurologist, psychiatrist, philosopher, author, and Holocaust survivor. He was the founder of logotherapy, a school of psychotherapy that assumes the central human motivational force is a search for meaning. Frankl believed that humans are motivated by a "will to meaning"—a longing to find purpose in life. He suggested that life can have meaning even in the most adverse of circumstances and that the motivation for living comes from discovering that meaning.

One of Frankl's most memorable metaphors is the "human existential vacuum." If meaning is what we need, meaninglessness is an empty hole in our lives. Whenever you have a vacuum, of course, things rush in to fill it. Frankl suggests that one of the most evident signs of an existential vacuum in modern society is boredom. In his book *Man's Search for Meaning*, Frankl describes how he survived the Nazi death camps in Auschwitz, Germany. While many people may view Victor Frankl as a victim of circumstance, he defined freedom intriguingly: "To choose a response to a given set of circumstances is to choose a way to live." Frankl continued, saying, "Between stimulus and response, there is a space. In that space is our power to choose our response. In our response lies our growth and our freedom."

During his four years in a concentration camp, Viktor Frankl had every opportunity to overcome feelings of hopelessness and despair. In 1942, the Nazis sent him and his family to the Theresienstadt concentration camp and later transported those who survived to the infamous Auschwitz camp, where Frankl remained until his rescue. Despite the inhumane conditions that surrounded him, Frankl found meaning and documented everything he went through. In his now-famous work, *Man's Search for Meaning*, Frankl proved how finding meaning, even in the most horrific of circumstances, helped him to mentally and physically survive the process and aftermath of his experience. "Every day, every hour," he wrote, "offered the opportunity to make a decision, a decision which determined whether you would or would not submit to the powers which threatened to rob you of your very self, your inner freedom; which determined whether or not you would become the plaything of circumstance, renouncing freedom and dignity to become molded into the form of the typical inmate."

Faced with the concentration camp atrocities, Frankl was forced to decide whether to be crushed by his experiences or use them as a foundation on which to build his future. He ultimately chose the latter option and established a form of psychology called "logotherapy." According to this psychological theory, the search for meaning in life is the main motivation of most people. Like Frankl, we can each decide what our lives mean. Some people may feel crushed by their experiences, so much so that they bind themselves to patterns of unhealthy thinking and behavior. However, hardship bears no meaning until we decide it does.

Some of your coachees may need support in interpreting the meaning of their life experiences in a helpful way, but it's not your job to determine what this is. Life Coaches don't need to answer the question, "What is the meaning of life?" Instead, they ask their coachees, "What changes must you make today that will make your life more meaningful?"

**PRINCIPLES INTO PRACTICE QUESTIONS:**

1. What role might hardship have played in influencing what you view as purposeful in life?
2. What role have your past experiences played in shaping how you relate to certain people?
3. What aspects of your past could you leverage from to shape your own unique style and attitude toward delivering Life Coaching?

# THE POWER OF BEING RELATABLE

*"Relatability is often accepted as a criterion of value, even by people who might be expected to have more sophisticated tools at their disposal. The modern meaning of 'relatable' is to describe a character or situation in which an ordinary person might see himself reflected."*

—IRA GLASS

Let me tell you a story about an ex-soldier. After serving in the army for over a decade, he terminated his service, packed his bags, and started his train journey home toward re-entering civilian life. En route, he was plagued with doubts regarding his future. What would civilian life be like? What would he do for a living? Immersed in a world of daydreams, the soldier reached his hometown and started walking home, only to fall into a huge pothole. He wasn't hurt, but when he gathered his thoughts and pulled himself up, he was horrified to see how deep the pothole was. It was too deep for him to physically climb out of.

With no hope of getting out by himself, he sat on his bag and waited for someone to pass by. After a few hours, he heard footsteps, so he called for help. It just so happened that a therapist was passing by, who stopped, leaned over the hole, and called out, *"My goodness, what a nasty predicament you're in; is there anything I can do to help?"*

*"Yes,"* the soldier replied. *"I can't get out of this hole by myself. Can you help me?"*

"*Certainly, I'd be happy to!*" The therapist started the timer on his watch, pulled out a notebook from his pocket, and sat beside the hole. Then in a comforting voice, he asked, "*And how does it feel being in the hole? Have you experienced a traumatic experience like this before? And what is your relationship like with your parents?*" The soldier spoke about his feelings, relationship with his parents, and concerns about transitioning from the military to civilian life.

One hour of therapeutic discussion later, the soldier had forgotten what hole he was in and had now become focused on the myriad of emotions he was experiencing toward the different aspects of his "messed up" life.

A moment before the soldier began talking in more depth about his insecurities and occasional anger management issues, the therapist's watch beeped. The therapist immediately stood up and brushed the dirt from his trousers. "*That will be it for this week,*" he said. "*How about I stop by next week, and if you remain in a hole, we can speak again soon?*"

"*Okay. Thank you!*" said the soldier, not knowing what else to say. The ex-soldier was alone again until finally, an hour later, he heard more footsteps. After calling out for help once more, a doctor then leaned over the hole and said, "*Is there something I can do to help?*"

"*Yes,*" the soldier replied. "*I've fallen into a hole. Can you help me to get out, please?*"

The doctor smiled. "*I have just the solution you need,*" he said, reaching into his bag for a notepad and pen. He asked the soldier several questions about his health, symptoms, medications, and allergies. After the soldier responded, the doctor scribbled some words onto a page, tore it out, and dropped it in the hole. The soldier caught the paper and looked at what the doctor had written. "*What am I supposed to do with this?*" he asked.

"*Take this prescription once a day with food,*" the doctor advised. "*If you still have concerns about being in your hole after a few weeks, please get in touch with me again, and I'll be glad to write you a repeat prescription.*"

After four more hours of being in the hole alone, the soldier became desperate. The rain had started, and he was cold, tired, and hungry. Once again, he heard footsteps nearby and, this time, cried out for help with a greater depth of intensity to his tone. This time, a minister leaned over and looked into the hole. *"Oh, my poor child. What can I do to help you?"*

*"Please,"* the soldier exclaimed in desperation. *"Just help me out of this hole!"*

*"Of course,"* the minister replied. Then he knelt and began praying, *"Oh God, our Father, help this poor brother to find the inner strength and fortitude he needs to turn his situation around for the better. Amen."* After the prayer, the minister walked away and left the soldier alone, close to tears with fear and frustration.

Hours passed again before more footsteps came by; only, when he cried out for help, a familiar face leaned over the edge of the hole. It was one of his former army comrades, another ex-soldier who had discharged himself a few years prior. *"Mate,"* his friend cried out, *"What the heck are you doing down there?"*

*"I fell into this hole,"* the soldier replied, *"I've tried everything and can't get out. The therapists couldn't help me, the doctors couldn't do anything, and even a priest couldn't help."* Upon hearing the soldier's predicament, his old friend jumped into the hole with him.

*"What are you doing?"* the soldier who was stuck in the hole asked, *"Now we're both stuck down here!"* His old army friend smiled, winked, and replied, *"Don't worry, friend. I've been in this hole many times before, and I know how to get out."* Then, he picked up the soldier's bag and gestured for him to follow. *"Come on, let me help you out of here."*

People turn to Life Coaches after exhausting all other options. They have read the books, weighed the options, sought out different sources of pleasure, and come up wanting. They are in what I call "the hole" in life. Like the soldier, they are just looking for someone to give them some practical help to get them out. Most people love hearing inspiring stories of people who've overcome hurdles to get to where they are today. How resourceful you are when overcoming challenges will determine your effectiveness at helping others progress in life.

You don't have to have miracle cures or be light years ahead of your coachees to coach them or know all the answers: that's the beauty of coaching. All you need is your story, and all coachees need is someone who knows first-hand how to get out of the hole they're in. Sharing your journey with coachees can be a powerful tool in your coaching relationships, as it will make you seem more relatable, trustworthy, and grounded.

Back in 2007, I was the ex-soldier who fell in the hole, and I got stuck in it for years. At the time, my life seemed meaningless and without a sense of purpose. My hole was one of alcoholism, homelessness, financial destitution, and emotional bankruptcy, which no therapist, medical doctor, or priest was able to help me out of. And trust me, I tried all three options!

My life improved, however, on being befriended by Pete, a wise family man and wise role model at that stage in my life who, eventually, guided me out of the hole I was in one step at a time. Pete was instrumental in helping me develop a vision for who I wanted to become and how best to utilize my circumstances at the time. He helped me organize my thoughts, take responsibility for my actions, and set achievable goals for driving my life forward.

Pete didn't call himself a coach, nor did he have any ICF certification or accreditation. But Pete was a great coach because of his wisdom and experience. He could understand and relate to where I was in my life. Back in 2007, Pete knew exactly how to help me out of my hole because, twenty years earlier, someone else had compassionately helped him out of his.

**PRINCIPLES INTO PRACTICE QUESTION:**

1. How have the "holes" that you've historically found yourself in influenced you toward taking the life path that you are now currently on?
2. In what ways might your experience of falling into "holes" increase how relatable you are to those whom you eventually go on to Life Coach?

# COACHING FOR CULTIVATING AWARENESS

*"Self-awareness is the ability to focus on yourself and how your actions or thoughts align with your values. If you're highly self-aware, you can objectively evaluate yourself, self-regulate, and understand correctly how other people perceive you."*

—SHELLEY DUVAL

Self-awareness is like oxygen in your lungs: everyone has it, but how accurate this awareness is, is an entirely different matter. Most people believe they have self-awareness. They come to Life Coaches and list all their perceived "flaws": *I'm lazy; I'm unmotivated; I'm fat; I can't do anything right; I'm too depressed to get out of bed; I'm unlovable*; But having self-perceived flaws aren't the same thing as a person having profound self-awareness. For example, if you're dealing with someone who is struggling with their weight, their self-awareness isn't demonstrated by them acknowledging their weight issue; self-awareness is knowing WHY they over or under-eat and WHAT they need to do to change this behavior.

Self-awareness is more than skin-deep; it's about going beyond the basic understanding of a person and looking at how and why they are the way they are in the world. Self-aware people don't live on mindless auto-pilot; they know what they are doing, why they do what they do, know what they're feeling and why, and how they impact others.

Simply put, self-awareness involves understanding your own needs, desires, habits, and everything that makes up who you are. The more you know yourself, the better equipped you will be to navigate life transitions fluidly and adapt to seasons of unexpected change.

**THERE ARE TWO TYPES OF SELF-AWARENESS: PUBLIC AND PRIVATE**

As you know, self-awareness is developed through introspection, practice, and observation. Introspection involves reflecting on one's thoughts and feelings to gain an understanding of oneself. Practicing self-awareness can help people recognize their values and goals, which can give them heightened clarity when it comes to decision-making, acting, and behaving.

Public self-awareness refers to being conscious of how we might come across to other people through our attitudes, interactions, and behaviors. By being aware of these things, people tend to abide by social norms and conduct themselves in an acceptable manner. Though this can have benefits, it may also lead to self-consciousness. People who possess a high level of public self-awareness may become overly concerned with others' opinions about them.

Private self-awareness refers to the ability to reflect on one's inner state. Introspection is a form of private self-awareness where individuals examine their feelings and reactions with curiosity. For instance, if you feel tense while preparing for a meeting, recognizing this tension as nervousness about the meeting is an example of private self-awareness. However, when self-awareness becomes self-consciousness, people tend to hide certain aspects of themselves and develop an inauthentic persona *(otherwise known as a facade)*.

It's a common misconception that emotions should be suppressed or ignored. In reality, this can often do more harm than good. When we try to bottle up our emotions, they tend to come out in other, less productive ways. We might internalize them and end up feeling resentful, angry, and resigned. Or we might externalize them by blaming, discounting, or manipulating others. Obviously, neither of these approaches is helpful in the coaching process. Instead, it's important to acknowledge and accept our emotions, regardless of whether they are positive or negative. Only then can we begin to work through them in a constructive way.

Lack of self-awareness is a significant handicap for many new coaches who might have invested in a training course but who haven't yet invested in peer accountability and skill development. A study conducted by Adam D. Galinsky and colleagues at Kellogg School of Management found that often, as people enter into a position of influence or authority, they become more self-assured and confident. On the downside to this, they also tend to become more self-absorbed and less likely to consider the needs and perspectives of others. Again, this is an attitude that certainly doesn't serve the Life Coaching process.

As you know by now, Life Coaching is an intimate process through which a coach strives to help a coachee find clarity, direction, and a sense of purpose. In order for this to be successful, it is essential that a coach be self-aware. This means having the ability to look inward and reflect on one's thoughts, feelings, and behaviors. Without this self-awareness, a coach will find difficulty in asking appropriate questions that will encourage a coachee to do the same. Self-reflection is at the core of developing self-knowledge and insight, two things essential for anyone who hopes to create lasting change in their life. If a coach can't model this behavior, they will likely find it difficult to help their clients achieve the same.

Self-awareness allows us to see ourselves clearly, and it precedes all personal growth. Being self-aware means being conscious of different aspects of ourselves, such as traits, emotions, and behaviors. But is it something that can be learned? Yes, but understanding the following aspects of the self is necessary to achieve this:

## WHAT IS A SELF-CONCEPT?

Your self-concept is the way you view yourself, and it develops based on your interactions with others. Self-concept refers to how you evaluate yourself and your identity and how you compare or contrast yourself to others. Though similar, self-concept differs from self-esteem. Self-concept is your self-perception, while self-esteem is based on how you value that perception. Carl Rogers, a psychologist, theorist, and clinician, asserted that people's self-perception leads to the evolution of their personality, attitude, worldviews, and behaviors, which in turn, feed back into how people see themselves. People usually have a mix of positive and negative self-concepts. Here are some examples.

EXAMPLES OF POSITIVE (IDENTITY) SELF-CONCEPTS:
- A young person sees herself as being compassionate and caring.
- A man views himself as honest, hardworking, and trustworthy.
- A woman sees herself as a supportive friend to her husband.
- A man identifies as growing in integrity and character.

EXAMPLES OF NEGATIVE (IDENTITY) SELF-CONCEPTS:
- A person sees herself as incompetent and uncoordinated.
- A man views himself as unskilled, talentless and worthless.
- A woman perceives herself as a detestable spouse and friend.
- A man over-identifies with his sexual orientation or skin color.

Most people have multiple domain-specific self-concepts that constitute their collective self-concept (identity)—and some will always be more useful than others. Most people act according to how they view themselves (self-concept). So, when coaching, you might need to help some people shape a positive self-concept for themselves that doesn't restrict them unduly and will motivate them to unhesitantly work hard to attain their goals or objectives.

**WHAT IS SELF-WORTH?**

Self-concept is how you identify ("I am a good man"), while self-esteem reflects the opinion you have of yourself ("I'm proud to be a good man"). In other words, self-concept addresses the question: Who am I? Whereas self-esteem speaks to how you feel about how you identify. The dictionary defines self-worth as "the sense of one's worth as a person."

Your self-esteem will be determined by the value you place on yourself (your self-worth), as your self-worth will be founded on the virtues you reflect throughout your daily interactions, such as how honest, sincere, creative, kind, or generous you choose to be. Although other people's opinions of you might matter sometimes, your self-perception is what will have the most significant impact on your self-worth and, consequently, your self-esteem.

I was an amateur rugby player who viewed himself as "pro" in my early twenties. In reality, much of this false self-concept was used to hide my lack of experience and physical strength. On the rugby field, I didn't survive long. An elite group of Fijians battered me hard in my first full game, leaving me broken-boned and bruised. Reality is rarely pleasant, but it can push us to look within and confront our inner demons. Back then, I overcompensated for my low self-esteem by inflating my ego on the rugby field—it took two black eyes and a broken collarbone for me to accept that I was hiding behind a façade of self-appeasing lies.

When coaching, you can identify people with self-worth issues when they focus more on creating outcomes rather than the coaching process. Many people confuse net worth for their self-worth, and mistake their talents as a reflection of their intrinsic value. But these things aren't true. While developing skills and abilities can aid the self-worth discovery process, understanding how to put skills and abilities to good use is how self-esteem grows.

## WHAT IS SELF-ESTEEM?

Self-esteem is determined by how a person sees themselves in any given moment. Years ago, I coached a man who was unemployed and looking for work. When we started working together, I could see that the man had no confidence due to over-identifying with negative terminologies which reflected his circumstances, such as "unemployed freeloader."

People who lack self-esteem usually doubt their character and question their abilities. As a result, they are less likely to risk attempting new things. A low sense of self-worth often leads to decreased confidence levels and can cause people to feel stuck in fear and inaction.

I've read many self-help books and psychology texts over the years, and I remember reading a passage that said, "People who want to feel better about themselves must work hard to improve their self-esteem." This isn't true. Self-worth always precedes self-esteem, and by this, I mean that it is not psychologically possible for anyone to feel better about themselves without first committing to the process of self-improvement and growth. Individuals who can identify their own growth, over time, will place greater value on themselves and their future growth potential. This helps people to increase their self-esteem and build confidence. It is a positive feedback loop that first starts with growing in self-awareness.

To conclude, personal growth is difficult to achieve for those without a healthy self-concept. Self-awareness lets people identify aspects of their character and psychology that need improving. Life Coaching will often involve helping people to see themselves clearly, quantify who they are, and also who they can work toward becoming. Without a clear picture of their growth potential, many people will never reach it. It's by committing to the process of personal growth and development that self-esteem will eventually blossom.

**PRINCIPLES INTO PRACTICE QUESTIONS:**

1. In what ways do you see that self-awareness enables you to cultivate strong self-esteem?
2. In what ways do you see the interconnectedness of self-worth and your self-esteem?

# EQ: A KEY PREDICTOR OF SUCCESS IN LIFE

*"If your emotional abilities aren't in hand, if you don't have self-awareness, if you are not able to manage your emotions, if you can't empathize and have effective relationships, then no matter how smart you are, you are not going to get very far."*

—DANIEL GOLEMAN

Emotional intelligence is the cornerstone for any successful Life Coaching journey. Invest in yourself to gain the right skills and tools to have meaningful conversations with your coachees and make a lasting impact on their lives. With an understanding of emotions, you can help others recognize their emotional triggers and manage them maturely when needed.

Daniel Goleman, the author of *Emotional Intelligence*, believes that emotional intelligence (EQ) is an important factor that determines people's success in life. EQ refers to the capacity people have to comprehend and manage their emotions maturely. It is a life skill that enables people to exercise effective social skills, empathy, and self-control while engaging with others, rather than their personality traits or habitual patterns of behavior.

If you have never developed your emotional intelligence, you might find it difficult to understand how someone else is feeling in a social situation. This lack of understanding could lead to ineffective interactions and difficulty relating to others. It's important to invest time in developing your emotional intelligence to avoid these challenges. So why is EQ important?

EQ plays a crucial role in maintaining good interpersonal communication by enabling you to connect with others on a more personal level. It helps you establish trustworthy relationships, handle difficult conversations, and find solutions in times of conflict. Therefore, EQ is vital for Life Coaches who want to make a positive impact in their relationships.

Typical Qualities of Emotionally Intelligent People Tend to Include:

- The ability to separate their perspective from reality.
- Awareness of their personal strengths and limitations.
- Self-assuredness, social confidence, and influence.
- The ability to let go of mistakes and learn from them.
- Tendency to accept and embrace seasons of change.
- A strong sense of curiosity and compassion for others.
- Sensitivity toward the needs and wants of other people.
- The ability to regulate emotions in difficult situations.
- Tendency to manage criticism and accept responsibility.
- Ability to read and interpret social situations accurately.

Is it possible to learn Emotional Intelligence? Absolutely. By using various methods on your own or through training and Life Coaching, you can improve your EQ for faster and more significant results. Emotional intelligence comprises emotional perception, emotional reasoning, emotional comprehension, and emotional regulation. Each of these elements contributes to an individual's overall emotional quotient. The capacity to recognize and label emotions in ourselves and those around us is known as emotional perception. By using our emotions as a foundation for decision-making, we can reason with them. Recognizing emotions necessitates comprehending their origins and how they affect our thoughts and actions. To deal with emotions, we must control them and react well to our circumstances.

Emotionally intelligent people know that, while emotions can be powerful, they are only temporary. Individuals with mature emotional intelligence consider the perspectives, experiences, and emotions of other people and use this information to discern why people behave as they do. This ability allows them to remain calm in tough situations, understand the cause of people's problems, solve complex challenges, and build healthy relationships; all of which are essential for a Life Coach to become socially influential.

To enhance your emotional intelligence, follow these four stages of self-improvement: self-awareness, self-discipline, social awareness, and social intelligence. Proficiency in all of these areas will help you adapt to coaching scenarios, connect with coachees, and ask suitable questions that can facilitate their growth. Usually, self-reflection, along with discipline, helps individuals to build EQ and resilience. With improved EQ, you will be better equipped to handle difficult conversations and support coachees in achieving their goals.

**SELF-AWARENESS MUST COME FIRST**

Without self-awareness, people are ignorant of their thoughts, the causes of their emotions, and the motivations for their behaviors. This lack of understanding can lead to a host of problems, both personal and interpersonal. For example, someone who is not attuned to the way their words might be interpreted by others is more likely to communicate in a way that regularly offends people. On a personal level, unaware people will often make the same mistakes over and over again because they do not understand the relationship between their actions and outcomes. In contrast, a self-aware individual will step back and reflect on their actions to gain insight into why they are experiencing life in a certain way. With this knowledge comes the ability to make positive changes in one's life. Thus, self-awareness is the initial stage of EQ and also the first stride toward all personal development.

**SELF-DISCIPLINE COMES SECOND**

Any area of life that you want to see improvement in requires self-discipline. Self-discipline is the engine that drives decisiveness, inner resilience, patience, and consistency. It's what challenges you to remain loyal to your commitments and persevere through challenging times. With self-discipline, all things are possible. Self-discipline begins with taking control of your thoughts. If you don't control what you think, you can't control what you do. Self-discipline allows you to think first and act afterward. It is often said that we cannot help others until we have helped ourselves. This sentiment is particularly true when it comes to Life Coaching. In order to effectively help other people achieve their goals, a Life Coach must exemplify the virtues and traits that they hope to instill in their coachees. Just as a grossly obese person could not congruently offer dietary or fitness advice, a Life Coach cannot authentically help someone develop discipline in an area of their life if the coach is not already disciplined in that same area.

## SOCIAL AWARENESS COMES THIRD

Awareness of oneself is the foundation from which social awareness grows. As you become more in tune with your own thoughts, feelings, and motivations, you will automatically become more attuned to the thoughts, feelings, and motivations of others. This process starts with learning to empathize with people, which requires listening to their perspectives and understanding their experiences. With self-discipline, you can experience people objectively and apart from your prejudices or biases. With this discipline under your belt, you can put yourself in someone else's shoes and visualize how they see the world. As your social awareness grows, you'll find it easier to communicate with people from different backgrounds and build connected relationships.

## SOCIAL INTELLIGENCE ALWAYS COMES LAST

Your ability to manage relationships will play a crucial role in determining your quality of life. Social intelligence is necessary for engaging in respectful conversations, positively impacting individuals, and understanding the intentions behind their words and actions. Discernment involves differentiating between truth and lies and right and wrong. It involves accurately judging which questions to ask and which not to ask. Discernment is key to recognizing individuals for who they are and fostering healthy relationships.

Social intelligence involves knowing how to say the "right" words in the "right" way at the right" time. Social intelligence entails empathizing with others, listening to them attentively, seeing people without prejudice, and consistently behaving in a manner that is honest and genuine. Socially intelligent people pay attention to how their communication style, perspective, and persona is impacting on others. A person's social faculty refers to their ability to be aware of how they come across to others and adapt their behavior accordingly. This allows them to maintain healthy relationships and influence the people around them.

Emotional intelligence isn't an area that a skilled Life Coach would typically primarily focus on. EQ should just be a natural byproduct of the Life Coaching process. As the person being coached talks openly and honestly about themselves, what they want out of life, and their internal struggles and challenges, EQ starts to develop naturally. Your opportunity as the Life Coach is to indirectly facilitate this process. Just as a pebble can create waves in a pond, your words and actions will create ripples of impact in the lives of other people.

**PRINCIPLES INTO PRACTICE QUESTIONS:**

Too often, people focus on their negative personality traits instead of their positive ones. Focusing on the positives allows us to appreciate our value and worth more accurately.

How would you fill in the blanks on the following five statements?

1. _____ is something I do that adds value to other people.
2. _____ is one of my main strengths that I often underutilize.
3. My ability to _____ is regularly respected by other people.
4. _____ is what allows me to impact other people the most.
5. _____ will allow me to achieve my goals as a Life Coach.

# SEVEN LEVELS OF HUMAN CONSCIOUSNESS

*"With self-awareness you grow more intelligent. In awareness you learn, in self-awareness you learn about yourself. Of course, you can only learn what you are not. To know what you are, you must go beyond the mind. Awareness is the point at which the mind reaches out beyond itself into reality. In awareness you seek not what pleases, but what is true."*

—SRI NISARGADATTA MAHARAJ

As you know by now, Life Coaching should aid people in furthering their personal growth, setting goals, achieving goals, growing in awareness, and achieving their potential. Another term for awareness is consciousness, which refers to the understanding you have of yourself and your surroundings. This awareness varies from person to person. Consciousness is a mysterious power that every human being has. Philosophers are still trying to explain it, psychologists are still trying to understand it, and many people don't even know that it exists.

There are seven different levels of human consciousness, each of which represents a different stage in our personal growth and development. As a Life Coach, it's important to be aware of these different levels so that you can gauge how effective your Life Coaching is in helping your coachees make sensible decisions that let them move forward in their lives.

**LEVEL 1. VICTIM CONSCIOUSNESS**

It is interesting to observe how different people react when they encounter difficulties in their lives. Some people immediately assume that they are the victims of some outside forces, while others take responsibility for their actions and work to improve their situations. This difference can be seen as a spectrum, with victim consciousness at one end and empowered consciousness at the other. People who fall at the victim end of the spectrum tend to have a general apathy toward life. They believe that any difficulties they encounter are due to other people and frequently engage in the blame game. In contrast, people with empowered consciousness take an active role in shaping their lives. They understand that they are ultimately responsible for their own happiness and take steps to create the life they want.

**LEVEL 2. CONFLICT CONSCIOUSNESS**

The second level of consciousness is conflict consciousness. In this state, people become aware of wrongs that they assume have been done to them. They are passionate about rectifying these wrongs or fixing the problems they see around them. This level of consciousness can be a powerful force for good in the world. It can motivate people to stand up against injustice and fight for what is right. However, it can also lead to division and conflict. When people are fixated on their own point of view, they can lose sight of the common good. They may become so focused on winning an argument or proving themselves right that they are willing to sacrifice relationships and even their own happiness. For those who wish to live in a more harmonious world, it is important to be aware of the dangers of conflict consciousness and to find ways to transcend it.

**LEVEL 3. RESPONSIBILITY CONSCIOUSNESS**

William James once said, "The greatest discovery of every generation is that human beings can alter their lives by altering their attitudes of mind." This certainly holds true when it comes to responsibility consciousness. When people reach this level of awareness, they realize that their problems are theirs alone. This is a major shift in thinking, as prior to this level, people would have blamed others for their problems or refused to take responsibility for themselves. At this level of consciousness, people recognize that they are the only ones who can resolve their conflicts and pursue their goals. This level of consciousness is empowering, as it allows people to take control of their lives and create the future they desire for themselves. However, it can be daunting, as it requires people to set goals, make difficult decisions, work diligently, and confront their challenges directly. Nevertheless, the rewards are worth it, for when people seize control of their lives, they often find that they can achieve anything they commit to.

**LEVEL 4. CONCERN CONSCIOUSNESS**

The fourth level of consciousness is known as concern consciousness. This is a state of mind where people commit to serving a purpose greater than just themselves. People who reach this level are typically driven by a desire to make a positive difference in the world. They may use their past experiences to help other people or leverage their strengths to build something meaningful or worthwhile. In many ways, this is an exciting stage of the coaching relationship. The coachee is typically passionate about making a difference and is eager to use their experiences to benefit others. As the coach, it's rewarding to support this level of mindset growth and development, as those who reach this level of consciousness will often go on to achieve great things and make a positive impact in some way.

**LEVEL 5. RECONCILIATION CONSCIOUSNESS**

Most people only ever scratch the surface of their potential. They live their lives within the confines of what they think is possible, never questioning the box they have put themselves in. But there are those rare few who dare to push themselves to new heights. These are the people who step into reconciliation consciousness—a state of mind where they learn to collaborate with others for the benefit of all parties. In this level of consciousness, people accept others' talents and weaknesses, and they play to their own strengths for a shared common purpose. As a result, they are able to achieve things that few people believe possible. They become a force to be reckoned with and united in their quest for growth. This is the power of reconciliation consciousness. It is a state of mind that can change the world!

**LEVEL 6. SYNTHESIS CONSCIOUSNESS**

The sixth level of consciousness is synthesis consciousness. This mindset is characterized by profound inner peace and empowerment. Many people live in constant stress, always toiling to meet their goals. But synthesis consciousness is the opposite of this. People who reach this level of consciousness still set goals and create plans, but only because they can, not because they need to. This deep inner peace comes from the realization that they cannot control the outcomes of their efforts. They work hard toward a goal, knowing they cannot determine the results. And it is this knowledge that gives them peace. While it may seem like an impossible state of mind to achieve, synthesis consciousness is something that all people are able to reach. It is only through mastering their mindset that people can hope to attain it.

**LEVEL 7. CREATIVE FIRE CONSCIOUSNESS**

The seventh and last level of consciousness is creative fire consciousness. This mindset is characterized by pure, raw, and unabridged creativity. The mindset is liberated in every way possible, and a person is committed to one meaningful, long-term purpose. Creative fire consciousness operates outside of reservation or fear and is fully, authentically expressive. People who push their way through the seven levels of awareness can enter this stage of life, knowing that any day could be their last, which leaves no minute available for wasting. This level of consciousness is a place where people are excited about what they're creating, without attachment to any outcome. They know that the process is just as important as the end result. When this highest level of consciousness is reached, people look back on their life and see how their every life experience brought them to this moment—

grateful for all of the ups, downs, and bumps along the way. People who arrive at this level of consciousness have made building, creating, and making a difference their only priority in life.

These seven levels are the stepping stones that all people must take toward becoming elevated in their thinking and fruitful in their action-taking. This teaching is an important one that isn't commonly taught in most coaching training courses. By guiding people through the process of looking higher and thinking bigger, you will make a transformational impact in anyone's life whom you coach.

**PRINCIPLES INTO PRACTICE QUESTIONS:**

1. Which of the seven levels of consciousness do you see yourself as being at currently?
2. What new disciplines might you need to develop to move up a level?
3. How might understanding these levels of consciousness inform your Life Coaching?

# THE HUMAN BEING IDENTITY CRISIS

*"Most people are parts of others. Their thoughts are other people's thoughts, their lives a mimicry of other people's behaviors, their passions little more than a quotation."*

—OSCAR WILDE

Who are you? It's a question we all must ask at some point in life. And it's no easy question to answer. Self-identification is a process that we all undergo as we grow, mature, and develop throughout life. It is how we make sense of ourselves and the world, and it's what lets us connect with the people groups we are most drawn to. Self-identification might begin with race, skin color, social status, net worth, or sexual orientation, but it cannot end there.

As English philosopher James Allen once wrote, *"As a man thinks, so he is; as he continues to think, so he remains."* This is never more apparent than in how people identify. Have you ever met someone who identified as "worthless" and acted for years as if this were true? A woman who identifies as powerless might never make bold decisions. Someone who identifies in sexuality might end up over-obsessing with their gender for a lifetime. Identity is often arrived at by the way in which people interpret and use their life experiences. If you view yourself as able and competent, you are more likely to take risks and pursue goals. On the other hand, if you see yourself as dumb, powerless, or unworthy, you are more likely to give up easily when the going gets tough. The good news is that, by growing aware of the words you use to self-identify, you can break free from unhelpful self-labeling, see yourself in a more accurate light, and open up new growth opportunities for your future.

All identity is in relationship to something else. People draw their identities out of their environments and life experiences. A person can only identify as "good"—"I'm a good person"—if they have first experienced what they perceive as a "bad" person. Life-defining moments such as unexpected success, rejection, loss or trauma are formative. How closely a person identifies with something is what shapes who they think they are. For example, if someone associates with a country, they might identify as that nationality; if they associate with a preferred sexuality, they might identify or obsess with that sexuality. While identity can be a powerful statement for many, there's also an insidious side to it. As an example, a woman who identifies as a "mother" may feel guilty if she doesn't spend every waking minute with her children. However, if she includes other aspects of herself in her identity—"wife," "business woman" or "friend"—she'll likely feel more balanced. A man who bases his self-worth on his career may feel like a failure if he becomes unemployed. However, if he also identifies with the other roles he fulfills—"husband," "father" or "community leader"—again, he will likely feel more balanced and self-assured.

By expanding their "self-labeling" to include a variety of other traits and characteristics, people give themselves the freedom to pursue goals without worrying about straying from who they think they are "supposed" to be. Without self-awareness, many people naively identify with abstract ideas, inconsistent emotions, or random life experiences that undermine their ability to become more. By growing aware of the words they use to identify with, people can divorce their perceived limitations and start living growth-oriented lives.

While some identity labels empower people, others have the opposite effect. The reality is that all people become who they choose to be and carry an identity around with them that sits in the balance of who they are, how they see themselves, and how they think other people see them. Identity can be weak or robust; but often, it's only in moments of truth—when forced to confront themselves—that people gain insights into their true potential.

| | |
|---|---|
| I'm smart. | I'm non-binary. |
| I'm artistic. | I'm a criminal. |
| I'm Muslim. | I'm an alcoholic. |
| I'm athletic. | I'm widowed. |
| I'm a mother. | I'm uneducated. |
| I'm Christian. | I'm different. |
| I'm a Democrat. | I'm a soldier. |
| I'm heterosexual. | I'm a candlestick maker. |
| I'm Conservative. | I'm homosexual. |
| I'm happy-go-lucky. | I'm capable of anything. |

As a coach, one of the most important things you can do is help your coachees to take responsibility for being who they really are. This can be a challenge because many people never take the time to think about who they are or what makes them unique. As a result, some of your coachees may struggle to answer a simple open-ended question such as, "Tell me about who you are?" When asked this question, like a deer caught in the headlights, some people will respond with confusion, "What do you mean?" or "What do you want to know?" Often, people will reply with generic statements that still provide no insight. This represents the human identity crisis. People struggle not because they don't know how to answer but because they genuinely don't know who they are and how they fit in with society.

Most people experience some form of identity crisis in their lives, and for the vast majority, articulating that experience can be challenging. Many of your future coachees might over-identify with negative characteristics, traits, or nouns that limit their growth capacity. Your opportunity is to help them recognize their ability to outgrow who they were yesterday and commit to the journey of identifying and expressing themselves in responsibility, integrity, maturity, and creativity today. It is nearly impossible to go through life without encountering adversity. Challenges and hardships are an inevitable part of the human experience, and how we respond to them says a lot about our character.

People who are able to persevere in the face of adversity and come out stronger on the other side are said to have "good character." While some people are born with qualities that allow them to respond well to difficult situations, character is something that all people can grow in over the course of a lifetime. And unlike many other things in life, growing in character is significantly more empowering than deciding to over-identify with singular terminologies and otherwise restrictive nouns. After all, when our character is tested, it is our core values and principles that will see us through—not our labels. In the end, character is something that we all have the power to cultivate, regardless of our circumstances or background.

In his book, *On Becoming a Person*, psychologist Carl Rogers suggested, "The most powerful motivational function of the human mind is the need to be true to one's identity." In other words, people don't achieve major life goals by accident. People who live confident, wealthy, and fulfilling lives do so because they hold themselves to high identity standards. People who see themselves as overweight are likely to stay overweight. People who see themselves as wealthy are likely to stay wealthy. And people who consider themselves principled will do whatever it takes to uphold their integrity.

A story that illustrates this point is that of the circus elephant. When breeding animals in captivity and showcasing them in circuses wasn't frowned upon, a baby elephant was born into a circus training arena. From the moment he could stand on his legs, the circus master chained him to an anchored stake in the floor. The baby elephant would try to break free with all his might, but at that stage of his life, he physically wasn't strong enough. So, after weeks and months of trying, he gave up. But as the years passed, the baby elephant grew into an adult who was more than capable of breaking free from his restraints and marching his way out of the circus, but he never did. Why? Because the elephant had been conditioned to not even try. His memories of being chained up as a baby had cemented his "inability" to break free. "It's who I am; that's just how life is for me." The elephant continued to be trapped by his identity beliefs, certain that he wasn't strong enough to escape.

Most people have a solidified sense of identity by the time they reach adulthood (even if this identity isn't always accurate). People typically adopt the beliefs and values of their parents, family, and peer groups. For better or worse, these become our truth, and we base our lives around them. The challenge comes when people want to change their lives for the better, but their identity beliefs hold them back.

When your coachee says, "I am...," this presents an ideal opportunity to ask questions and determine if this identity positively serves them. It stands to reason that those who raise their standards and hold themselves accountable to a more responsible, integral, creative, and wiser identity will start seeing real, lasting change in their lives. The kind of questions a Life Coach can ask at this stage of a coaching conversation are reflective in nature and intended to provoke thought about what matters in life. "What do you want your legacy to be?" "What kind of person do you want to be remembered as?" These kinds of questions can help a person to realign their identity with their goals and create lasting change.

**PRINCIPLES INTO PRACTICE QUESTIONS:**
1. What terms or phrases do you use to define yourself narrowly or conservatively?
2. How does deductive self-identification impact your readiness to pursue positive goals?
3. How might deductive self-identification impact your coachee's readiness to pursue goals?
4. What noun virtues could you use to identify in a liberated or unrestrictive way? *(For example: "I identify in integrity, kindness, generosity, honesty, creativity or sincerity.")*

# PSYCHOANALYTICAL IDENTITY COACHING

*"One of life's primal situations: the game of hide and seek. Oh, the thrill of hiding while the others come looking for you, the terror of being discovered, but what panic when, after a long search, the others abandon you! You mustn't hide too well. You mustn't be too good at the game. The player must never be bigger than the game itself."*

—JEAN BAUDRILLARD

Coaching is less of a process-based methodology than it is a healthy, connected relationship. There are many skills to learn as a Life Coach, but the real key is your ability to initiate truth-centered discussions and authentic relationships with people.

Are you aware of what the game of hide-and-seek is? Hide-and-seek is a popular children's game in which at least two players conceal themselves in a given environment to then be sought and found by one or more seekers. Each individual game is played by one chosen player who will count to a predetermined number with his or her eyes closed while all of the other players find creative and innovative places to hide.

You might be wondering why I am discussing this popular age-old children's game. Well, individuals who fail to develop a healthy sense of identity in their younger years can end up playing a "grown-up" version of hide-and-seek throughout much of their adult life. People often use their future life pursuits, historical lifetime achievements, self-quantifying identity terminologies, their sexual orientation, professional persona, celebrity status, net worth, career success, academic qualifications, and sometimes even their diagnosed or self-diagnosed mental disorders to hide who they truly are behind. This phenomenon is often referred to as the "masks people wear," or the "facades people hide behind." Much of what you see initially in people who you don't yet know can be a mask-wearing social persona—with an insecure human being hiding somewhere in the background who's desperately waiting to be noticed and "found." As a new Life Coach, it can be useful for you to understand this because the goals that some people will claim to be passionate about pursuing will serve no greater purpose than stroking their ego and fortifying the mask that they're hiding behind.

**WHAT MASK OR SOCIAL PERSONA DO YOU HIDE BEHIND?**

Who do you know who regularly conducts themselves in an overtly false or superficial way? Do you ever do this? If so, in what contexts do you conduct yourself in a false or superficial way, and why? In what contexts do you remove all masks and just be fully yourself? Some people reading this will be used to living their life without wearing masks, and for others contemplating this idea for the first time, it might seem both provocative and challenging.

The masks and facades people hide behind are just socially serving constructs. A social construct is a persona that exists not in any objective reality but as a result of assisting human-to-human interactions. Human beings hide behind their social constructs until they decide to mature their identity and base their personality upon virtuous characteristics rather than ego-edifying behavioral patterns. Some typical examples of social constructs could be masculinity and wealth. It is often easier to see how masculinity could be a social construct than it is to see how wealth is also one. Masculinity would not exist were it not for human interaction; therefore, groups of people must come together in agreement that masculinity exists and then also agree on what masculinity is. Without this agreement, masculinity cannot exist.

In order for a person to decide whether wealth is a worthwhile life pursuit, they must decide whether they like how the idea of wealth is constructed in their mind or not.

Another example could be young homosexual men who have been bold enough to "come out of their closets." Within days, weeks, or months, these men might come together and start collectively frequenting LGBTQ nightclubs, attending gay pride events, and before long, some of them will be wearing make-up, high-heeled shoes, dancing around flying rainbow flags and talking in an overtly "feminized" voice. Granted, some people might take this example as inappropriate, but others will just see yet another socially constructed pattern of behavior in motion. Human beings are social animals before all things and will readjust their attitudes, priorities, goals, and life ambitions in hope of being socially accepted.

Another example could be the aggressive world leader who invades nations with the intent to prove to the world how "powerful" he or she is. Or the middle-aged man who, after years of bodybuilding, still isn't content with his body mass. Or the multi-billionaire business mogul who doesn't yet have enough money or material possessions. Or the men and women who spend a fortune on surgically modifying their physical bodies to be seen as more beautiful or socially acceptable. Yes, even beauty is a social construct. But all of this is just a society-wide, worldwide game of "grown-up" hide and seek. There are many other examples I could give, but you are now most likely starting to understand the principle.

The purpose of Life Coaching certainly isn't to make psychoanalytic assumptions about what reasons might underpin the masks that people wear, the personas they display, or the superficial goals they claim to be passionate about pursuing. But it is important that you understand that social constructionism exists—and ALL people buy into it to some degree or another. The social constructs we each accept as valid determine what life pursuits, attitudes, and general patterns of behavior we accept as being "normal."

So, why is this important for you to know? This is important for you to know as a Life Coach because some of the goals people set will be more geared up to serve their fake social persona than their authentic innermost priorities and needs. Please allow yourself a few moments to ponder over this big idea. Some of the goals people set will be more geared up to serve their fake social personas than their authentic innermost priorities and needs. Please allow yourself a few more moments to ponder over this REALLY BIG idea.

Be prepared to take some of the goals people claim to be passionate about pursuing at face value in the same way you might take people's fake social personas at face value. So what is the purpose of this chapter, then? It is to simply raise your awareness that the goals some people claim to be passionate about pursuing are not the same kind of goals that will give their lives a true sense of meaningful direction and purpose.

There's an old saying that goes, "Those who play silly games win silly prizes." This expression means that those who take part in valueless life pursuits will win valueless prizes. Normally, this phrase is used to refer to people who make reckless lifestyle decisions. And in the same way, people who commit to living their life in a superficial way might end up achieving goals and prizes that typically aren't the same ones that would otherwise bring them the satisfaction, fulfillment, and inner peace that genuinely motivates them. Any goal a person sets that isn't propagated by something they truly value will unlikely be compelling enough to inspire them to fulfill it. So, while a shallow person might find themselves winning meaningless accolades, ultimately, they won't find contentment until they commit to pursuing something with greater depth or substance. On the other hand, if a person is motivated by something they believe in and value deeply, then they're more likely to not only achieve their goals but also feel a sense of satisfaction and inner peace—even if their accomplishments aren't externally recognized or lauded by others. So, while the superficial pursuit of empty prizes might appear to succeed on a surface level, in reality, it's a shallow and unfulfilling existence that always leaves people craving for something more.

# LOOKING FOR THE ANSWERS WITHIN

*"Look inside yourself for the answers—you're the only one who knows what's best for you. Everybody else is only guessing."*
—CHARLES DE LINT

This chapter wraps up this section of the handbook, and I'd like to share a story that conveys an idea to carry with you into section three. People throughout the centuries have questioned the meaning of life—from the Sumerians to the Mayans and from modern scientists and philosophers to believers and atheists.

Until this moment in history, humans had depended on the gods to reveal the truths of humanity. However, as societies began to advance, the gods were afraid that they would start to find these truths independently and would no longer need the gods. The gods summoned one another to a great assembly to discuss what to do with the truths. After much debate, they decided humanity's truths would need to be hidden.

Artemis, the goddess of the hunt and nature, offered to hide the truths in the depths of the deepest forest, inhabited by ferocious crocodiles, giant baboons, poisonous spiders, and venomous snakes. If they were not enough of a deterrent, then the savage tribesmen would surely keep them out. No man would dare venture there.

"No, no, that won't do. That won't do at all." A voice came from the edges of the assembly hall. A squat, balding man with a crooked brow walked toward the great Zeus. It was Koalemos, the often-forgotten God of stupidity.

Artemis rolled her eyes and gave a long sigh at his approach. "And why won't it work?" she demanded, her eyes red with anger. She raised her hand to strike down the imbecile. "Perhaps I should turn you into a rabbit and feed you to my dogs."

"Let him speak," commanded Zeus. His voice shook the assembly hall. Artemis, scowling in contempt for the lesser God, reluctantly lowered her hand.

Koalemos stepped forward. "I don't think that will work. Man is too smart for that."

"And whose fault is that?" murmured Artemis as she turned her back to the council.

Koalemos let out a nervous laugh. "Yes, well, I just wanted to point out that man has built large boats to sail deep into the jungles and large machines to trample down the trees. Man no longer fears nature."

Poseidon then stepped forward, tapping his trident down with booming thunder. "If men do not fear nature, then perhaps he will fear the depths of the unknown. Entrust the truths of humanity with me, and I will bury them in the deepest depths of the sea."

A commotion broke out among the council. Hades scoffed at his brother Neptune. "No one fears water. Allow me to bury them in the earth where no hand can touch them."

Angered by his brother's insolence, Poseidon thrust his trident toward Hades. Amid the commotion, Koalemos pushed aside the trident and stepped between Poseidon and Hades, not having enough sense to stay quiet. "No, that won't do either," he said.

Dumfounded, both Hades and Poseidon stared down at the little God as he continued to speak. "Man is much too smart for that. He has vessels that can carry him to the deepest reaches of the sea. And he fears not the Earth. Man has dug to the greatest of depths to retrieve Earth's riches." "Then what do you suggest?" snapped Hades.

"That's the real conundrum, isn't it?" Koalemos replied. The old God scratched his head as he paced the floor, drawing the council's full attention, including Zeus. He paused several times in his pacing to speak, only to stop himself and begin again with the pacing and head-scratching. Just as Zeus was about to lose patience and zap the impudent imbecile from existence, Koalemos exclaimed while thrusting his finger in the air, "That's it!"

Zeus and the council leaned in to hear what suggestions he might have. Koalemos scanned the crowd as if unaware they were waiting for him to speak. "Well, isn't it obvious?" he said. He leaned against Poseidon's trident with a grin. "We hide the truths in mankind."

Poseidon pulled his trident away, making Koalemos stumble. "What do you expect from the god of stupidity?" he scoffed. "Strike the fool from our presence. I'm tired of him."

"Just a minute," said Athena. As the goddess of wisdom, she had been silent until now, understanding that true knowledge is found less by talking and more by listening. "Even a fool can stumble upon wisdom while fumbling in the dark."

Zeus turned his attention to his daughter. "Please, share your wisdom, Athena."

Athena took a moment to compose her thoughts. "Koalemos is correct about mankind's advancements. Man has spent millennia conquering nearly every frontier around him. If we placed the truths anywhere else, even to the reaches of Selene's throne upon the moon, man would eventually find a way to reach it. Thus is the pride of man. He has conquered every frontier set before him but has neglected to seek that which lies within."

The council was quiet. All understood the wisdom of Athena.

"It is decided," said Zeus. "We shall place the truths of humanity within man's heart and see if he can find them in those depths where few in their lifetime even dare to tread."

I share this story to illustrate a point that Life Coaches need to remember when working with coachees. Human beings tend to hunt for life's solutions almost everywhere except within themselves. A typical coachee will seek answers to questions troubling them and look to you for help. But it is not the role of a Life Coach to give solutions or provide answers. You may think you have an answer to their problem, but this is your answer, not theirs. The Life Coach's role is to help the coachee orient themselves toward sourcing the answers they need—for themselves. By doing this, coachees become less dependent on your Life Coaching guidance, more self-sufficient, and reliant on their own inner compass.

# SECTION TWO SUMMARY

Coaching is less of a methodology than it is a wholesome, interconnected relationship. There are many skills to learn and tools available as an aspiring Life Coach, but the real key is your ability to initiate truth-centered discussions and build trust-based relationships with people. You will work with individuals who each have a different set of circumstances, goals, passions, interests, self-sabotaging tendencies, and motivations for wanting to improve.

In a handbook of this nature, we can only talk in general terms about the areas that people might want to improve on in life, such as career advancement, personal growth, life transitions, performance improvement, or relationships, but only in the broadest terms. Add to this picture the fact that people's priorities change over time as they clarify what motivates them and start thinking about who they want to grow to become for other people. There is no single, authorized reference manual with standardized coaching solutions that can be universally applied to all human beings. And this is what makes Life Coaching so inherently dynamic and is the reason for its effectiveness as a medium for positive change.

**IMPORTANT LESSONS TO REMEMBER:**
- People with a strong sense of direction are more likely to pursue their goals.

- People draw their identities out of their environments and life experiences.
- By drawing on your own life experiences, you will relate to people naturally.
- A person's self-esteem improves when they identify and accept their self-worth.
- Self-awareness precedes personal growth, and growth precedes social awareness.
- Without self or social awareness, you cannot gain insights into another person's life.
- How a person self-identifies will directly influence how they act and behave.
- There is no standardized coaching model that can be applied to all human beings.

**SECTION TWO NOTEWORTHY IDEAS**

Use this space to note down any ideas that have struck you as important throughout this section of the handbook. Also, write down any questions that might be beneficial for your future consideration and self-reflection.

........................................................................................................................

........................................................................................................................

........................................................................................................................

........................................................................................................................

........................................................................................................................

........................................................................................................................

SECTION THREE

# UNPACKING THE HUMAN EXPERIENCE

The human mind is a complex and fascinating thing. It is the seat of our consciousness, the engine of our thoughts, and the storehouse of our memories. In many ways, it is what makes us who we are. Given its importance, it is not surprising that psychologists have devoted centuries to trying to understand how the mind works. In this section of the handbook, we will take a shallow dive into the basic psychology of the human mind. The ideas throughout this section will benefit you most through self-reflection. By gaining a deeper understanding of how your own mind works and how you make decisions, you will be better equipped to positively influence people in their thinking and, ultimately, in their decision-making.

# ACKNOWLEDGING THE HUMAN EXPERIENCE

*"Why am I as I am? To understand that of any person, his whole life, from Birth must be reviewed. All of our experiences fuse into our personality. Everything that ever happened to us is an ingredient."*

—MALCOLM X

How do we make sense of the human experience? This is a question that has been asked throughout history, but it is one that remains as relevant today as ever. With almost 8 billion people on the planet, each with their own unique perception of the meaning of life, it can be difficult to come to a consensus about what it all means. Neuroscientists often reduce the human experience to brain function, leaving little room for personhood. Religious and spiritual people might believe in divine power or influence, while other people believe there is no such thing as free will. With so many professional and well-researched theories about the human experience, who are we to believe? The answer, of course, lies within each of us. We must each find our own way of making sense of the human experience. What works for one person may not work for another, but that doesn't mean that any single way is wrong.

Many people today like to side with science, but even science has its limitations. Despite sending billionaires into space and landing robots on Mars, they haven't cracked the riddle for human existence, nor have they found the answer for how exactly we came to be beyond the big bang theory and evolution. While these theories answer many questions, there is still much more we don't know. What's more, science can only take us so far, especially when it comes to understanding each other on a social and personal level. We need something more than science to help us make sense of the world around us and our place in it.

One of the greatest things about being human is that we are all so different from one another. We come in all shapes, sizes, and colors. We have different talents, interests, and experiences. And yet, in spite of all of our differences, we are all united by our shared humanity. The recent upsurge in gender non-conforming individuals has shown us that it is impossible to develop a neat, all-encompassing theory about what being human means.

We can't put people into boxes because even those who seem to fit into the same box on a surface level will experience reality differently from each other on an experiential level. Therefore, any attempt to pigeonhole human beings will always be flawed. We are complex, multi-dimensional beings, and any theory that tries to explain us must reflect that complexity.

So, to open up this new chapter in this handbook, let us keep an open mind about how people make sense of their lives, decisions, thoughts, beliefs, world views, and life experiences. Science or physics can't define human experience altogether, so let's not even bother to try. Our human experience is governed by a series of interrelated principles that are only accessible once we are ready to understand them, apply them, and benefit from them.

**PRINCIPLES INTO PRACTICE QUESTIONS:**

1. Through telling and hearing stories, people become more aware of themselves and their human experiences. In what ways has this statement been true or untrue for you?
2. By understanding other people's life experiences, human beings gain an understanding of their own unique qualities and emotions. How is this statement true or untrue for you?
3. Historically, what have you learned most from listening to other people's experiences?

# MAKING SENSE OF THE HUMAN EXPERIENCE

*"Many people spend their time, money, and energy trying to change their experience on the outside, not realizing that the whole thing is being projected from the inside out."*

—MICHAEL NEILL

There's truth to the saying, "He who has the most fun, wins." Look at most children. They are naturally optimistic and believe they can do anything. No challenge is too insurmountable. They live in a world of possibility. Their hopes know no bounds. So it makes sense that people who want to live productive lives remember how to think as they did as children. Without identity labels! Stoic and Roman emperor Marcus Aurelius wrote: *"A man's life is what his thoughts make of it."* Philosopher Ralph Waldo Emerson wrote: *"A man is what he thinks about all day long."* Author Earl Nightingale said: *"We become what we think about,"* and Mark Twain wrote: *"Life consists of the storm of thoughts that forever flow through one's mind."*

All of these men seemed to understand the following three life principles;

1. Human beings live in a world of thought.
2. Thoughts create our human experiences.
3. People experience what they think most.

Thoughts create the quality of all human life. It really is that simple. The secret to living a purposeful and productive life is to think about what we want most, and put a plan in place to get it. This is, in essence, all that Life Coaching helps people do—focus their thoughts on what is compelling, wholesome, and worth pursuing. Since everything is a reflection of our minds, everything can be changed by our minds.

Anything a person can imagine, they can make real. The main problem for most people, however, comes in their lack of discipline and ability to manage intrusive thoughts. Intrusive thoughts are unwanted notions that can pop into our heads without notice. They're often a repetitive thought pattern that crops up time and time again. The content of intrusive thoughts can vary, from mild anxiety-inducing to outright bizarre. But regardless of their content, these thoughts can have a real impact on the quality of people's lives.

Many intrusive thoughts come in the form of our inner critic: the voice that tells us, "You'll never get that job, you're not smart enough," or "Don't try that, you'll only fail." Having random thoughts is a natural human phenomenon and can help us to anticipate problems, plan ahead and remember things we might have otherwise forgotten. However, when these thoughts become fixated on certain topics or themes, they can start to interfere with the quality of people's daily lives.

For example, Sarah attended a Christmas work party in 2016 for a company she had just joined. She knew no one at the party, and every time she tried to participate in a conversation, she was shut down. Sarah spent the majority of the party in a corner by herself, feeling lonely, and until 2022, hasn't attended another one since. Every time a colleague invites her to a gathering, Sarah declines the invite. Despite being an integral part of the company and having made friends with many of her colleagues, she can't help but remember how she felt at that first-party and so avoids work socials, even though doing so costs her opportunities to connect meaningfully with her colleagues and develop new relationships.

Sarah's case is an example of how past experiences influence human behavior. How people think creates what they view as reality. How people view reality impacts how their body reacts to everyday experiences. This unconscious cognitive cycle results in the emotional states people experience. Although thoughts do not have inherent power, they can feel real when people invest their attention in them. When people engage with certain thoughts, they will start to feel the emotions associated with these thoughts and enter a new emotional state. This change in emotionality then affects how those individuals behave.

To live a wise life, people must learn to master their mind before it masters them. Mind management is a result of self-control, which happens through self-awareness and self-discipline. People need to learn how their thoughts form their reality. Only after becoming aware of the relationship between thoughts and emotions can people deliberately decide which thoughts to believe and which ones to ignore.

Every thought people have links to an emotion. When people identify with ideas such as, "I'm a loser," "I'm not smart enough," "I'll never be good enough," or "I'm a fraud," they might consequently feel disheartened or inferior. In a similar way, a person who identifies with positive ideas such as "I'm growing," "I can learn," and "I'm creative," will have fewer problems when it comes to tackling life's challenges.

"I have the worst luck in the entire world. I'm going to lose."

"I failed my last major exam, so I might as well quit now."

"She's late. It's raining. She's probably dead in a ditch somewhere."

The above statements are three examples of common cognitive distortions. Cognitive distortions are exaggerated or irrational thought patterns involved in the onset or perpetuation of unhealthy emotional states. Cognitive distortions that are repeated over time turn into beliefs. Due to our human nature to fall prey to cognitive distortions, many people wrongly attribute their emotions to external circumstances or even other people. Some people blame social media for their body image dilemmas, society for poor employment prospects, or the economy for their own undisciplined financial management. But nearly all of the emotional issues that people experience stem from irrational thinking and believing problems.

The pain some people feel about their financial failures, relationship issues, etc., is only based on how they perceive their immediate circumstances. It can be interesting to consider that human experiences are neither good nor bad—they're only perceived as good or bad once people decide if they like them or not. Don't get me wrong—emotions are real things, and the impact they can have on some people's lives can be debilitating, but regardless, emotions are just the product of the quality of people's thinking. Those who engage in negative patterns of thinking will experience emotional consequences that are also negative and undesired.

In essence, people create their own definitions of reality. What people believe to be true is influenced by many factors, including their perception, assumptions, and expectations. Perception is based on what an individual looks for and pays attention to. Assumptions are based on past experiences and current beliefs. And expectations are based on what an individual wants or needs from a given situation. All of these factors influence how an individual interprets their immediate circumstances and everyday life events, which in turn influences what they believe to be true. While objective reality does exist, it is often overshadowed by people's subjective reality and ignorant guesswork. As such, it is important to be aware of the factors that influence perception so that you are best equipped to support individuals in making wise decisions about how they respond to the world around them.

One Merriam-Webster definition of crazy is "insane." Another is "extravagantly or illogically foolish." The word crazy can also be used when referring to intense enthusiasm or fear. When it comes to achieving different or better results in life, however, "crazy" can simply mean continuing to act, think, or behave in the same old habitual ways while naively expecting new or improved outcomes. The truth is, if nothing changes about one's thinking processes, then nothing else is likely to change. In order to achieve the positive new life results they want, people typically need to first understand and upgrade their attitudes, mindset, and underlying self-beliefs.

It's not the thoughts that pass through people's minds that impact the quality of their life the most; it's the ones they take ownership of and focus their attention on. Once people agree to give their attention to a thought, it becomes more and more real to them over time and has more and more power over their life. The start of a new coaching relationship is an ideal time to peel back the accumulated layers of identity and old ways of unhelpful thinking to uncover the authentic person within. A Life Coach can help with this process by providing clarity and direction, as well as accountability and support. Through coaching, clients can learn how to break free from old and outdated thought patterns or self-defeating behaviors.

**PRINCIPLES INTO PRACTICE QUESTIONS:**
1. When was the last time you changed your mind about a person or situation?
2. How often do you openly change your mind about people or situations?
3. What could happen if you changed your mind about people or situations more often?
4. How important might flexible thinking be within a Life Coaching relationship?

# HOW PEOPLE SEE AND INTERPRET LIFE

*"What you see and what you hear depends a great deal on where you are standing. It also depends on what sort of human being you are."*

—C.S. LEWIS

Consider some of the issues that people bring into a Life Coaching relationship: they might be uncertain about their future, frustrated for a reason unbeknown to them, or lack confidence about their skillset. Other people may be searching for something meaningful to commit their time to, or just want to better understand their own motivations and goals. Some may want to become more innovative or influential, resolve relationship conflicts, manage their time better, or increase their professional performance. All people have different goals and priorities and manage life's obstacles differently because all people see and interpret life differently.

During my first three years of practicing Life Coaching, I voluntarily delivered over 1 thousand pro-bono hours to other ex-military veterans who lived in various veterans hostels throughout Scotland. I knew from experience that adapting to civilian life is no easy task, especially for those who'd experienced war or life-changing injuries. Like anyone transitioning into a new season of life, many of my coachees were blindsided by future uncertainty, a sense of current disorientation, and sadness for the friends and comfort zone that they'd left behind.

So let me share a story. During my time in the Army, I knew of two brothers. The older of the two brothers served nine months in Afghanistan and lost a limb in combat. Two years later, the younger brother served for nine months in a different Afghanistan province and also lost a limb upon triggering an improvised explosive device (IED). The Army paid for both brothers' treatments and resettlements, and Army charities helped where they could. In other words, both brothers had the same childhoods, were from the same area, experienced comparable injuries later on in life, and even received equal support (including aesthetic legs). Despite this, the two brothers responded to their life circumstances entirely differently.

The first brother had been an athlete before his accident, so his disability had no significance to him. Yes, he undoubtedly had to go through a mental shift that most people will never experience, but he persisted with his athletics, and for the next twelve years, he represented the Great British team at the paralympics and won several medals before starting a charity to help disabled children participate in track sports. The last time I heard, the brother and his wife were due to give birth to their third child.

In contrast, the second brother took a different path. For five years after his medical discharge, he attended veteran support groups and became a familiar face in British Legion bars. He spent the money that was granted to him—including his compensation payout—on alcohol and gambling. His wife left him and remarried. This brother can now be found outside the main Glasgow train station begging for change, alleging that he was inadequately supported by the British military after being medically discharged from his service.

Is the first brother living life as he would have done had he not lost his limb? Most likely not. Did losing a limb stop him from living his life, though? No. People see the glass as half-full or half-empty. How people perceive their circumstances depends on what they focus on. How people act depends on how they interpret their circumstances. A person's quality of life isn't based on what happens to them but, rather, on how they respond to what happens.

It's easy to form an opinion and judge another person's behavior. But we all see, interpret, and experience life in our own way. What might seem outrageous to you might seem perfectly justifiable to another person. This is what makes the Life Coaching relationship so unique. A Life Coach understands that everyone perceives reality differently and behaves accordingly. Instead of judging another person's behavior, a Life Coach asks the right questions to help that person understand their own behavior and take actions that are healthy and growth-oriented. Sometimes people behave in ways that are nothing but detrimental to their own personal growth and development, but a Life Coach knows that with the right understanding and guidance, everyone has the potential to grow and thrive.

Change is life's only guarantee, and the level of complexity people experience in life often reflects how effectively they navigate through change. The more dramatic the change a person must make, the more complex the process of transition usually is. Some people manage transitions better than others, and this is influenced by how they perceive things.

## HOW PEOPLE PERCEIVE "THE WORLD" CAN BE CATEGORIZED IN THREE WAYS
### THEA (ΘΕΑ): UNCONSIDERED OBSERVATION

The word θέα comes from the Greek word θεώμαι means "I watch." Θέατρο (theater) has also the same origin. Thea-orientated observations generally happen with little effort being made. Think of the last film you watched. While you may have enjoyed it, you possibly didn't take time to appreciate the reality of all you were seeing, such as videography, actors' costumes, CGI, video editing, scripts, etc. You maybe came away from the film with an idea of what you witnessed, but all you could relate to was what you saw through your eyes. Your perception didn't include the cost of production, the hours of work, intensive creative disputes, actors' sick days, the money earned and spent, production extras, sets, props, and so on.

People who "interpret life" in this blinkered way are like social media critics, who lend an occasional upvote or downvote to content that "makes them" feel something. They are swayed by emotions, pleas, propaganda, narrative spins and invest no time into exploring facts or understanding the views of others. They react to preconceived biases and prejudices.

### THEOREO (ΘΕΩΡΕΩ) CRITICAL CONTEMPLATION

Those who "interpret life" through reason and logic often sift through experiences and information to formulate conclusions and dismiss any notion that does not fit comfortably into their methodical (or ideological) framework. In other words, people who observe life in this way only accept ideas that make sense to them.

While those of *theoreo* are not easily swayed by emotion, they are not without bias. Their worldview can still be skewed by false data or inaccurate premises. Critical thinkers tend to have an exaggerated sense of righteousness, which can blind them to new possibilities and opportunities. Due to this tendency, *theoreo* observers don't always see other viewpoints as being as valid as their own. Because of this, critical observers can end up overwhelmed by divisive and fruitless debates about irrelevant beliefs or ideological worldviews.

### HORÁŌ (ΌΡΑΩ): CONTEMPLATE TO UNDERSTAND

If I were to summarize the most important principle I've learned in the field of Life Coaching and interpersonal communications, it would be this: Understand first, then be understood second. This way of relating to people can be represented by the Eastern term of "new mind" illustrated in the Buddhist "empty cup" story.

A swordsman heard rumors of a wise man who was a legend with his sword. The swordsman, who was determined to be the best in the land, went on a journey to find this wise man and learn from him. His journey led him to a secluded village at the top of a mountain. When he reached the wise man's home, he was invited in for tea. The swordsman kneeled before a table. As the wise man prepared the tea, the swordsman spoke of his travels and the other swordsmen he'd trained under and out-performed. His boasting lasted for hours while his cup of tea sat in front of him. The wise man smiled and let him finish his stories.

Eventually, the hour grew late, and the wise man had not spoken a word. The wise man brewed fresh tea, filled his empty cup, and proceeded to fill the swordsman's cup, which was still full. The tea ran over the lip of the cup onto the table and the swordsman's lap. With a disgruntled growl, the swordsman leaped from the floor.

"What are you doing, you old fool?" he demanded. "My cup was already full."

"Precisely," replied the wise man. "Until you empty your cup, I cannot teach you."

Those who take a *horáō* approach toward interacting with life's circumstances and people are simply curious about gaining understanding before all things. Facts matter, but facts don't always tell a complete story. They want to know how people interpret their experiences, let people be heard, and view all people as just being at a different stage of their life journey.

*Horáō* listeners offer input where they can. *Horáō* is how a Life Coach must interact with people. As a context for coaching, *Horáō* curiosity may be the quality that starts the process and the energy to keep it going. Always strive to stay open-minded and ask questions that will enable people to interpret the world around them in the most useful way possible.

**PRINCIPLES INTO PRACTICE QUESTIONS:**

1. What is your habitual way of looking at and interpreting your life?
2. How might your life change if you viewed life from a *we'll discuss* perspective?
3. How might you help other people see the world from a *horáō* perspective?

# PERSONAL BELIEFS AND WORLD VIEWS

*"People's beliefs become the thoughts that influence their behaviors and decision-making. By learning to question their thoughts and identify their irrational beliefs, people can free themselves from the self-imposed prison of their own minds."*

—DR. ALBERT ELLIS

In all the years I have studied psychology, philosophy, personal development principles, and theology, I have concluded that beliefs are simply the best assumptions people make about themselves and the world around them. A person's beliefs are the invisible foundations on which they build their lives; they are a person's best assumptions about how the world works, good and bad, and whether something is moral or immoral. All people hold beliefs about how skilled and attractive they are, how rich and sensible they are, what government should look like, and what religious ideologies are right, wrong, worthy of praise, and ridiculous.

The beliefs people adopt act like little internal "thinking maps" that guide their thinking, assuming, decision-making, and action-taking. The trouble is that beliefs are oftentimes based on very little evidence—if any evidence at all. People believe things because they were told something as a child or because their peer group shares the same or a similar worldview. As such, some people's beliefs can often be ill-informed, irrational, and downright silly. But the good news is that since beliefs are nothing more than assumptions, it's possible to reassess and replace them with more useful ideas at any given moment. If your coachee recognizes that they aren't navigating their life too effectively, they can always choose to draw a new map. And this sweet little truth also applies to you.

Beliefs are at the core of everything. They spawn from various sources, including everyday life experiences, wins, rejections, failures, family interactions, cultural ideologies (such as religious or political views), or even through education or parenting. But beliefs aren't always reliable. After all, what people see and how they interpret things, whether accurate or inaccurate, often determines what they eventually believe. Most people don't care whether their beliefs are true or false because they're usually just the best assumptions they've been able to conjure up about themselves, or about life in general, to date.

As a result, people form limiting beliefs, especially about themselves. A limiting belief is a false and valueless notion that originates inside of a person's mind that negatively impacts their goals and intentions by manifesting detrimental attitudes, habits, and behaviors. You might be wondering what limiting beliefs might currently be holding you back. Most people find it relieving to learn that limiting beliefs don't exist to destroy people; on the contrary, growing out of limiting beliefs is how people mature throughout life. That's why it's beneficial to question your beliefs regularly. If you're not careful, your assumptions about life can become like a prison cell that confines and restricts your potential.

The first step to breaking free from a limiting belief is to be aware of the kinds of limiting beliefs that exist—and how they might impact your thinking and decision-making. Once people are aware of the beliefs that hold them back, they can then start to challenge and change their mind about them. In the same way that a child can change their mind about who their best friend is every day, adult human beings can change their minds about what ideas they accept as factual and which ones they accept as falsehoods. In short, all self-improvement and life transformation begin when human beings decide to change.

Thus, the most powerful outcome that a coachee can arrive at through your Life Coaching efforts, is making a decision that will enable them to become more fruitful in any area of their life *(we'll discuss this in much more detail later on in this section of the handbook)*.

People waste years of their lives going around in circles because they allow inaccurate beliefs to hold them back without ever challenging their validity. In *Rational Emotive Behavior Therapy* (REBT), psychologist Albert Ellis identified several dysfunctional beliefs that people often hold, known as "Thirteen Irrational Beliefs." These irrational beliefs and attitudes lead some people into years worth of unnecessary struggle and hardship.

Ellis's definition of an irrational belief is that: it distorts reality; it is illogical; it prevents people from reaching goals; it leads people into unhealthy emotions and self-defeating behavior. Take a few moments to reflect upon each of the following irrational beliefs, and see if you can identify any that might currently be at play in your life.

### BELIEF 1. "I MUST GET THE APPROVAL OF EVERYBODY, OR I WILL BE WORTHLESS."

Some people assume this is true—instead of focusing their efforts on developing their own self-worth, becoming a wiser and more self-respecting adult who proactively seeks out new ways to add value to people's lives, and becoming more attractive in other people's eyes. Seeking approval generates a servile attitude that's forever at the mercy of other people's opinions.

### BELIEF 2. "OTHER PEOPLE MUST TREAT ME NICELY, OR ELSE THEY ARE BAD."

Some people assume this notion is true instead of accepting the truth that people are separate from their behaviors, and that no one is entitled to anything in life—especially being treated "nicely" by people. This naive belief gives birth to a disempowered attitude that insidiously assumes the world must be a "safe place" for people to function effectively.

### BELIEF 3. "LIFE MUST BE EASY AND PAIN-FREE, OR I CANNOT ENJOY LIVING AT ALL."

Some people assume this notion is true—instead of taking responsibility for themselves and charge of pursuing the outcomes they want more of. People who think like this are like perpetual Peter Pans, who refuse to grow up and mature in life. In truth, it's via embracing life's challenges that people develop resilience, not through trying to avoid or ignore them.

### BELIEF 4. "I MUST BE A HIGH ACHIEVER AND SUCCEED, OR I'M A WORTHLESS PERSON."

Some people assume this notion is true—instead of realizing that their self-worth is in no way a reflection of their productivity or net worth. No one can be fully competent in all aspects of life. People who perpetually seek success at all costs often end up obsessing and submitting to a continuous state of comparison with others that often only generates frustration and feelings of incompetence and uselessness.

### BELIEF 5. "NOBODY SHOULD BEHAVE BADLY, AND IF THEY DO, I MUST CONDEMN THEM."

Some people assume this notion is true—instead of realizing that people react impulsively at times and don't always measure the consequences of their actions. People make mistakes without realizing it. In most cases, those who behave poorly are not fully aware of the consequences of their actions on others. Tending to be more tolerant and rational in your interactions with people generally wins friends and has a positive influence on others.

### BELIEF 6. "IT IS INTOLERABLE WHEN THINGS DON'T GO AS PER MY PLANS."

Some people assume this notion is true—instead of realizing that no one in the world is entitled to having their life follow a smooth and uninterrupted plan. This limiting belief sets people up to be intolerant of other people who don't align with their idea of "how things must be."

This belief generally evolves into a manipulative or controlling attitude that most people find exhausting and do not want to be around.

### BELIEF 7. "WHEN CHALLENGING THINGS HAPPEN, I MUST ALWAYS FEEL SAD."

Some people assume this notion is true—instead of realizing that all people can make a decision to change how they're behaving the very minute that their longing to change becomes greater than their desire to remain exactly as they are and not change. Many people refuse to accept responsibility for managing their emotions and, thus, remain emotionally inconsistent, self-oriented, and untrustworthy in many areas of their life.

### BELIEF 8. "I MUST ALWAYS BE CONCERNED ABOUT SOLVING PEOPLE'S PROBLEMS."

Some people assume this notion is true—instead of realizing that all people are solely responsible for their own lives. No one is entitled to anything, and each person must address their own difficulties. Solving people's issues does nothing to help them become mature and responsible adults. Rather, it is beneficial not to take on the problems of others because it allows individuals to make wise decisions for themselves.

### BELIEF 9. "I CAN BE IRRESPONSIBLE, AVOID LIFE'S DIFFICULTIES, AND FIND FULFILLMENT."

Some people assume this notion is true—instead of realizing that the only route to personal growth is through taking responsibility for one's life, attitudes, habits, and behaviors. To avoid life's difficulties is to avoid opportunities for personal growth. While it might be possible to avoid taking personal responsibility for a season in life—it's impossible to find fulfillment and satisfaction through anything other than hard work and achievement.

### BELIEF 10. "THE PAST IS CENTRAL TO MY WHOLE LIFE. IT MUST DICTATE HOW I FEEL."

Some people assume this notion is true—instead of realizing that while some experiences mark us throughout life, this doesn't mean they must become a burden that people have to drag around with them forever (like martyrs). Some people use the past as an excuse to avoid facing the changes of today and not make the effort necessary to move forward. The past should be viewed as a valuable life experience, not an area to camp in indefinitely.

### BELIEF 11. "I ALWAYS HAVE TO MAINTAIN CONTROL AND STRIVE FOR PERFECTION."

Some people assume this notion is true—instead of realizing that there is no such thing as perfect, and perfection is nothing more than a subjective preference. The truth is that, at all times, people will behave and conduct themselves in alignment with the highest personal standards they have developed (for the stage of life they are in), or they won't. The only thing human beings can control is the attitude they take toward their circumstances.

### BELIEF 12. "IT'S OK TO RELY ON OTHERS. ALL PEOPLE NEED SOMEONE STRONG TO TRUST."

Some people assume this notion is true—instead of realizing that people only grow upon taking responsibility for stretching themselves, learning new things, and pursuing the goals they hope to achieve for themselves. The more people rely on others, the less they choose for themselves. The more people avoid making important decisions, the fewer opportunities they have to learn. Thus a vicious cycle of dependency and insecurity is created.

According to some self-help and new-age beliefs, people can manifest their dream lives and outcomes by focusing on what they want and projecting their wishes out to the universe. This idea has led to many unhappy people sitting at home, still waiting to receive their unrealized fortunes. While laziness and irresponsibility are appealing to many people throughout modern society today, the truth is that nothing good comes about in life apart from effort and sacrifice: mindset can only get you so far; action creates results.

Ellis's beliefs are deliberately extreme, highlighting that human beings often take irrational and unreasonably exaggerated viewpoints. He called this approach "awfulizing," as people generalize the various aspects of their life pessimistically. As a Life Coach, this is where you need to step in. Your opportunity is to help people identify smarter ways of thinking and liberate themselves from their false, destructive beliefs by encouraging them to stop blindly trusting the legitimacy of external opinions and the "meaning" of life events.

**PRINCIPLES INTO PRACTICE QUESTIONS:**

1. How might limiting beliefs negatively influence your decisions and outlook on life?
2. Which of these unhelpful beliefs resonate the most with your current worldview?
3. Would it be OK for you to change your mind about something you believe each day?
4. How might you support a coachee in evaluating how their beliefs are serving them?

# PARADIGM SHIFTS AND THE KUHN CYCLE

*"People see the world in terms of their personal theories and assumptions. The historian of science, however, might be tempted to exclaim that when paradigms change, the world itself changes alongside them."*

—THOMAS KUHN

Claudius Ptolemy was an astronomer and mathematician who wrote several scientific treatises essential to later Islamic and Western European science. His seminal work, the *Almagest,* was one of the most influential scientific texts in history, as it canonized a geocentric model of the universe that was accepted for more than 1,200 years and was a key source of information about ancient Greek astronomy. Although the tenets of Greek geocentrism were established by the time of Aristotle, Ptolemy was responsible for establishing the details of how the system worked in the second century CE.

For generations, Ptolemy's model was considered a masterpiece and influenced astronomical thought and Christian dogma. Still, the over-complication of the model did not sit well with all scientists. Having none of the modern instruments or understanding at their disposal, people would look at the heavens and believe they saw it moving while the earth, by all perceivable means, remained stationary. As time went on and measuring techniques improved, Ptolemy's model no longer held up to observation. Some tried to repair the old model by adding more complications, while others pursued other possibilities. Eventually, Ptolemy's geocentric model of the solar system was superseded by the heliocentric solar system of Copernicus.

In his book, *The Structure of Scientific Revolutions*, Thomas Kuhn looked at the history of science and argued against the idea that science progressed in a linear fashion according to the accumulation of theory-independent facts and neutral observations. Instead, Kuhn claimed that the history of science is characterized by revolutions in scientific thinking and human understanding. Kuhn explained that all scientists have a certain worldview or, as he called it, a "paradigm." A paradigm, he explained, is a universally recognizable scientific achievement that, for a time, provides model problems and solutions to a community of thinkers. However, when anomalies within the paradigm occur, which leads to thinkers questioning the basis of the original paradigm, a new theory and paradigm are created. As such, Kuhn's work offered an insightful look into how scientific progress is actually made and how our understanding of the world around us is constantly evolving. Kuhn argued that the process of deconstructing and reconstructing scientific paradigms occurs over several stages.

While this astronomy and science talk may seem completely off-topic, it perfectly demonstrates how people's paradigms, beliefs, or perceptions are adopted and eventually changed. Some individuals hold onto certain beliefs because they associate them with truth rather than seeing that these beliefs are merely perceptions. Just as the geocentric model was based on observable facts, beliefs are also based on observable truths. The observable facts remained when the paradigm changed to the heliocentric model, but the lens through which they were seen had changed. Let us use the stages of the Kuhn cycle to help us understand how paradigm shifts naturally occur and how negative (or unhelpful) belief systems can change over time through the adaption of new data and information:

## NORMAL SCIENCE

According to Kuhn, this is the stage where a paradigm is working well. An individual in this stage has no motivation to change because they have not reached a point where change has become necessary—at least not in their view. However, they may start to be confronted by information that contradicts their beliefs.

## MODEL DRIFT

At this point, the individual has seen discrepancies in their paradigm. For the most part, the person can ignore these contradictions, labeling them as one-offs. But as more of these contradictions accrue, it will become more difficult to shrug them off as coincidences. Doubt will begin to creep in, and the individual may explore other ways of reconciling these contradictions.

## MODEL CRISIS

The contradictions become overwhelming and may be perceived as attacks. The individual may choose to go on the defensive, closing themselves off and refusing to listen to anyone who provides an opposing view. Confusion is a big part of the crisis. The individual is still not ready to adopt a new belief. The pain in this stage is compounded by how the individual aligns their identity with the old belief. They will struggle to resist until the pain of remaining the same is greater than the pain of changing. When confronted with information that conflicts with long-held beliefs, some people may reject the data and those who present it, a rejection which you, as a Life Coach, will face more than you anticipate.

## MODEL REVOLUTION

Out of the chaotic confusion of the crisis, a new day breaks as more revelations come to light that finally demonstrate the flaws of the old belief. With the help of this newly released understanding, a new, more constructive belief is adopted, ending the crisis. This stage is a revelatory, enlightening breakthrough. There is a sense of freedom from limiting beliefs and excitement toward a future of endless possibilities. As people solidify the new paradigms and beliefs over time, they return to experiencing a new sense of normality.

As a Life Coach, it is important to be aware of the different stages of belief development that your coachees may experience and possibly even struggle with—especially if they've held tightly onto a specific limiting belief for many years. This will help you to understand their reactions to any provocative questions that you might ask them. If your coachee shows signs of defensiveness within a Life Coaching session, this can often be because they are struggling to break out of an old paradigm. In this case, it is important to give them time and space to reflect on the ideas they are struggling with. Ultimately, no matter where your coachee is in the belief development cycle, it is crucial to listen and understand their current paradigm before assuming how you might best question it. Asking your coachee about their past experiences can give you valuable insights into their current paradigms. It is only by understanding these hidden paradigms that you will be able to help your coachee effectively challenge and change them. Later on in the handbook, we will explore the different questioning models that you can use to achieve this.

**PRINCIPLES INTO PRACTICE QUESTIONS:**

1. Can you relate the Kuhn cycle to how you have evolved in your thinking over the years?
2. What beliefs aren't you prepared to change your perspective on yet? If so, why is this?
3. In what ways could understanding the Kuhn cycle benefit your practice as a Life Coach?

# LOCUS OF INTERNAL AND EXTERNAL CONTROL

*"Locus of control is a term for how people view their autonomy in life. People with an internal locus know they are responsible for their outcomes and feel in charge of their lives. Those with an external locus see themselves as pawns in a greater game that's played by others. Those with this external locus assume that other people, environmental forces, deities—basically any external events, have full influence over their lives."*

—PHILIP ZIMBARDO

Who is ultimately responsible for your fulfillment, progress, and contentment, you or someone else? What influences your future: fate, politics, mysticism, the universe, or an influential deity? The term "locus of control" refers to how much control a person feels they have over their behavior. Julian B. Rotter coined the term in 1954, and it has since become an integral part of personality psychology, bridging the gap between behavioral and cognitive psychology. Rotter believed that behavior was primarily determined by external factors like rewards and punishments (reinforcements). He argued that external factors influenced people's emotions, habits, outcomes, behavior and, in turn, determined a person's lifelong attitudes and beliefs.

There's much in life that happens outside of our control: such as the weather, global warming, pandemics, how people treat us, and so on. However, that doesn't mean human beings are helpless in life. Whilst we can't control being made redundant due to global recession or getting cheated on by our spouse, we are in control of how we choose to respond to these circumstances—which is otherwise referred to as an internal locus of control.

Those with an external locus of control, however, will tend to blame other people, their parents, politicians, God, or events for their feelings, such as "she irritated me," "that put me in a bad mood," "you offended me," and so on. The people who hold an external locus of control refuse to hold themselves responsible for the condition of their lives. They blame external factors, other people, or past traumas for why they "couldn't" or "can't" do something rather than acknowledge that they are the only ones responsible for holding themselves back.

## THE EXTERNAL LOCUS OF CONTROL

People with an external locus of control generally accept statements such as:

"Things happen to me that I cannot control."

"I must always be kept safe and secure."

"I will always be a victim due to my past."

"My past determines what my future will be."

"I need people in my life to make me happy."

"My partner doesn't meet my deepest needs."

To illustrate this mindset, let me tell you about a girl named Marta. Born in a small village in late-seventeenth-century Lithuania, she was the daughter of two peasants who died of the plague when she was three years old. She was taken in by a pastor in Marienburg and served as a scullery maid who never attended school and grew up completely illiterate.

Marta could have accepted the circumstances of her life and deemed herself a lifelong victim. It would have been justified—she was orphaned at such a young age and became an illiterate servant. She had no reason to think that she would ever be anything more. A person with an external locus of control would justify a bitter attitude and anger toward the things that happened to them. If Marta had an external locus, she might have pushed others away with her anger and bitterness and ended up miserable and lonely.

Marta was married to a Swedish military officer at the age of seventeen, but only for eight days. The Russian army invaded, and the Swedish troops were forced to abandon the city. Consequently, Marta was left without a husband or any job prospects. She joined the household of one of the Russian generals as a housemaid before leaving her home country of Lithuania to be sold to the household of Prince Menshikov. There, she met her husband, Peter, converted to the Eastern Orthodox church, and changed her name to Catherine.

Peter the Great and Catherine I ruled Russia as their most beloved emperor and empress. The French writer and philosopher Voltaire praised Catherine for saving the life of Peter the Great, whose army was overwhelmed by Turkish troops. She offered her jewels as a bribe to the vizier Pasha to ensure a safe retreat for Peter and his men. Voltaire spoke of Catherine in great esteem, considering her life story nearly as remarkable as Peter's. Some people might say that Catherine's fairy tale rags-to-riches story was a matter of luck. Those with an external locus are likely to have this kind of reaction. People with an external locus might also see Catherine as a manipulative opportunist, using her good looks to get ahead. They often attribute others' success to dishonesty and manipulation and believe their lack of success results from their "upstanding character." This type of generalization is simply a means of rationalizing the disparity between their situation and other situations.

## THE INTERNAL LOCUS OF CONTROL

If you believe that you hold the keys to your future, you have an internal locus of control and are more likely to take action to change your situation when needed. People with an internal locus of control generally accept statements such as:

"I make things happen and choose how I respond to things."

"I am responsible for building the life that I want."

"I must take risks and face uncertainty to progress."

"I can overcome any obstacle that comes my way."

"The quality of my future will be whatever I make it."

If you believe that you hold the keys to your fate, you are more likely to take action to change your situation when needed. On the other hand, if you believe that the outcome is out of your hands, you may be less likely to work toward change. People who place their locus of control internally take responsibility for their thoughts, emotions, and actions. They can't control what happens to them, but they can choose how to respond despite external threats. They recognize that none of life's storms last forever, that the present and the past have no bearing on the future, and they will always have opportunities in front of them. While there is no way for me to know what kind of person Catherine was, I like to think she was a person with an internal locus of control who simply waited out the storms of life and took advantage of the opportunities when they eventually came along.

It's human nature to be drawn to stories of rags-to-riches, overnight successes, and lottery winners. We love to hear about people who have beaten the odds because it gives us hope that we might be able to do the same. But the reality is that most successful people achieve their goals through many years of hard work and personal sacrifice, not luck. This is not to say that dishonest and manipulative "successful" people don't exist or that everyone will hit hard times at some point in their lives. But I believe that most people who are successful have an internal locus of control. That is, they believe that they can control their own destiny, and they aren't afraid to work hard to achieve their goals. They also understand that success seldom comes easy and that personal sacrifice is often required.

People with an internal locus of control understand that fulfillment in life is not exclusive to a few lucky individuals. It is just a matter of believing that we are each responsible for captaining our own ships, steering the direction of our own lives, and working hard to actively pursue our desired ends. When we take this mindset, we open up a world of possibilities for ourselves. No longer are we at the mercy of luck or fate. We are in control of our own destiny. And that, indeed, is a powerful paradigm and a useful way of thinking that all people can adopt, if they choose it, and keep as a companion throughout the journey of life.

**PRINCIPLES INTO PRACTICE QUESTIONS:**

1. Where do you place your locus of control, internally or externally?
2. What has having an external locus of control historically cost you?
3. How might you encourage a coachee to become internally focused?

# NAVIGATING THROUGH CHANGES AND TRANSITIONS

*"It isn't the changes that do you in, it's the transitions. Change is not the same as transition. Change is situational: the new site, the new boss, the new team roles, the new policy. Transition is the psychological process people go through to come to terms with the new situation. Change is external, transition is internal."*

—WILLIAM BRIDGES

As a Life Coach, your *Horáō* curiosity will lead you to understand your coachees from the inside out. You will only learn about those things, people, and situations that you are curious enough to ask questions about and take the time to understand. A coachee will respond to your curiosity by looking inside for their own answers, trying to understand their world and how they function. Once you understand their interior workings as a coach, you can then ask questions that they themselves would ask if they knew how to. As a Life Coach, you will be in a strong position to ask them challenging questions because you're not distracted by their current paradigms, self-sabotaging talk, past history, biases, or what the opinions of their loved ones might be. As your questions grow more intriguing, your coachee will learn what it's like to be less judgmental of themselves. A coachee who is LESS likely to judge themselves will be ready for a paradigm change.

As mentioned in section two, change is life's only guarantee. Transitions are a necessary part of life, but they don't always come easy. For some people, change is hard to adjust to and can be quite stressful. Others seem to take change in stride and navigate their way through it with ease. The level of difficulty people experience during a transition usually reflects how wisely they navigate their way through the change. The more dramatic the change a person must make, the more complex their transition usually is. Some people manage transitioning better than others, and this usually determines how receptive a person is to receiving Life Coaching. Some people learn the hard way that change isn't the same as a transition. Change relates to external circumstances, whereas a transition is a cognitive process.

No one ever said that change was easy. In fact, it's often quite difficult to adapt to a new situation, whether it be a new job, a new home, or even a new baby. And while some people seem to transition effortlessly, others find themselves struggling to keep up. That's where the support of a Life Coach can come in handy to assist people in successfully navigating their way through a career change (such as a layoff or firing), the early stages of marriage, first-time parenting, a problematic divorce, moving to a new city, retirement, empty nesting, or even a business or organizational restructure. These different expressions of transition might have been voluntarily chosen by a person or imposed by another. No matter the circumstance, with the right support system in place, anyone can weather the storm and emerge on the other side of a major life change stronger and more resilient than before.

**THE DIFFERENCE BETWEEN CHANGE AND TRANSITION**

Change is an inherent part of life. At every moment, our cells are dying and being replaced by new ones. Our thoughts and emotions are constantly in flux. Even the world around us is always changing as the weather shifts and the seasons come and go. As anyone who has ever experienced it knows, change is not always easy. It can be disruptive and unsettling, forcing us to leave the familiar behind and adapt to new ways of doing things. But as difficult as it may be, change is essential for growth. Just as our bodies need exercise to stay strong, our minds need to be challenged in order to stay sharp. Adapting to change requires flexibility.

We are always in transition, whether we realize it or not. Birth is a transition. So is growing up, leaving home, getting married, having children, changing jobs, and retiring. Even death is a transition. Each of these life events brings new challenges and opportunities, which we must learn to navigate in order to successfully move from one stage of life to the next. The ability to adapt to change is an essential part of being human. The key is to be aware of the process and to understand that it's normal for people to feel uncertainty or doubt during times of transition. With this knowledge, a Life Coach can help people to transition with confidence and grace. Here, let me explain the four types of lifestyle transition;

ANTICIPATED LIFESTYLE TRANSITIONS

An anticipated lifestyle transition is something people naturally expect to happen in adult life, such as; going to school, changing careers, getting married, moving home, or starting a family. When these transitions happen as expected (or planned), much can be learned within a Life Coaching relationship about how the change either meets or supports a coachee's needs.

UNANTICIPATED LIFESTYLE TRANSITIONS

An unanticipated lifestyle transition is that which was unplanned for. Experiences such as; redundancy, illness, COVID-19 lockdowns, car accidents, or even a marriage breakdown. Unanticipated transitions are often more stressful for people than anticipated transitions. However, the potential for personal growth and reward is also significantly higher. Think about the story of the two brothers in a previous chapter. Both brothers underwent the same unanticipated lifestyle transitions, but how they individually perceived their circumstances determined how smoothly they each navigated their transition.

## NON-EVENT LIFESTYLE TRANSITIONS

Non-event transitions refer to when something that was supposed to happen, doesn't. This can be because the event didn't occur at all, or it simply didn't happen when expected. Examples of this could be; not getting promoted, not being able to start a family, not finding a life partner within a given timeframe, etc. Managing grief and dealing with loss (often of an expected lifestyle) can feature strongly within this transition.

## SLEEPER TRANSITIONS

Sleeper transitions are the ones that happen without much awareness surrounding them. They sneak up on people quietly. Examples of this can be: gradually gaining competence at work, understanding human behavior, developing parental wisdom, learning a new language, the speed at which you run a marathon, or developing great Life Coaching skills. All of these things happen over time, with patience and practice. But sleeper transitions can also have a negative impact; like the lessening of intimacy in a marriage, a father becoming estranged from his son, becoming lackadaisical and demotivated at work. Sleeper transitions catch people off-guard and are often the source of people's regrets.

People who *resist* transitions tend to focus more on the emotional impact they cause, and rather than focusing on growing, evolving, or making some positive lifestyle changes, their productivity quickly declines. When people view transitions as a natural human occurrence, they will readily engage with the disruption, humbly accept the loss, and focus on the future. The wisest questions people can ask upon being caught off guard by a transition are: "What part did I play in this?" "What do I have access to that will allow me to navigate this change?" and "What changes must I now make within myself and also in how I'm living my life?" With competent Life Coaching support, these are the kind of questions that can provoke people to undergo huge breakthroughs within their thinking, perceiving, and action-taking.

People often see change as if it's something that happens overnight.

And sometimes, it can be, but other times it's just a consequence of failing to notice the lesser changes that happen gradually over time. Transitioning is the process that bridges the gap between what people had and what they get next. It can be a tough process, but it's one that everyone goes through at some point in life—and without it, people would never grow or learn. As a Life Coach, your opportunity is to assist people in breaking through the experience.

**PRINCIPLES INTO PRACTICE QUESTIONS:**

1. When was the last time you navigated your way through a difficult life/career transition?
2. What were the main lessons that this transition taught you about yourself?
3. Which of these lessons could you draw from and integrate into your future Life Coaching?
4. If you were to break your transitioning process down into a series of simple action steps that another person could take, what would they be?

# LIFE COACHING BREAKTHROUGH SESSIONS

*"A great breakthrough in life comes when people realize they can learn any skill, navigate any storm, move through any transition, and achieve any goal they set for themselves. This means there are no limits on what anyone can be, have or achieve."*

—JOEL ESTEEN

The purpose of a breakthrough session is to help facilitate a positive shift in perspective for a coachee. Some people get stuck in a particular (and usually an unhelpful) perspective because they don't see another possible (more positive) way of looking at things. As we discussed in the previous chapter, it's not changes that cause people their main difficulties in life, it's navigating their way through transitions. And this is when people hire a Life Coach.

In recent years, coaching as a practice and profession has taken hold in a range of settings. Life Coaches operate from home offices, within businesses, from within jail cells to cubicles at large corporate offices. Some coaches work as independent contractors for businesses and integrate consulting into their coaching practice. Some coaches work with private clients. Others specialize in working with teams, people in relationships, or organization systems. Coaching today is cross-cultural and covers endless demographic categories, such as; vocation, income, education, and ethnic background. Coaches can specialize in select areas and focus on working with CEOs, immigrants, expatriates, entrepreneurs, parents, or teenagers. The environment in which coaching takes place is also varied. Some Life Coaches work with people by phone, with regularly scheduled appointments. Other coaches deliver coaching in-person or online via zoom technology. Coaches may contract with their coachees for a fixed block of time, such as two or three months. Other coaches establish ongoing, open-ended relationships. There is no right or wrong way of delivering Life Coaching.

Within this framework, coaches bring their own life experiences, wisdom, coaching competency, and a wide variety of coaching models. Yet, regardless of what form coaching takes place in, it will be most effective when coach and coachee create a space for both parties to consciously agree on what the purpose of the alliance is.

People seek coaching because they want to achieve their ideal outcomes, which usually involve a breakthrough in their thinking or understanding of how to attain what they desire. This breakthrough could be reaching a goal or performing better at something. For some people, a breakthrough may require adopting new habits or disciplines. In a Life Coaching relationship, a breakthrough could mean that a person recognizes how their negative attitude is hindering their desired quality of life, career, or relationships. The coachee's "ideal outcome" should be the primary focus of all Life Coaching efforts, regardless of how they may define it.

A Life Coaching breakthrough session is about helping a coachee identify a way to think, behave, or see things differently from how they are currently doing so. In other words, it's about helping them come to terms with their present circumstances, explore what needs to change, and decide on the specific next steps for making that change happen. But before we can construct a breakthrough, we must understand what a breakthrough session is. Life Coaching breakthrough sessions aren't about setting far-distant future goals or delving into people's past experiences; they're simply about helping a coachee understand their current situation and find a wise way forward. By taking the time to explore all three of the following stages, you can give your coachee the best possible chance at creating a change in their life.

There is no one-size-fits-all approach to Life Coaching, but this particular model can be extremely helpful for those who are new to the field. The aim of the model is to help people create a change in their lives by empowering them to take responsibility for themselves, solve their own problems, and make the most of their opportunities. As a Life Coach, one of your key roles is to help people help themselves, and this model provides a simple yet effective framework for doing just that. By using this model, you can help your clients make lasting changes in their lives that will have a positive impact on their overall well-being.

**STAGE 1. ASSESS A COACHEE'S CURRENT SITUATION (CURRENT STATE)**

*"Know thy enemy and know yourself; in a hundred battles, you will never be defeated. When you are ignorant of the enemy but know yourself, your chances of winning or losing are equal. If ignorant both of your enemy and of yourself, you are sure to be defeated in every battle."*

—SUN TZU

The purpose of this first stage of a breakthrough session is to explore a coachee's current situation or circumstances. The goal of this stage is to build rapport within the relationship and help the coachee clarify what the main deficit in their life currently is, and then decide on what their main opportunity for personal growth is. Asking probing questions and helping a coachee explore different perspectives is key at this stage, as sometimes they can be resistant. Your opportunity is to question any negative patterns of thinking, irresponsibility or excuses, and help them to identify positive reasons that will empower them to take decisive action.

KEY QUESTIONS YOU CAN ASK IN THIS STAGE OF THE BREAKTHROUGH INCLUDE:
1. What is the main area that you need to improve in your life?
2. What are the main opportunities you have for growth and improvement?
3. What specifically must change about your current circumstances?

4. Which aspect of your life isn't working out quite so well for you?
5. How could you summarize your problem in one simple sentence?

> An important point to remember here is that your role ISN'T to act as an agony aunt, grief counselor, or therapist. Your aim is to ask reflection-worthy questions and create the "head space" for your coachee to decide what positive changes must be made.

### STAGE 2. DEFINE IDEAL OUTCOMES AND POSITIVE GOALS (IDEAL STATE)

*"The ultimate reason for setting ideal outcomes and positive, clearly defined goals is to entice a man to raise up his thoughts, grow disciplined in his person and become the man that it takes to achieve them."*

—ANDREW CARNEGIE

The purpose of this second stage of a breakthrough session is to assist a coachee in taking full responsibility for their current circumstances. This stage is geared up to assist the coachee in turning their focus away from what the main problem is and establishing the truth about what they want or need instead. During this stage of the session, you will encourage your coachee to consider new opportunities, realistic possibilities, and perspectives that might allow them to start moving forward somehow. This stage of a breakthrough is characterized by the coachee defining ideal goals and positive outcomes that will incentivize them to start action planning.

KEY QUESTIONS TO ASK IN THIS STAGE OF THE BREAKTHROUGH INCLUDE:

1. What would allow you to feel like you are making progress in this area?
2. What would the best possible outcome be that you could work toward?
3. How will you know that this area of your life has vastly improved?
4. How would defining what an ideal outcome looks like in this area?
5. How could you summarize an ideal solution in one simple sentence?

> An important point to remember here, is that your role ISN'T to make suggestions or come up with any answers or possible solutions here. Your aim is to ask thought-provoking questions and create space for your coachee to choose what outcomes are right for them.

## STAGE 3. DEFINE A STRATEGY AND NEXT STEPS (ACTION STATE)

*"You've got to think about all the important big things while you're doing all the small things, so that all the small things go in the right direction."*

—ALVIN TOFFLER

The purpose of this third stage of a breakthrough session is to define what the most practical and wisest next steps are that will allow your coachee to do some work, break through their circumstances, and start moving forward right away. It's usually interesting at this stage to see how resourceful your coachee is. During this stage, you will invite your coachee to consider all of the best options they have available to them and decide on one, two, or three action steps they can take between now and the next time you speak with them. This process is designed to help your coachee move from their current situation to one they would prefer.

KEY QUESTIONS TO ASK IN THIS STAGE OF THE BREAKTHROUGH INCLUDE:

1. What is the first and best step you can take to move forward today?
2. Who else can you ask to support you in taking this action step?
3. What else can you take control of doing NOW to keep moving forward?
4. Once you've started moving forward, what's the next step you can take?
5. If there's only ONE step you can take responsibility for taking, what is it?

> A point to remember here, is that your responsibility as a Life Coach is never to make suggestions, come up with a strategy or recommend action steps for your coachee. Your sole aim is to ask questions and create space for your coachee to decide what they will take responsibility for doing next to start moving their life forward right away.

A coaching breakthrough session is typically a 90- to 120-minute conversation that's dedicated to addressing one specific area or challenge in your (or your coachee's) life. This will often just be a one-time session or, once you become competent in leading people through the process, can lead to subsequent coaching sessions. This Life Coaching breakthrough model is one of the most basic, yet most powerful, coaching models you can master and apply. Yes, there are many other more complicated coaching frameworks out there, but always remember that your coachees don't need you to give them complicated—they just need you to help them break through their circumstances and generate positive results—which this three-stage coaching framework is more than capable of delivering.

# THEORY DETERMINES WHAT YOU CAN SEE

"Whenever a theory appears to you as the only possible one, take this as a sign that you have neither understood the theory nor the problem which it was intended to solve."

—KARL POPPER

The foundations of Life Coaching are deep-rooted in principled psychology-based change theories. Like all skilled helping disciplines, coaching is a process that's mainly concerned with facilitating changes in people's lives; changes in mindset, changes in attitude, changes in productivity, efficiency, effectiveness, fruitfulness, and changes in how people interpret themselves, other people, and the world. While often overlooked, this latter type of change is pivotal to the success of Life Coaching. Nurturing a heightened state of responsibility, decisiveness, consistency, and resilience within a coachee is crucial if coaching is to evolve into something more than just a quick fix for people's issues. Only by strengthening a coachee's capacity to make sensible decisions can the potential of Life Coaching be realized.

During my years of coaching people, I have found that the coachees who underwent the most significant long-lasting changes were not necessarily those who achieved the most impressive short-term results. Instead, they were the ones who took time to carefully reflect on what goals were congruent to them and weighed out these goals in light of what they saw their medium- and long-term priorities as being. Time after time, I have seen people who use coaching as an opportunity for personal growth achieve the greatest and most sustainable long-term results. While short-term results are important, it is the long-term personal growth of the coachee that leads to positive lifestyle changes that sustain over time.

Have you ever had the experience of suddenly noticing a particular model of car after you've started considering buying one? You may have been driving along, minding your own business, when you notice a sleek sports car zip past you on the highway. Or, you may be walking through a parking lot, and suddenly every car seems to be the same color as the one you're thinking of purchasing. This phenomenon is known as the Baader-Meinhof effect or frequency illusion, and it occurs when our minds are focused on a particular thing, causing us to notice it more often than we would if we were thinking about something else. The Baader-Meinhof effect is a result of expanded awareness: when we pay attention to something, we become more conscious of it, and it becomes more prominent in our lives.

When I was studying psychology, I learned assumptions, theories, techniques, and models that all became part of my repertoire of Life Coaching resources. Like many other skilled helping professionals, I have studied many schools of psychological thought and have adopted principles from a range of different theoretical approaches. In the 2010s, I was very fortunate to benefit from the wisdom of Gerard Egan's mentoring. Gerry was the author of *The Skilled Helper* book (among endless other coaching-related resources) who sadly passed in May 2022. As he once explained to me, a common way psychologists define themselves, when asked what "school of thinking" they practice, is eclectic. In my view, the same eclectic approach should be true for the discipline of Life Coaching, as it should never be overly reliant on techniques and models or be limited by one single theoretical approach.

Being "eclectic" is an important lesson, especially for new Life Coaches. This approach helps people make wise decisions by blending together the valuable lessons, models, life principles, theories, and disciplines that have personally impacted them the most. The process is similar to learning how to drive a car. When people first learn to drive, they are observant of the pressure on the gas pedal, the turn signals, and all the rules and regulations of the road. They are constantly thinking about the techniques and details of driving. However, as they become more proficient drivers, driving becomes a set of automatic habits. They no longer think about the techniques or details—they just drive. In the same way, eclectic Life Coaching allows you to focus on the personal growth and development of your coachee rather than getting bogged down in the specific details of every theory or approach.

As Albert Einstein once said, "Theory is useful, because your theory determines what you can see." In other words, the beliefs and assumptions you have about the world will impact how you perceive and interact with it. This is especially true for coaches, who often come from a therapeutic background. Much of what they have learned about the mind and human behavior can be useful to their coaching; however, it is always good practice for coaches to examine the assumptions they hold as ongoing professional development.

This self-awareness can help you to better understand your coachee's outlook on life, the priorities they hold, and the challenges they face. After all, if you don't understand your own mental models, you will be limited in your ability to understand (and empathize) with those belonging to other people. By taking the time to reflect on your own beliefs and assumptions, you can become a more influential and "human" Life Coach to those people whom you serve.

**PRINCIPLE INTO PRACTICE QUESTION:**
1. How might your current knowledge and experience influence the depth that your Life Coaching goes to and also the direction that it takes?

# QUANTIFYING THE LIFE COACHING ALLIANCE

*"It is not love or money that makes the world go around, but rather those supportive alliances in which people grow and receive support for the achievement of purposeful goals."*

—DAVID LLOYD GEORGE

Until now in the handbook, we have discussed different principles that will help strengthen and sustain the relationship between a Life Coach and a coachee. Here, I'd now like to briefly outline how important an initial coaching conversation is for the coach and coachee to sit down and deliberately design what their future collaborative alliance will look like. This way, the coaching relationship can be redesigned as necessary until it meets both parties' needs. This designed alliance is what will become the container in which all future Life Coaching sessions take place. By taking the time to thoughtfully design a Life Coaching alliance, the Life Coach and coachee can both ensure a productive and supportive coaching experience.

The shape that a coaching relationship becomes will be unique to each individual coaching relationship. The initial stages of a coaching conversation will define the purpose of all subsequent coaching and also create a target for the coaching relationship to reach. This foundation-setting process familiarizes a coachee with the Life Coaching process, creates an opportunity to discuss what the alliance must be, will clarify what a coachee's main goals are, and also provide an honest forum for the coach and coachee to negotiate the future direction of their relationship. There is no standardized way of doing this. This opening conversation is vital in order for both parties to understand what they both want and need from each other in order for the coaching relationship to be successful. Furthermore, it allows for explicit discussion of any limits or boundaries that either party may have, which is important in ensuring that the coaching relationship remains professional and comfortable for both parties. By having this open and honest conversation at the start, it paves the way for a more effective coaching relationship that can produce better results.

The early stages of an initial coaching conversation are part "coachee orientation" and part "self-discovery" work; your goal with this is to define what the coaching alliance must be by inviting your coachee to honestly answer some questions (in no particular order):

- What specifically are you hoping to achieve through Life Coaching?
- What are your expectations of coaching and of me as your Life Coach?
- What relationship conditions must exist for us to work together effectively?
- What potential obstacles stand in the way of this relationship being valuable?
- What questions must be answered for you to get the most out of this process?
- What factors must be in place for this coaching relationship to be impactful?
- What reasons exist that might stop you from making life-changing decisions?

These questions (or questions like this) will allow you to set the stage for a healthy and purpose-oriented Life Coaching relationship, in which you and your coachee will both feel confident to move forward together. As your coachee becomes transparent about what they hope to accomplish, you can then make a well-informed decision regarding your competency level to effectively deliver upon what the coachee expects from you. Ultimately, by initiating this honest conversation about what your coachee wants from you within the relationship, and also from participating in the Life Coaching process, you can then set accurate expectations for building a realistic, focused, and productive Life Coaching alliance.

**PRINCIPLES INTO PRACTICE EXERCISE:**

As previously mentioned, there is no universal or standardized way of initiating an initial coaching conversation, or delivering a Life Coaching session. As you reflect on the prior list, what other questions do you feel could be asked in an initial Life Coaching conversation?

# THE FOUNDATIONS OF FACILITATING CHANGE

*"Change is the only constant in life. In order to mature, men and women must be willing to change—there's no other way to grow up. To mature mentally and emotionally, people must change how they speak, how they think, and the way they make decisions."*

—EDWIN L. COLE

When people start maturing in their thinking and take responsibility for what they do (or don't do) and the results they have created (or the messes they have made), people transform from irresponsible delinquents into responsible adults. This lifestyle transformation takes some people longer than others. It often seems difficult at first, but making a decision to change and taking full personal responsibility in life is worth the effort because perpetual childhood is costly, and as many people learn the hard way, is just an unsatisfying way to live life.

You can tell when a person hasn't matured because they use the same words they've always used, express the same opinions they've always expressed, think the same thoughts, and are guided by the same motivations. People who refuse to grow up engage in the same behaviors, display the same attitudes they've always displayed and continue to make the same lifestyle decisions that have never even served them. It takes much reflection and self-awareness to change as a person, and many people never make that effort. They stay stuck in their ways, refusing to consider that there might be a wiser way to think or do things. Some people get locked into ways of thinking that don't serve them, but they're comfortable, so they don't bother changing. As a result, some people never grow up or move forward in life. They just exist in a stagnant state, going through the motions of life but not really living. It is human nature to avoid change. Some people get comfortable in chaos and resist anything that threatens to disrupt their routine. But as anyone who's ever been stuck in a rut can attest, refusing to change has consequences. But before people can change, they must be honest about their words, motivations, actions, and attitudes. Only then can people make principled decisions that are based on values rather than on emotional whims.

Values are what people prioritize most in life. They're what people stand for, live for, and even die for. In extreme cases, values are what some people pay the ultimate price for. Behind every decision people make is a value. You could say that values are the fuel of all decision-making. Principles are different from values, though, and are the moral guidelines that help people determine right from wrong and wise decisions from unwise ones. Principles help you to define what adds value to your life and avoid what detracts from your life. Some life principles are easy to become disciplined in; others are not.

It's easy to make decisions when the options are clear and choose the right path when the facts or future consequences are certain. But as you probably know, most of the tough decisions that people need to make in life exist somewhere between black and white, with the lines between wise and unwise being blurry. And this is when people usually need someone to speak to (i.e., a Life Coach). The principles that people need to sensibly navigate their way through life aren't deep, dark secrets—nor are they hard to understand. On the contrary, the principles you will share with your coachees are the same basic rules for life that you were likely taught as a child by your parents, teachers, grandparents, friends, and significant others who cared about you. Not surprisingly, these are often the same "positive psychology" concepts you will encounter when reading almost any personal growth book. These principles are so timeless that most world cultures develop "sayings" that summarize them, such as;

"The more you give out, the more you get back."

"Don't focus on faults; only focus on solutions."

"Your actions speak louder than your words."

"There's no time like the present moment."

"Look before you leap, not after!"

"Honesty is always the best policy."

These are just a handful of principles that, while they may appear "too simple" (because you've heard them all before), provide invaluable guidelines for life that many of your future coachees will benefit from being reminded of. You might see these principles as "tools" that formulate part of your Life Coaching "mental" toolkit, which you just carry around with you wherever you go. As with all artisan trades, the better the tools, the better the tradesperson (can be), and in more relevant terms, the greater the outcomes of your Life Coaching can be.

One reason why wise Life Coaches are in high demand is that many people need a sound basis for making big decisions. The 2020s have witnessed many cultures around the world plummet into senselessness. People the world over are making many social media-influenced decisions that are resulting in a spectrum of disastrous consequences. As a Life Coach, the more wisdom you cram into your cognitive toolkit now, the more wisdom you will have to positively influence your coachees when the time comes to make an important decision or resist making a disastrous one. The difference between wise decisions and disastrous ones can often be traced back to the principles that guide the individual who's deciding. And this is possibly the greatest responsibility that you have as a Life Coach—to influence your coachees in making sensible and principle-based decisions.

*"Look before you leap, not after!"* A seasoned Life Coach will know what principles they stand for and always think about the long-term consequences each decision might incur. They consider not only the

potential benefits of the decisions their coachees make but also the potential pitfalls, consequences, and costs.

It's not enough to know what's right or to talk about what's right; as a Life Coach, your opportunity is to consistently do what IS right and showcase your life as a living example of wise and principled living. So don't be satisfied just to learn or quote wisdom from across the ages. Make whatever changes are necessary to live by those rules, seven days a week and twenty-four hours a day. Make "practice what you preach" a principle you live by. While you're at it, take an honest look at the habits and attitudes you've been embracing. If change is required, make those changes today. Model the attitudes that you want your future coachees to exhibit. Become the kind of "role model" human being that other people might want to emulate. Let your life become a living example of what it means to live life wisely and well.

Albert Einstein once famously said, "Insanity is doing the same thing over and over while expecting new results." If you'd like better results in your own life, relationships, family life, business endeavors, or in the effectiveness of your Life Coaching, you might need to make some changes and do some things differently than you have done in the past. To do things differently, you might need to start thinking or acting differently—which brings me to what I want to share with you in the next chapter, a set of governing principles to influence wise decision-making.

**PRINCIPLES INTO PRACTICE EXERCISE:**

Think about What values and principles matter the most to you. Reflect upon a recent time you made a major life transition or decision. Which values or principles helped you to navigate that transition wisely and effectively?

# THE PRINCIPLE OF COUNTING OPPORTUNITY COSTS

*"The percentage of mistakes in quick decisions is no greater than in long-drawn-out vacillations, and the effect of decisiveness itself makes things go and creates confidence."*

—ANNE O'HARE MCCORMICK

I have always found that the best decisions are those that are made intuitively and with confidence. My grandfather was a man who never hesitated to make a decision. He always seemed to know exactly what he wanted and where he was going. As a result, he was always successful in whatever he undertook. On the other hand, I have also encountered people who lack decisiveness. They are the ones who struggle to make decisions, second-guess themselves, and hesitate to act. In my experience, indecisive people are usually not as successful in life as intuitive and decisive people are. People who are indecisive tend to be those who end up missing out on opportunities or taking a path that doesn't suit them.

Decisiveness isn't a quality that all people possess. It takes a special kind of person to see what needs to be done and have the courage to do it. This is why making wise decisions is such a crucial element of a coaching relationship. Individuals who make quick decisions have a higher chance of getting what they want than those who stall and procrastinate. When a Life Coach is decisive, it shows that they are confident and in control. This confidence will usually inspire a coachee to follow suit and can help build a fruitful coaching relationship.

Decisiveness is an important personal quality that shows a person is willing to take responsibility for his or her actions. A coach who is afraid to make bold decisions is not a coach that people can trust. Trust is the key ingredient of any wholesome Life Coaching relationship, and it is earned when a coach demonstrates decisiveness. Decisiveness is wisdom in action. It's the ability to know what a wise decision is and also having the preparedness to follow through and make it. Decisiveness is a life skill that many people never bother to develop. Decisive people make great Life Coaches because they tend to arrive at accurate conclusions about people's readiness for coaching early on. Decisive people tend to dislike unnecessary delay; when a decision needs to be made, they make it.

In a world where we are constantly bombarded with choices, it can be difficult to know which ones are the right ones to make. Unfortunately, it seems that, more often than not, people are making reckless decisions without considering the consequences. As a result, destructive behavior and emotional bankruptcy have become all too common. Just scroll through your social media feeds, and you'll see examples of people all over the world making careless choices without a thought for the future.

This isn't just an issue in far-flung corners of the globe; it's happening closer to home as well. If you take a look around your hometown, you'll likely see the consequences of poor decision-making everywhere you turn. From drug and alcohol abuse to promiscuous sex, gambling addictions, overflowing prisons, and violent crime, the evidence of poor decision-making is all around us. And while it's easy to point the finger of blame at others, the truth is that we are all susceptible to making unwise choices from time to time. Many young people who need the benefits of a wise education treat school as a decade-long vacation. We see an ongoing disintegration of family values depriving children of the wisdom they need to make sensible life decisions. Politicians are corrupt, and the institution of politics is broken; global economies are collapsing, young people are being manipulated by deceptive adults into thinking that gender is in some way interchangeable, and religion has been reduced to little more than song-singing and discussion forum debates.

So what is the answer? Let us remind ourselves of a principle; *give a man a fish, and he eats for today; teach him how to fish, and he feeds himself for life. Teach a man how to teach his friends to fish, and we start ending world hunger.* As a Life Coach, you might support parent groups in their efforts to raise children with wisdom and discipline. You might host workshops to educate teachers on how to help young people make wise lifestyle decisions that will lead to them living satisfying and fruitful lives, instead of ones overflowing with apathy and regret. You might never go on to become a Life Coach, and that's OK. But you can become a wise role model who can help people replace bad habits with better ones, replace impulsivity with wisdom, and guide people in making the best possible choices at a given time. Indecision leaves people in a state of mental paralysis and tied up in emotional knots—which eventually evolves into depression if left untouched for long enough. William James, one of psychology's forefathers was right when he said, *"There's no more miserable person than the one in whom nothing is habitual but indecision."*

Perhaps you view decisiveness as a trait given to only a few, but this is untrue. Decisiveness is a practical life skill that can be scaled up, matured, enhanced, improved, and refined over time. Decisiveness reflects a person's self-discipline and commitment to ongoing personal betterment. It's important to state, though, that until a person knows what is important to them (i.e., their values), it will be impossible for them to make consistently wise choices. Values, as I have already stated, are the "most important" things that people live and die for. You may think your values are the same old clichéd values that many people post on their Facebook pages: mantras like "family must come first," "live everyday as if it's your last," "be a source of love and light in the world," etc. But here's the actual truth: your true values will be reflected through what you do and in how you spend your time—not in the words that you say.

Although we often deceive ourselves into thinking we know what motivates us, the truth is that we often have only a vague understanding of our inner drivers. This is why taking "time out" for self-reflection is central to personal growth and development. By examining our actions and considering how we spend our time, it's possible to get a clearer picture of what motivates us. This process is essential if we want to understand ourselves. What do you value most in life? Is it money, time, or something else entirely? Your answer to this question can say a lot about you. If you value money above all else, you will likely be very strict with your spending and try to save as much as possible. On the other hand, if you value time more than anything, you will be strict with how you spend it and make sure that you are always doing what is important to you. So, if you want to know what someone values, ask to look at their bank account and schedule. You will see the truth for yourself.

How we spend our time and money reveals what we value most in life. If our calendar is filled with activities that don't align with our "stated" values, then we must reevaluate how we're spending our time. The same is true of our money. If we're not spending our money in a way that reflects our values, then we need to reevaluate our priorities. By taking a close look at how we spend our time and our money, we can get a clear picture of what we value most in life. And when we align our values with our actions, we can live a life that is both congruent and fulfilling. For example, if you say that you value your health, but you spend your evenings sitting on the couch watching TV instead of going for a walk, then it's clear that your actions don't reflect your stated values. Similarly, if you say that you value family, but you're never home because you're working long hours, then again, your actions are not in alignment with your values. In order to live a fulfilling life, it's important to take stock of your values and make sure that your actions reflect what you truly care about. When your actions and your values are in alignment, you can live with purposeful intentionality.

You can think of values as "what people stand for." They're the things people live and are sometimes willing to die for. Principles are timeless, universal truths, the rules of the game that human beings must play by—or reap the consequences. Principles show you how to apply your values and how to accomplish your goals. It's useful to note here, however, that NOT all life principles are healthy or equal. When you begin interacting with a new coachee, she might tell you that her aim is to "turn her financial situation around" and "find a new way of generating income for herself." As a principle, generating income for oneself is generally a good thing. However, your coachee might, during an earlier stage in her life, have subscribed to some unhelpful ideological concepts (UICs), such as; "I'm entitled to something for nothing," or "I shouldn't need to work too hard to earn good money."

I'm saying here that setting goals is just a small part of the Life Coaching process—and one which we'll cover in significantly more depth later on in the handbook. The greatest challenge that many Life Coaches face within a Life Coaching relationship, is either their coachees UICs or their own UICs. Decision-making is an invaluable life skill that gets developed over time. It requires wisdom, discernment, sound judgment, and learning lessons from our past mistakes. Principles are your roadmap to Life Coaching success because they will help you to help people distinguish between the things that will ADD value to their life (assets) and the things that will TAKE AWAY from their life (liabilities). At all times, every decision people make will add value to their life or take value away from it. This principle is called "counting the cost," and is a valuable life discipline people tend to only learn after navigating their way out of the school of hard knocks.

Nobody sets out with the intention to fail in life, but unfortunately, many people do due to not counting the cost of their decision-making ahead of time. Setting goals with your coachees is like planning out a new building project. As with all new things, new building projects can often seem exciting for people, but the "counting the cost" principle insists that before a person begins to pursue a goal to build anything, they ensure they are willing and able to pay the full cost of the project. As a Life Coach, your opportunity is to help people become aware of this "counting the cost" principle so that they can make the best possible decisions for themselves in any given situation. Always be practical, never hypothetical. When people learn to "count the cost" of their choices, they'll become far more likely to make choices that will generate the "right" long-term outcomes or lead them in a direction that they genuinely want to take.

Many people have distorted values today, employ unhelpful ideologies, and make disastrous lifestyle decisions that lead them into states of financial poverty, mental confusion, and sickness through losing their marriage, health, sanity, and even their children. Life is like a big fight for territory. People will come to you for Life Coaching to help them take new territory or reclaim lost territories. When people stop fighting for what they want in life, what they *don't want* might end up taking over and completely consuming whatever territory, however little, they have left. And this is the potential cost of indecisiveness.

**PRINCIPLES INTO PRACTICE QUESTIONS:**
1. What are some areas of your life in which you struggle to be decisive?
2. What can you do to gain clarity about what is most important to you?
3. How do you currently spend the majority of your time and money?

Write honestly about how you spend the majority of time and money, and see if you can identify any positive changes you will benefit from making—doing this will allow you more clarity to make wiser decisions that reflect what's actually important to you.

*(Side note: These questions can also serve as a really useful framework for coaching people who state that they're uncertain about what their priorities are.)*

# FACTORS THAT INFLUENCE DECISION-MAKING

"It doesn't matter which side of the fence you get off on sometimes. What matters most is getting off. You cannot make progress without making decisions."

—JIM ROHN

Every day, people are faced with an endless array of choices, big and small. What to wear? What to eat? What to watch on television? But sometimes, the stakes are much higher. People might be considering a change in career, a move to a new city, or starting a new business. While you should never make people's decisions for them, your value as a Life Coach resides in the input you give when helping coachees make their life-changing decisions.

According to research by behavioral psychologist Dan Ariely, human beings are predisposed to making irrational and emotionally-based choices. One major reason for this is that, at some point, instead of following sound logic or "common sense," people embrace their unconscious instincts, urges, and impulses. Human beings often fail to consider all facts when making important decisions and, instead, are influenced by their biases. As a result, some people make unwise decisions that fail to align with their best interests.

In his book *Thinking Fast and Slow*, Daniel Kahneman explains that there are two systems in the human mind that affect judgment and choice. The first system is fast, emotional, and instinctive. It is the "gut feeling" people have when choosing between two options. The second system is slow, logical, and deliberate. It is the ability people have to evaluate information before reaching a conclusion. Some people become obsessed with their intuition and emotions, and they ignore important facts—that, if considered wisely, would allow people to distinguish between their emotional and logical responses to a situation. In other words, some people let their feelings dictate their actions instead of using logic and reason to think things through sensibly. This can lead to impulsive decision-making and poor choices in life. As a Life Coach, it is your role to guide people in making slow, logical, wise, and deliberate decisions—and to assess the pros and cons of all options before making a choice.

In this chapter, I want to share with you the conflicting options that are available to all people as they face making decisions. Wisdom is not the same as having intelligence or being smart. Intelligence requires processing information in a logical way. However, having intelligence is not enough for effective decision-making. What is needed in addition to intelligence is wisdom—the capacity to see the whole picture, to understand what is most important, and make choices that align with those priorities. By helping people make wise decisions, you help them in the process of aligning their decisions with their priorities. In this way, you can help people avoid the pain of regret and the suffering that comes from making choices that are out of alignment with what is most important to them.

As any experienced Life Coach knows, there is no magic bullet or one-size-fits-all approach to Life Coaching. Exactly the same is true of decision-making. There is no "master methodology" you can call upon that will turn unwise decision-makers into wise ones. How people make decisions is influenced by many factors—some within their awareness, and others are not. Therefore, it is important to be aware of all the dynamics that influence decision-making in order to help people make the best decisions possible. The best that you can do is become more conscious of the choices YOU make, and as this happens, you will become naturally more equipped to challenge the decisions that your coachees might make.

## WISE RESPONSIBILITY VS. FOOLISH IRRESPONSIBILITY

I read *The Road Less Traveled*, by M. Scott Peck a few years ago, and it got me thinking about the difference between wisdom and foolishness. Wise people see what's true and adjust their lives accordingly. Foolish people, on the other hand, insist that truth adjusts itself to their reality. In other words, wise people meet the demands of life, while fools expect life to meet their wants and preferences. Wise people ask for feedback from trusted sources, own their attitudes, life's outcomes, mistakes made, and never make excuses for the state of their lives. Fools get offended by truth, refuse to accept their imperfections, and blame other people for the circumstances they face.

People who take responsibility for their mistakes and shortcomings are more likely to make the changes necessary for living a more satisfying and rewarding life. Irresponsibility breeds disempowerment, and responsibility cultivates empowerment. People who take responsibility for themselves, pursuing their goals, and working on their weaknesses and shortcomings become empowered. When people are empowered, they live life with a greater sense of purpose and actively direct their energies toward their desired outcomes. Responsibility or irresponsibility is a decision that all people make every single day.

## DELIBERATE HUMILITY VS. SELF-CENTERED OBSESSION

Humble people realize how little they know and accept the importance of ongoing self-improvement. Pride-driven people, on the other hand, are egotistical and typically concerned with just themselves. Pride is the desire to move past one's current position. When people lose sight of a meaningful purpose, a psychological inversion occurs in which their mental attention shifts from a sense of social contribution to an internal focus. This is when people become self-obsessed and distorted in character. Humble people tend to be more open to feedback and ready to learn from their mistakes. Prideful people often have a hard time admitting when they're wrong and resist feedback that could help them improve.

Peeling an onion is a good analogy for the process of developing humility. Just when you think you've removed all traces of pride, you find another layer lurking beneath the surface. In much the same way, forsaking pride and choosing to be deliberately humble is a lifelong process that requires patience and dedication to develop. Humble people tend to go far in life, as they remain open to correction and improving themselves wherever necessary. Proud people don't want to change because, in their view, they're already 100 percent "right."

### EMOTIONAL DECISIONS VS. RATIONAL DECISIONS

There are two competing mental processes at work when it comes to making decisions: logic and emotions. Understanding whether your decisions are based on logic or emotion is essential for ensuring that your short-term decisions serve your long-term goals and progression. Some people assume that the decisions they make are based on facts and "common sense" logic—these same people might also naively assume their perception to be a reality in actuality. The logical mind aids people in visualizing what the long-term results of their behaviors might be, allowing them to act accordingly. Many people, on the other hand, overly rely on emotions when making major decisions, and because emotions are prone to change, they seldom provide a solid basis for sensible decision-making.

For example, some people make snap judgments due to anger or fear rather than taking time to weigh up all other options that are available to them. Deciphering whether your choices are "generally" driven by logic or emotion is a vital first step in ensuring that your decision-making is geared up to support your long-term personal growth and satisfaction. This same step is equally valid in the context of Life Coaching, as you question the role that emotions might play in overriding your coachee's better judgment.

### MOTIVATED BY UNITY VS. DRIVEN BY DIVIDE

There have always been a plethora of causes for human division. While some people may claim that humanity is "progressing" scientifically and technologically, I would argue that mankind has been depleting in wisdom for decades. In the 2020s, humanity is a century removed from World War I, but it's still trapped in divisive ideas that claim black is better than white, male is superior to female, old is wiser than young, or rich is preferable to poor. And these manifestations of human difference only scratch the surface of why individuals quarrel with one another. Attitudes of division are propagated in how we interact with strangers and are visible within politics, religion, schools, workplaces, and even family homes.

Unity is hard to build, and division is easy because, as humans, we are naturally inclined to gravitate toward those who are like us. However, this tendency toward division leads to all intolerance and broken relationships. The attitude of division is rooted in fear and insecurity, and is fed by the need people have to feel superior over others and find a group to belong to. Ultimately, division is born out of disinterest in understanding differences. People make decisions to unite and divide with others every single day, and it's the outcomes of these decisions that commonly fuel the states of loneliness and sadness that people suffer in.

**GROWTH ORIENTATION VS. GRATIFICATION ORIENTATION**

We live in a world where many people (especially within the self-improvement industry) make a lot of money by selling people quick fixes and miracle cures. Even within the Life Coaching industry, there are, sadly, endless con artists who sell "high ticket" coaching training programs under the premise that delegates will exit a fourteen-day training course with a successful six-figure "business in a box"—only in exchange for XXX number of £££££s or $$$$s.

Some of your coachees will expect your coaching to somehow, miraculously "heal their woes" and "address their challenges" with little or no effort invested on their part. It is easy to do "easy" things that require little effort and provide immediate gratification. Long-term personal growth, business success, and healthy marriages, on the other hand, rarely come easy. The sad reality is that some people would rather pay for a quick fix than put in the hard work required for creating the positive changes they want in life. Achieving anything substantial in life requires hard work, investment, discipline, and delaying gratification. In nearly every field, those who achieve great feats are rarely those who take the easy route.

**FAITH FOR FUTURE GAIN VS. FEAR OF FUTURE FAILURES**

We live in uncertain times. Uncertainty often opens the door to fear, stress, and scarcity thinking. Even something as benign as checking the news or scrolling through social media raises the heartbeat when we're assailed by everything that is (or could be) wrong with the world. Your coachee always gets to choose how they respond to the events that happen in their life. They can choose to look to the future with fear or look to the future with faith. Fear looks to the future and assumes what "might" happen. This is the negative guesswork that plunders the present moment and steals its inner peace. Anxious people look to the future and catastrophize rather than put actionable plans into motion to prepare for the best.

Faith looks through history and provokes people to remember the challenges they've already overcome and learned from. Faith precedes all progression. People who won't take risks, step out of their comfort zone and work hard to create the changes they want would be foolish to expect more tomorrow than what they've already achieved today. So, encourage your coachee to have faith in themselves and hope for a positive future, but ONLY if they're prepared to do everything within their power to achieve the outcomes that they hope for.

Decision-making never happens in a vacuum. There are always situational circumstances that influence our every decision. Without acknowledgment and understanding of these factors, the decisions people make can be ineffective and even unwise. The next time you find yourself having to make a decision, big or small, before all other things, take a step back and assess all of the different factors that come into play. Only by doing so will you be able to arrive at a well-informed and thoughtful decision that will increase the chances of success for whatever it is you or your coachee need to achieve.

**PRINCIPLES INTO PRACTICE QUESTIONS:**

1. Which attitudes above have hindered your personal growth the most?
2. Which attitudes above have hindered your career advancement the most?
3. In your eyes, how important is coachee decision-making in the Life Coaching process?
4. How might your response to the last question inform the caliber of your coaching?

# SECTION THREE SUMMARY

A Life Coach's main goal is to help people improve their quality of life. This happens as people become conscious of the factors that influence their decision-making. Think about the decisions you have made today. How many of them were the result of thoughtful analysis, sorting through options, considering their potential effect on others, or setting aside your biases? How many were based on your desire to prove yourself, take the easy option, ignore how your choice might impact others, or succumb to peer pressure? In truth, everyone wants to believe they're capable of sound judgment, yet most people can use a little help to make wiser decisions that reflect their values and priorities. A Life Coach can provide this help by serving as a sounding board, challenging assumptions, and asking thought-provoking questions. In doing so, a Life Coach can help people gain greater clarity about what they want and why they want it. As a result, people are able to make decisions that are in line with their values and priorities, leading to a more rewarding and satisfying life.

**IMPORTANT LESSONS TO REMEMBER:**
- People who refuse to challenge their perspective on things become closed off from reality.
- The shape a coaching relationship becomes will be unique to each coaching relationship.

- A breakthrough session should help facilitate a positive shift in perspective for a coachee.
- The "ideal outcome" of Life Coaching is the reason why people want coaching to begin with.
- All people are only ever one paradigm shift away from transforming how they see things.
- Life Coaches don't offer solutions. They assist people in making well-informed decisions.
- The greatest coaching outcome is a coachee growing in responsibility and decisiveness.
- A coachee will become automatically empowered on deciding what they must do next.
- Mind management is a result of self-control, which happens through self-awareness.

### SECTION THREE NOTEWORTHY IDEAS

Use this space to note down any ideas that have struck you as important throughout this section of the handbook. Also, write down any questions that might be beneficial for your future consideration and self-reflection.

## SECTION FOUR

# THE MOTIVATIONS FOR HUMAN BEHAVIOR

In this section of the handbook, we will explore human values and consider what role they may play in influencing a coachee's decisions within a typical Life Coaching conversation. Values are the guiding principles that help people make choices between what is instantly gratifying and what will best serve their long-term goals. By understanding values, individuals can make better-informed decisions about how they live their lives. People who contemplate their values before making important decisions are more likely to act in ways that will benefit them in the long run.

# VALUES: THE DRIVING FORCE OF BEHAVIOR

*"Values are like fingerprints. Nobody's are the same, but you leave m"em smudged all over everything that you do."*

—ELVIS PRESLEY

Values are what guide our actions, thoughts, and behaviors and are the cornerstone upon which human beings make their every decision. Our values shape who we are as individuals, and everyone has their own set of values that carry varying degrees of importance to them. For example, one person might value achievement before all things, while someone else might see security as being of utmost importance. Benevolence might be a priority to one person whilst being completely unimportant to another. Some people spend their days in pursuit of happiness, while others lead social movements that transform endless people's lives. Our values are what make us who we are. Our values are the reason why we have what we have. They are the foundation upon which our entire lives are built.

In my early years of studying psychology, there was a training instructor who I found very easy to connect with. I would regularly ask her questions and be met with provocatively reflective responses—I possibly appreciated these dialogues more than the endless hours I spent listening to curriculum-based instruction. A few days after the course ended, I was invited for a break-out session with my instructor to discuss how the course had impacted me or influenced my thinking in any way. I was a man of ideas at that point in my life and would take any opportunity to discuss my future hopes and aspirations. The first words that exited my instructor's mouth were, "Kain, you seem to be a highly driven man." I agreed as I proceeded to detail the endless goals I hoped to achieve. After listening to me monologue for five minutes, she raised her hand, gesturing to me to stop talking.

"What you say is interesting, and you are unquestionably a highly-driven man. However, I'm curious to understand what specifically drives you. What is the real motivation behind your high energy and actions?" The question struck me hard. Until this precise moment in my life, I had been referred to, many times, as a high-energy individual with uncapped potential and a huge inner drive. My main issue back then was that I had never stopped to consider the true reasons "why" I had so much "inner drive" or the honest reasons "why" I wanted to do anything meaningful with my life at all.

Trying to understand the values that motivate human behavior is like trying to unravel a big ball of knotted string. All human beings share the same values, to some degree, and this is what allows people to relate to each other. It's impossible to relate to any other human being, other than through the decisions they make—which are all fuelled by values and what people deem as important to them. What one person considers to be imperatively valuable, another may just view as a mere preference. Some people place greater weight on certain values than others do, and this is what makes values so complex. And yet, despite their complexity, values are the reason why people get out of bed in the morning, get married, get divorced, build businesses, go to war, play it safe, take risks, write books, or even commit crimes. Values are what make people human. They are what connect us to each other and drive us forward. In a world that is ever-changing and increasingly complex, our values are what anchor us and give our lives a sense of meaning.

People are often quick to judge the decisions that others make without taking time to understand the true motivations behind those decisions. We all carry exactly the same values, but we each prioritize our values depending on what we deem to be of utmost importance.

Some values are based on moral principles, while others are based on performance, aesthetics, or social interactions. The degree of importance that people place on each of these categories is what determines their behavior.

**MORAL VALUES**

Most people have a sense of "right" and "wrong," even if they don't always follow their own moral compass. But where do these values come from? Some people believe they are innate, while others argue they are learned through experience. There is no easy answer, but it's clear that moral values play a vital role in our lives. They provide a framework for making decisions, and they help to motivate us to act in a certain way. As we navigate the challenges of life, our moral values can guide us toward a path that is honest, compassionate, integral, and sincere. Though they may sometimes be difficult to follow, living by a set of moral values is what lets people live strong and consistent lifestyles.

**PERFORMANCE VALUES**

If you've ever been a part of a team, you know that not everyone works the same way. Some people are natural leaders, while others prefer to stay in the background. Some people work best under pressure, while others work best when they can take their time. And some people are able to accomplish a lot in a short period of time, while others are more careful and methodical in their approach. These output differences reflect the "performance-based values" that people view as important. Performance values influence how we work, creatively express ourselves, or perform tasks. And they play an important role in determining how fruitful we are in life. Some performance values, such as efficiency and productivity, are prized by many organizations. Others, such as self-discipline and perseverance, are more internalized values that we each need to develop on our own. But all of them contribute to our overall effectiveness as human beings.

## AESTHETIC VALUES

When we think of aesthetic values, it can be easy to only see things such as order, structure, or proportion in balance. Aesthetic values assist us in perceiving the natural world around us. However, aesthetic values go far beyond what we perceive as being attractive. They also include our personal preferences and biases. What one person finds attractive is often different from what another person does. Beauty is subjective. This is because our individual experiences and perspectives influence what we perceive as being aesthetically pleasing. Aesthetic values help us to connect with the world and appreciate what we see, hear, feel, taste, and smell via our representational systems. People connect to what they can experience. For example, if you take the time to enjoy a landscape, you will see and understand it better—giving you a broader perspective of the world in general.

## SOCIAL VALUES

Social values deal with interacting with others and include qualities like cooperation, courtesy, and loyalty. We learn these values from our family and friends, and they shape how we think about and relate to others. People who act in accordance with social values tend to be more successful in their relationships and pursuits while simultaneously making life more pleasant and orderly for those whom they keep company with. Social values offer guidance regarding how we should behave toward others. Of course, not everyone shares the same values. And sometimes, our own values conflict with those of others. But even when there is disagreement, taking time to understand and respect people's values is an essential part of living in a harmonious society.

A unique blend of all four values types makes us who we are. For example, I might place a high value on integrity because I believe it is morally imperative to live life in an integral way. I might also value efficiency because I view time as being one of life's most valuable commodities. I might prioritize connected relationships in which I can be myself with people because I find little value in superficial relationships. And I might place a high value on balance because I see it as important to maintain harmony throughout the various areas of my life. What is important to me might not be important to you, and vice versa. This is OK, though, because it's this degree of difference that gives us a reason to understand each other.

Values are the guiding principles that help us to make choices between what's instantly gratifying and what will best serve our long-term goals. By understanding values, we can make wise decisions about how we live our lives. People who consider their values before making important decisions are more likely to act in ways that will benefit them in the long run. In this section of the handbook, we'll explore values further and consider what role they might play in influencing the decisions a coachee might make within a typical Life Coaching conversation.

**PRINCIPLES INTO PRACTICE QUESTIONS:**

Values function like compass points. A compass needle points toward the true north and acts as a guide for travelers. Values serve us in a similar way, guiding us in the direction of our life.

1. What has really motivated you in the past? What motivates you more today?
2. What characteristics are common to the people whom you respect the most?
3. In what ways have your priorities changed as you have gotten older and matured?

# THE FREEDOM VS. SECURITY CONUNDRUM

*"You will work at your Freedom or accept your bondage. None are more hopelessly enslaved than those who falsely believe they are free."*

—JOHANN WOLFGANG VON GOETHE

Values are motivational constructs that inspire the goals people aspire to attain. Values transcend specific actions and situations. We all hold numerous values that shape our decisions and actions, each with a varying degree of importance. Values are abstract, "conceptual" goals and are often thought of as constants, but they aren't. Values, and especially how we prioritize them, will change constantly as we progress throughout the different ages and stages of life. For example, men in their twenties might value excitement and risk, whereas men in their forties or sixties might be more motivated by security and home comforts. Values can also be influenced by our culture, family, friends, religion, and life experiences.

As previously mentioned, we all have values that give our lives a sense of purpose. All people have a set of values that get prioritized based on what people view their current life deficits as being. These priorities change over time as people find new ways to get what they want and fulfill their values. Think about it this way, no one is motivated to work hard to pursue something that they already have. As a Life Coach, your opportunity is to help people set goals that are aligned with their values and current priorities in life (this is otherwise referred to as congruent goal setting). This will not only increase the likelihood of four coachees achieving those goals but also help them to find more fulfillment in the process.

Values act as a compass that guides us through life's ups and downs. When our values align with our actions, we feel satisfaction and fulfillment. Even amidst challenges, when our values are guiding us, we can still find inner peace and contentment. But when our values are out of sync with our actions, it can lead to feelings of frustration, dissatisfaction, and even despair. People who make decisions that go against their values, or act in a way that is inconsistent with what they believe in, typically end up feeling conflicted and confused. Inner conflict and confusion are among the most common challenges people bring to a Life Coach.

The values that people prioritize actively pursuing will often be influenced by their immediate life circumstances. For example, a man with a top-end salary and plenty of money away in savings accounts might not value financial stability as much as those who have little financial stability would. Another example could be a freelancer who values self-direction more highly than those who work in a traditional office setting. Life circumstances often impose constraints against pursuing or expressing values. Having dependent children, for instance, may lead a parent to stop pursuing stimulation-based values and avoid high-risk sports that might jeopardize their ability to parent. In other words, life circumstances make pursuing some values more (or less) rewarding or potentially costly. Another example could be a woman who lives in a society where certain gender stereotypes prevail. On one hand, she may be rewarded for pursuing benevolence values and, on the other, undermined for pursuing a position or role of authority. Values are central to our lives, and it's important to be aware of how they shape our decisions and also our inner conflicts. The following story will hopefully serve as an example of this.

**THE FREEDOM VS. SECURITY CONUNDRUM**

When I was a child, I would take holidays to a fishing village on Scotland's northern coast with my parents. My father often worked in this area, so during our vacations, we would visit the hotel he stayed at whilst working away. The hotel was owned by a lady named Margaret and had been a family business for decades. My sister and I looked forward to these hotel visits for a few reasons; the first reason was Margaret would always bake us fresh cakes, and the second reason was that we could spend time with her talking Mynah bird, Tweety.

Margaret lived in a small apartment flat above the hotel, and Tweety was in a birdcage in her living room during the winter months; he had all the mirrors and trinkets he could ever want and enjoyed flying around the living room when Margaret let him out of the birdcage to stretch his wings. In the summer, however, Margaret moved the birdcage to the kitchen, which had sea views for her bird to enjoy. Margaret thought she was spoiling her little bird on those days when, in actuality, these times were like torture to him. He lived a life of blissful ignorance for nine months a year, but when summer rolled around, he got to see everything he was missing out on: the sunshine, trees to build a nest in, woodlouse (among other bugs) to eat, and, of course, other birds he could fly around with. He was never more aware of his cage than when he sat there, trapped behind his bars, watching the other birds swoop past the window and perch with each other in the trees and on the lawn.

One summer day, Margaret decided to go grocery shopping. She packed her bags, opened the cage to let her little bird fly around whilst she was gone, and left her home, unknowingly leaving her kitchen window open. Tweety hopped down onto the ledge of the birdcage and looked longingly at the open window. This was his chance for freedom, once and for all. He could finally find out what the wind felt like; he could eat berries all day, bathe in puddles, and hop around in the dirt to dig for worms. Perhaps, he thought, he could even try to build himself a nest and find himself a little girlfriend to start a family with. Then doubt and fear crept into his mind. What if none of the other birds liked him, or what if some of these birds were dangerous? If there were birds, there were surely other beasts out there that could harm or even kill him should they want to. What if he couldn't find any berries or worms or build a nest? How would he survive? Then finally, he thought, what about poor Margaret? She'd spent years treating him kindly, feeding him well, and she didn't have anyone else in her life. Surely she'd get lonely and upset.

Tweety spent hours procrastinating, contemplating all the potential pros and cons of his freedom. He desperately wanted to be free, but he was also terrified at the idea of leaving behind his security and home comforts. He was so lost in his thoughts that he didn't hear Margaret return from the shops. It was only when he heard the window closing that he grew aware of his situation. Margaret, relieved, closed the door of the birdcage and said, "Who's a pretty boy then?" She draped a blanket over the birdcage and vowed to never make that mistake again. For the rest of her life, Margaret double-checked that the birdcage was locked before leaving her apartment, and Tweety never got another opportunity to explore the world beyond it.

We have all been there before: at a crossroads, unsure of which path to take. One path leads to the safety and comfort of the known, while the other path represents the unknown, full of excitement and possibility. It can be a tough decision to make, especially when both options are appealing in different ways. This situation is often referred to as a values conflict, where having one good thing comes at the cost of having another good thing. For example, you may long for the excitement of a new relationship, but that means giving up the comfort and security of your current relationship. Or you may yearn for the freedom of being your own boss, but that means giving up the stability of a regular paycheck. Your future coachees might sometimes struggle with exactly the same conundrum as Margret's bird did.

It is often said that the only constant in life is change. And yet, so many of us resist change, preferring instead to stay in our comfort zones. Of course, there is nothing wrong with feeling comfortable and safe. But if we allow our comfort to become a prison, we will never experience the growth and freedom that comes from stepping outside of our comfort zones. Values are at the heart of every decision we make. They drive our choices and shape our actions. And so, when faced with a choice that needs to be made, it is important to ask ourselves what we value most. If we value comfort and security, then we will stay within our comfort zone and not risk everything for something new. But if we value growth and opportunity, then we will be willing to sacrifice everything for a chance to experience something new. There is no right or wrong answer—only the answer that is right for you. And exactly the same will be true for all of your future coachees.

Most people eventually learn that something better might be attained tomorrow by giving up something of value today. This is partly what it means to pursue meaning over appeasement. No coach can predict if a coachee will make enough money to survive if they abandon the job they hate or if leaving the marriage they're unhappy in will lead them to a happy life with someone new. Life Coaches aren't fortune tellers, but they can help people to evaluate the congruence of their decision-making. When decision-making isn't congruent, something must change. Nothing in life is guaranteed, even the comfort zone! Whether or not a coachee wants to face hard times is their decision, but the role of an effective Life Coach is to encourage them to grow, not remain the same. Just because the cage is comfortable doesn't mean there aren't even greater treasures and experiences outside the window.

**PRINCIPLES INTO PRACTICE QUESTIONS:**

1. In what areas of your life do you prioritize security and comfort over freedom?
2. What might happen if you started prioritizing freedom over security in your life?
3. How might you help others make intimidating or challenging decisions?

# A STOIC REMEDY FOR TIMES OF DIFFICULTY

*"See if you can catch yourself complaining about a situation you get into, what other people do or say, your life in general, even the weather. To complain is to undermine what is. When you complain, you become a victim of your own circumstances."*

—ECKHART TOLLE

There is a story about a complaining turkey who wanted to fly. You may think I'm a little obsessed with birds at this point, but bear with me; they're helpful allegories. This turkey, and his turkey friends, were fed up with watching other birds fly about in the sky while he and his turkey friends remained grounded. This was something that, together, they often complained about. He spent half his life watching other birds fly around and balance themselves upon the breezes. Having experimented with different wing flapping techniques, the turkey finally mastered one. Even with his unusual shape and size compared to the other birds, he learned to fly. The turkey, wanting to share his newfound joy, invited his friends to a gathering where he taught them how to fly. Soon, by the end of the meeting, all the turkeys had learned to take wing. The turkey was so proud of his friends for mastering this new skill; however, at the end of their first flight, he was left flabbergasted as he watched his other turkey friends walking back to their nests, complaining about how "easy" all the other birds "have it."

It's human nature to complain. We complain about the weather, our jobs, homes, our political leadership, financial affairs, families, and even "society" when there's nothing more specific to complain about. And many people hire a Life Coach for the purpose of complaining about the condition of their lives. Trust me when I say that this WILL happen to you at some point. But what might happen if, instead of letting people complain about their circumstances, you could redirect their energy toward focusing on what is within their power to change? Just imagine the possibilities! People could create their dream vocations, design their ideal homes, forge healthy relationships with family and friends, and make a positive difference in the world. All it takes is a shift in perspective from complaint-mode to creative possibility.

Values are the guiding principles in our lives. They dictate how we see the world and how we interact with others. If our values are out of alignment with our actions, it can lead to feelings of frustration and dissatisfaction. Some people spend their entire lives dissatisfied, forever complaining that life isn't working out for them as they want it to. When we complain about our lives or circumstances, it is often because we are not living in a way that aligns with our values. Those who want to improve their lives must start by examining their values. Values are the foundation upon which we determine our choices, decisions, actions and behaviors.

Suffering is part of life, and it's generally the things that people "suffer over" that they go on to complain about. All people have the choice to let suffering control them and, consequently, suffer more, or learn from suffering, grow and become more resilient through it. The latter is a lesson some of your coachees will have to learn the hard way, and to do so requires a sacrifice of giving up something valuable in order to gain something better. People who reach this stage of maturity in their decision-making will be ready to forego expediency and make those tough decisions that serve a greater form of good.

Socrates was a renowned Greek philosopher who was sentenced to death for the alleged crimes of heresy and false teaching, among other things. Prior to his execution, he wrote about perceiving death as a blessing rather than a curse. He realized that his life had been so rich and full that he could let go of it gracefully. Socrates maintained his calm and composure during his execution, which has continued to inspire many to rethink their attitudes toward death. Instead of seeking a quick way out, Socrates accepted his fate. By doing so, he exhibited bravery in the face of death. His example continues to teach us the significance of sacrifice and the value of living a meaningful life, lasting even 2500 years after his death.

The idea of "Amor Fati" or "love of fate" is taken from the Stoic philosophy book *Meditations* by Marcus Aurelius, a man who served as both a wise philosopher and Roman Emperor. In *Meditations*, Aurelius reflects on how to live a wise and values-oriented life based on the principles of courage, wisdom, and self-control. The main proposal is that we should accept what happens to us—good and bad—because it is all part of life. This doesn't mean we should be passive and expect negative things to happen, but rather that we should accept all of life's experiences—positive and negative—and learn from them.

"It is better to light one candle than to curse the darkness." This quote is often attributed to Confucius, but it is also found in the Bible, amongst other religious scriptures. The key message is simple but profound. It is better to do something good than to do nothing at all. If we all lit just one candle, the world would be a much brighter place. And this is life's very own remedy to complaining. The quote also reflects the idea that if we live according to our highest ideals (i.e., our highest values), we will be protected from fear, even fear of death. Death is inevitable, and so is suffering. But if we can face these things with acceptance of the truth that death and suffering are inevitable, positive meaning can be found in the midst of all life's challenges, trials, and tribulations. In other words, it is better to live a value-oriented and purpose-driven life than worry about the inevitability of death.

Some people fail to get started in life. Like Margaret's bird (from the last chapter), some people spend their lifetime staying connected with the same kind of people, keep going to the same places, stop learning after their school years end, never push themselves to master a skill set or way of thinking, and feel discouraged because their lives fail to move forward and progress. This can be likened to sitting in a freezer feeling sad about being cold.

Over the years, I've had people ask me about my time in the military and how challenging it was for me. My standard response is that the transition from one way of life to another is significantly more distressing than remaining stationary in a way of life that one is already comfortable in. And while it's true that the grass is sometimes greener on the other side of the fence, other times it isn't. The truth is that those who refuse to change their circumstances will never know the outcomes of exiting the comfort of sameness. I believe that personal growth comes from taking risks and pushing ourselves outside of our comfort zones. It's human nature to yearn for that which we do not have and focus on the faults of what we do have. We see a new car down the street and want it without stopping to think about the car payments we'll have to make or the repairs it might need. In the same way, we see people with "picture perfect" lives and want what they have without stopping to think about the struggles they might have that we can't see. It's easy to look at something else and think that it would be better than our current situation. But the truth is, change is never easy.

Moving from one way of living life to another is always challenging, even when we're moving closer toward something that we want. There are always adjustments to be made and things to learn through the transition of reprioritizing our values. Sometimes, the grass isn't greener on the other side of the fence. Sometimes, we're better off staying where we are. But those who never step outside of their comfort zone and take the chance to find out what they're capable of will never know what they're missing out on. Any fool can criticize their circumstances—and most fools do. If you don't like what is in front of you, change it. If you can't change it, change how you think about it. Just don't complain. Life involves taking risks and making choices that get us closer to what we want. Sometimes we make wise choices. Sometimes we don't. But if we don't move at all, nothing changes at all.

How we view hardships will determine how maturely we react to and overcome them. It is often said that what doesn't kill us makes us stronger, and those who face great adversity and suffering and come out on top know that it is through struggles that people find their greatest strengths. Those who have gone through tough times often emerge as stronger, wiser, and more resilient versions of themselves.

Some people take a rejection or challenge and never find their way back. Those who do, come back stronger with the muscle of their character proudly flexed. But what separates the comebacks from the casualties? As with all things, mindset. People who view hardships as an opportunity for growth and persevere despite the challenges they face are the ones who come out on top. They are the ones who learn from their mistakes and become better, smarter, and more resilient because of them.

**PRINCIPLES INTO PRACTICE QUESTIONS:**

As a Life Coach, you can use the following strategic questions to help your coachees gain an empowering perspective in times of difficulty. To appreciate how much value a coachee might find in answering these questions, first, take some time to answer them for yourself:

1. Who are you without your past achievements, rejections, and failures?
2. What have you learned from the hardship that you can't learn anywhere else?
3. What guidance could you offer a friend who is facing a similar situation?
4. What are your strengths, and how must you apply them in this situation?
5. What part of this story would you want to tell your grandchildren about?
6. In what ways will you grow stronger and wiser via these circumstances?
7. What is the simplest and most straightforward solution to this hardship?
8. What is the first step that you must take to begin moving beyond this?
9. What values have influenced your responses to these eight questions?

# A THEORY ABOUT HOW LIFE WORKS

*"On the whole, I think it fair to say that human history is a record of the ways in which human nature has been sold short. The highest possibilities of human nature have practically always been underrated."*

—ABRAHAM MASLOW

It is often said that wisdom is knowing what to do with what you know. This is true in many ways, but it also highlights the importance of understanding. To truly know what to do with what you know, you need to have a deep understanding of how life works. Your understanding of how life works will determine your experience of it and the outcomes that you produce. All human beings each act in accordance with what makes sense to them. When your understanding of how life works is based on inaccurate information, your experience of life will be artificial and unfulfilling. On the other hand, when your understanding of how life works is based on an accurate understanding of what motivates you, your experience of life will be rich and fulfilling. Here are examples of people doing what "made sense" to them.

In ancient Aztec culture, it "made sense" to sacrifice members of society to the gods in order to keep their communities thriving. *(This involved slaughtering them, by the way.)*

In England in the 1850s, it "made sense" for city managers and city waste management companies to dump raw sewage into the river

Thames—but only so long as local people carried small bunches of flowers around with them to protect against illness.

Throughout many western societies, it "makes sense" for people to work sixty-hour work weeks, sometimes for decades, to make money to provide for the families that they barely get to see and eventually divorce their spouse and become estranged from their offspring.

In the COVID-19 pandemic of the early 2020's, it "made sense" for political leaders to lockdown their countries, restrict people's social movements, stop all "non-essential" service providers from running their organizations, and wait for vaccinations to be rolled out to prevent a virus from spreading that killed fewer people than what the common flue does annually.

All people make values-based decisions all of the time, and there are no exceptions to this rule. When talking about motivation, the topic of goals inevitably comes up. As a cognitive mental event, a goal is a "spring to action" that directs human behavior in purposive ways. Goals, like mindset, beliefs, expectations, or self-concept, are sources of internal motives and cognition. Ironically enough, goals are generated by what is NOT, or in other words, a discrepancy between where we are and where we want to be. The saying, "If you don't know where you're going, any road will get you there," describes the difference in motivation between those who have goals and those who do not focus their attention in any specific direction. Put simply, having goals gives our lives purpose and direction, and without them, life is empty. It can be said that all decision-making is values-oriented because it is informed by what we hope to achieve in the future. Our values act as signposts that help us determine which actions are worth taking and which ones are not. In this way, it could be argued that the very act of setting goals is a value-based decision. Without goals, we would just be drifting through life without any real sense of purpose or direction.

The topic of motivation is frequently associated with the name of Abraham Maslow and his famous hierarchy of needs. Maslow was an American psychologist who explained motivation through the satisfaction of needs arranged in a hierarchical (triangular) order. As satisfied needs do not motivate, it is dissatisfaction that stimulates people in the general direction of fulfillment. A fascinating thing about Maslow's theory of motivation is how accurate it still is, despite being developed over half a century ago. His hierarchy of needs identified that humans are not motivated by a single need but, rather, by a complex web of interrelated needs. Once our basic physiological and safety needs are met, we seek out higher-order needs like love, belonging, achievement, and self-actualization (self-awareness). Maslow's theory offers a basis for understanding human motivation and defines values as conditions within all people that are essential for the maintenance of a fulfilling life and the nurturance of growth and well-being.

## ABRAHAM MASLOW'S HIERARCHY OF HUMAN NEEDS

Maslow's hierarchy of needs assumes that everyone has specific requirements, ranging from basic physiological needs to self-actualization. In Maslow's view, each lower-ranking need must be met before higher needs can be satisfied. You can likely meet your basic life needs, such as food and water, but very few people take the time to develop a sense of belonging or facilitate social reform. By understanding where a coachee falls on Maslow's hierarchy of needs, you can determine the next step in their pursuit of self-actualization. Furthermore, it explains why they may experience a sense of aimlessness after achieving some significant milestones. When going through the hierarchy of needs with a coachee, make sure they don't get hung up on one particular need. They need to satisfy it to a sufficient degree before moving forward, but many people aren't willing to be merely satisfied in the lower rungs of the hierarchy, which is what holds them back from achieving much greater things.

Maslow's legacy is his explanation of the order in which human needs progress in ever-increasing complexity, starting with essential physiological needs and ending with self-actualization. While basic needs are experienced as a sense of deficiency, the higher level needs are experienced more in terms of the need for growth and fulfillment.

**SELF-ACTUALIZATION**
You are living to your highest potential

**ESTEEM**
You've acquired the skills that lead to honor and recognition

**LOVE & BELONGING**
Achieving deeper, more meaningful relationships

**SAFETY**
Home, sweet home

**PHYSIOLOGICAL NEEDS**
Food, water, sleep

Maslow's hierarchy of needs states that five categories of human needs dictate an individual's behavior. Those needs are physiological needs, safety needs, love and belonging needs, esteem needs, and self-actualization needs.

PHYSIOLOGICAL NEEDS (BASIC HUMAN NEEDS)

Back in 1943, in his paper "A Theory of Human Motivation," Maslow proposed that all human beings have needs that must be met, from the most basic (physiological) to the most complex (self-actualization). According to Maslow, people will primarily focus on meeting their basic needs before moving on to higher-level, more advanced needs. For example, imagine that you haven't eaten food for three days; your hunger will serve as your motivation to source food. When you are hungry, it is improbable you'll be driven by budgeting your finances or doing an excellent job at work. Maslow supported this idea by saying, *"A person who is lacking food, safety, love, and esteem would most probably hunger for food more strongly than for anything else."* In short, not meeting a physiological need will typically dominate a person's thoughts, dwarfing any idea they might otherwise have of fulfilling higher-level needs like social or personal growth. Once a person's basic needs have been satisfied, the next level in the hierarchy will begin to emerge and become a driver of their thoughts and behaviors. A person will seek out ways to meet a higher need.

### SAFETY NEEDS (CONTROL AND PREDICTABILITY NEEDS)

Once a person's physiological needs are satisfied, the safety needs come into play and tend to focus on ensuring comfort, security, stability, and predictability—with as little potential risk of losing out on one's "basic physiological needs" as possible. These safety needs include feeling safe within the home, knowing their family is protected, and having enough funds to afford basic necessities such as food, water, and warmth.

The iconic Western genre depicts a romantic picture of the American frontier with legendary outlaws like Billy the Kid and lawmen like Wyatt Earp duking it out in the deserts of the rustic West. Whilst Western culture loves to glorify gunslingers and the mayhem of the Old West, no one likes living in those conditions. The Wild West lasted for about thirty years before the US government sent in enforcers. Contrary to what the movies showcase, there wasn't much debauchery or many bank robberies (in fact, only eight recorded cases between 1859 and 1900). The same holds true today. Movies celebrate gangsters and show the rough streets, but most people live in relatively quiet suburbs. Governments, Police HQs, and courtrooms are established to ensure that most people can enjoy safety and predictability. Politicians who best provide citizens' safety are most likely to be elected. Insurance companies carved out an entire industry based on selling people "security."

Much like the problem with the attitude that often accompanies materialism, the human drive for safety can become detrimental when people grow obsessed with keeping what they have. What once served as a means of security can soon become desperation to amass in greedy proportions. People often rely too much on security, and when this happens, become less self-reliant and more dependent on state-provided systems. People who prioritize security for longer than they should tend to compromise their future freedom and growth.

## SOCIAL NEEDS (LOVE AND BELONGING NEEDS)

When people have fulfilled their safety needs, a new need arises for connectedness, including love, social relationships, and a sense of belonging. Belonging is at the heart of every social group, whether a family, religion, community, or nation. Regardless of how introverted or independent a person may claim to be, our social psychology drives our innate desire to have close connections and people to rely on. People who lack social connection are easy prey to cults, gangs, abusive partners, scammers, and extreme fringe groups who, although toxic, offer a sense of belonging in return for loyalty.

Before the 2020 global pandemic and its social distancing laws, loneliness was already viewed as a global health crisis. A 2010 study found that not being socially connected was as harmful to one's health as obesity in those aged fifty-plus. Despite technology's ability to connect the world, it has inadvertently become a wedge in people's ability to forge meaningful relationships. If you ever spent time with a coachee who claims to suffer from extreme sadness, ask him what part loneliness might play in the suffering, and learn the relationship between social destitution and sadness for yourself.

The average American spends five hours and forty-two minutes on their phone every day. Of this time, they are only interacting with other people 58 percent of the time. That leaves 42 percent of the time where they are engaged in other activities such as playing games, working, watching TV, reading books, or browsing the internet. Even when people are interacting with others on their mobile phones, studies have shown that these interactions are shallower and have less emotional significance than face-to-face interactions. Although technology has made it convenient to communicate with others, it has also caused social isolation and loneliness to rise, especially in many western societies.

## ESTEEM NEEDS (EGOCENTRIC NEEDS)

A need for self-esteem refers to a person's sense of self-worth and typically aligns with a person's ability to live up to their expectations or standards in some regard. In every society, there are always some who seek to stand out from the rest and be recognized or esteemed by others. Some people will go to great lengths to achieve this goal. According to Maslow, people have a deep need to feel respected and valued. This need can manifest itself in many different ways, from seeking fame to striving for power and status. The need for esteem is a powerful driver that can lead people to accomplish great things—or do society great harm.

Those who are raised in emotionally stable environments learn to develop a secure sense of self-esteem and not be reliant on the approval of others. However, many grow up in environments that stifle self-esteem and lead to self-validating behavior, such as people-pleasing, self-comparison, and an inability to set wise boundaries. Just log onto social media to see what people resort to for social validation: from death-defying stunts to aggressive social posts and obscene content creation: all in the name of notoriety and followership.

Celebrities often make spectacles of themselves on the world stage for the amusement of others. Business people sacrifice their integrity for corporate advancement. Politicians tell lies and make false promises to garner votes for reelection. People with low self-esteem can often be so desperate for a sense of purposefulness in their lives that they'll risk their health, long-term reputation, relationships, and potential, all for a fleeting moment of external validation.

## SELF-ACTUALIZATION (PERSONAL GROWTH NEEDS)

In order for a person to reach their full potential, which Maslow referred to as self-actualization, they must first satisfy the lower level needs that we've already mentioned, including physiological needs such as air, water, and food; safety needs such as employment and shelter; love and belonging such as friendships and family; and esteem needs such as self-worth and respect. Once these needs are met, then and only then can an individual begin to focus on self-actualization. It is important to note that this process does not happen overnight, and oftentimes an individual will regress back to a lower level need if they do not feel like their higher level needs are being met. For example, if someone loses their job, they may go back to focusing on safety needs before turning their attention back to social needs.

Maslow studied a group of people whom he categorized as "healthy" to identify their characteristics and compare them to other, less fulfilled, individuals. Maslow described his work as "a study of psychological health" (Maslow, 1970: 125) and selected his subjects from his social circles and peer groups. However, he also included a selection of public and historical figures that he studied through biography. Among these were Greek philosophers Spinoza, Plato, Aldous Huxley, Eleanor Roosevelt, Abraham Lincoln, and Thomas Jefferson. Maslow's study highlighted a range of significant personality characteristics that his selected group of people all seemed to share. These include the following:

- The ability to perceive reality clearly and not be deluded.
- The ability to judge people fairly and situations accurately.
- Self-accepting without obsession over personal imperfections.
- Spontaneity in thinking and behavior, as well as a sense of humor.
- The ability to look beyond oneself to the problems of the outside world.
- A quality of detachment and an ability to be self-contained when alone.
- Ability to resist social pressure without being intentionally unconventional.
- Capacity to be solution-oriented rather than ego-driven and self-obsessed.
- The capacity to appreciate all of life's everyday experiences as they are.
- Genuine interest in social issues and the progressive well-being of others.
- The capacity for a reflective, heightened, and transcendent experience.
- The ability to form deep and satisfying relationships with other people.
- Originality, creativity, and a willingness to experiment with new ideas.
- The ability to function optimally when facing uncertainty or doubt.

Maslow did not hold that only an elite few could attain the state of self-actualization. On the contrary, he pointed out that often people living in strikingly similar circumstances experience enormously different outcomes in life. The hallmarks of self-actualized people include their ability to unconditionally accept others, flaws, and all. They see the potential in people and are quick to forgive. This acceptance doesn't just extend to other people—self-actualized people are also accepting of themselves. They know that they are not perfect, but they don't dwell on their flaws or try to hide them from the world. Instead, they embrace all aspects of themselves, warts and all. This allows them to build deep, meaningful relationships with others—relationships based on honesty and authenticity.

One reason, Maslow suggested, why people resist self-actualizing is because it's easy to do nothing and not grow, even if unhappy, because this lets people know what to expect. This idea explains why some of your future coachees might have spent years in a career that they hate, and it's the same reason why some people commit years to a toxic relationship. Aiming for one's full potential requires boldness and a willingness to fail. And those who only do what's necessary to get by in life will never, ever find true fulfillment.

**PRINCIPLES INTO PRACTICE QUESTIONS:**

1. Which of Maslow's sets of needs resonates the most with you?
2. What role does the need for self-actualization play in your life?
3. How might you portray the importance of self-actualizing to a coachee?

# HUMAN VALUES: THE LAW OF CONSISTENCY

*"Motivation gets you going, but discipline keeps you growing. That's the Law of Consistency. It doesn't matter how talented you are. It doesn't matter how many opportunities you receive. If you want to grow, consistency is key."*

—JOHN C. MAXWELL

It's often assumed that effective decision-making involves having the right information and the right resources in the right place at the right time. In my experience, these things are just part of the equation. The second and more critical part of the equation is consistency. Consistency is firmness of character and the ability to make good decisions time and time again, facing down the inevitable temptation to take the easy path. And when it comes to mature, consistent decision-making, here's a principle worth remembering: decisions are not circumstantially based; they're born out of people's character. In other words, good decision-making isn't about what you do in a given moment; it's about how mature you are. It's about your values, your priorities, and your commitment to making wise decisions to the best of your ability.

Stephen Covey once famously said, "Character is who you are in private when no one else is watching you." Covey seemed to understand that it's easy to maintain positive character traits when conditions are good, and other people are looking on. But a real test of character is how people conduct themselves in private. Consistency of character is reflected through the congruence between your values and actions. When your actions align with your values, you can confidently look people in the eye, knowing what you stand for. When your values match your actions, peace will occur naturally in your home, in your relationships, and also deep within you. Inconsistency and incongruence are the two main sources of angst—even though some mental health "experts" might claim otherwise. When there's congruence between what you say and do, your conscience is clear, and your confidence can be high. Covey's words ring particularly true in today's society, where many people put on a false persona for social media or for work and create a version of themselves that may look good on the surface but doesn't accurately reflect who they are as people.

But the reverse is also true. When you engage in activity that is out of your character (i.e., robbing a bank or physically abusing someone), it steals your inner peace. Consistency involves living your life without superficiality, double standards, manipulation, deception, or falsehood. People are often surprised to learn that "being consistent" is a remarkably easy way to conduct oneself and is also the only self-respecting way to live life. People who live their lives inconsistently live without self-respect. A husband's consistency gives his family security, and a business leader's consistency gives an organization stability—because consistent people are reliable people. Consistency allows business partners to maintain trust in each other and stay loyal—even when the going gets tough. So ask yourself this question: Are you the kind of person who people can count on to be the same tomorrow as you are today? And if so, will you be the same next week? If not, why not?

On the day you start coaching people, your coachees will watch you closely and constantly. Within a few sessions, they will have recognized your patterns of behavior, attitude, language, questioning, and decision-making. If you deviate from any of those patterns, you can be sure of two things: firstly, your coachee has already noticed; secondly, they will come up with an explanation for it. This is why it is essential to be authentic and transparent with your coachees from the beginning. If you try to present yourself as someone whom you are not, eventually your coachees will see through it and lose trust in you. As you consistently show up for your coachees, their trust and respect for you will naturally grow.

The coaching relationship centers around helping people to make sensible decisions and each of those decisions presents a crossroad where we can choose a positive path or a negative one. Today's decisions always create tomorrow's results, and these results will be either ideal or otherwise. It's up to your coachees to make decisions that align with the results that they actually want. Those who choose wisely will build a bright future for themselves, and those who choose poorly will inevitably end up on a very different path. Of course, making wise choices is not always easy. People are often tempted to put off making hard decisions today in favor of immediately gratifying experiences. But as Abraham Lincoln once wisely said, "You cannot escape the responsibility of tomorrow by evading it today."

Anyone who has ever been employed knows that, ultimately, we are all servants. We may be servants of our bosses, our clients, or our customers, but we are still servants. And while there is nothing wrong with being a servant, it is useful to be aware that the decisions we make determine who or what we end up serving. People who make wise choices find themselves serving something worthwhile. But people who make poor choices end up serving things and people that cost them time, effort, and inner peace. And that is a waste of a life.

The American educator Frances E. Willard observed, "Sow an action, you reap a habit; sow a habit, you grow in character; grow in character, you reap a destiny." Willard understood that the habits people develop today become their masters tomorrow. So when urging your coachee to choose their next steps carefully, remind them never to experiment with things that they wouldn't want as permanent features on their personal life landscapes.

To ensure that your Life Coaching efforts are fruitful, you must rely on values to guide your decision-making process. Principles accumulate over time as you grow to understand what they are (which we will explore in the next chapter), as you observe life, read books, work with mentors, take training courses, and experience the ups and downs of everyday life. Acquiring wisdom takes time, and you will learn good judgment through reflection, observing the outside world and your own internal one: thoughts, motives, biases, and attitudes.

Your personal blog may be filled with quotes about integrity, courage, and grit, but if you're not outworking these principles in your own life, then they're nothing more than empty words. The same goes for values. If you talk about the importance of authenticity, honesty, and hard work, but your actions don't reflect these values, then they hold no weight. When your actions match your words consistently, people will see what you stand for. And just as important, you will know what values and principles you stand for. So if you aspire to become the kind of Life Coach who's intent on leaving a positive, lasting legacy in your wake, you must decide every day to be exactly the same person in private that you'd want anyone else to see in public. This is referred to as integrity, and it's by practicing and consistently prioritizing integrity that you will positively influence other people the most.

**PRINCIPLES INTO PRACTICE QUESTIONS:**

1. If you have wisdom and integrity but lack consistency, what might happen as a result?
2. How do you relate to people who demonstrate inconsistency? Why?

# THE CONNECTEDNESS OF HUMAN VALUES

*"A highly developed values system is like having an internally built compass. It serves as a reference to point you in the right direction when you are lost."*

—IDOWU KOYENIKAN

What do you need? Your response to this question will depend on who is asking and why they are asking. If you were stranded in the desert and dying of thirst, you might answer, "I need water." If your boss asked the same question, and especially if he said, "What do you *really* need?" You might say, "A pay raise would be good!" If, however, you ask a coachee this within a coaching session, the answer could be anyone's guess: respect, connection, significance, someone who listens, self-esteem, a better husband, more money, a safe environment for one's children, control, excitement—the list is only limited by creative imagination and desire.

It is easier to make a list of things you want rather than identifying what you truly need in life. While our wants are typically superficial, our needs are more profound and are harder to define. The purpose of Life Coaching is to help people gain clarity on their genuine needs so they can make informed decisions that align with their values. In other words, if someone has a clear understanding of their values and priorities, they will be better equipped to make informed life decisions rather than being swayed by every passing trend. Often, people lack a personal vision for their self-improvement or growth, and without guidance, they may make decisions that contradict their values and goals. Before making any major decisions, a competent Life Coach will assist individuals in gaining clarity about their values and priorities.

The ultimate goal of any Life Coach should be to help the coachee identify their core values and learn how to live in alignment with them. This means that when it comes time to make decisions and take action, the individual will be able to do so with confidence and clarity.

### VALUES: LIKE MARKERS ON THE FLOOR

No more than a moment's reflection is required to connect us with the truth that we value certain things. We want to feel a certain way; we want people to treat us well; we want a career and financial opportunities that give us security; we want to know we matter to someone and belong somewhere; we want warm weather for our summer vacation. If we could stop time at any given point in our day, it wouldn't be hard to pinpoint the specific values that truly motivate us to do what we do and say what we say.

When was the last time you went to see a movie? Can you remember how the floor markers in a theater show you which way to walk? Floor markers serve the purpose of keeping people moving in the right direction and stopping them from falling down stairs. Now, imagine there are no floor markings. What might happen? People might end up tripping themselves up, falling down the stairs, or mistakingly watching a rom-com when what they paid to see was sci-fi. This is just everyday life for those people who want to "go with the flow" and not think too much about what might make their lifestyle become more meaningful. People who never figure out what their priorities are will end up aimlessly traipsing through life without ever knowing where they're going. They would rather follow the crowds instead of blazing their own trail. And that's a shame because, as anyone who has ever found their way knows, life is better when you're living it on your own terms. So, in a really practical sense, values can be thought of as markers on the floor which help guide your decision-making.

People who follow the crowd rarely give thought to the direction in which they're headed. Crowd followers tend to naively assume that if *"the majority of people are doing it,"* then *"it must be OK."* As a result, the kind of people who tend to follow the crowd might mistakenly assume that they're speeding down the highway of life when they're actually just driving headfirst down a dead-end street. Those who follow the crowd usually get lost in it and overpowered by it. In truth, most crowd followers are lost. They may not feel lost, think they're lost, or act lost, but they're definitely lost. So it's no wonder that many people have trouble finding their bearings and deciding what is important to them. The crowd is constantly pulling them in one direction while their true innermost needs are tugging their hearts and minds in a totally different direction.

**VALUES: INTEGRITY AND INNER STRENGTH**

Another term for character is inner strength, and inner strength is a matter of integrity, not toxic masculinity, feminine masculinity, or muscle mass. Inner strength involves cultivating the courage required to live out your convictions and stand loyal to your values—in spite of what the crowd is or isn't doing. Strength is standing up for the principles you believe in, even if everybody else is traveling in an opposite direction. Strength is the determination to become the caliber of human being you need to be, not the inconsistent, career-changing, gender-fluid, unprincipled follower that much of society wants you to be. The kind of strength that matters is hard to find in a world that values conformity over individuality.

Before I started Life Coaching as a freelancer and selling my services to the public, I worked in B2B car sales. I worked throughout my studies as a means of funding them. I was always a pretty good salesman. I had a natural knack for it, but more importantly, I loved helping people to make a big financial decision that was right for them. My management team at the time, however, didn't share my agenda—all they cared about was making as much money as possible. It didn't matter to them how we did it, as long as we hit our monthly and quarterly targets. And if we didn't? Well, let's just say there were consequences. That wasn't an environment I wanted to be in. I didn't want to be driven by greed or motivated by fear.

One day, my boss pulled me into his office. It had most likely become evident over the passing months that my heart wasn't in the job anymore; I wasn't generating the volume of sales that I'd done in the past and wasn't willing to compromise my integrity to sell people cars that paid the highest commissions rather than helping people to make decisions that were right for them. "Kain," my boss said as I sat down in his office, "give me one good reason why I should keep you on as part of my team?" One good reason? I mulled over the question for a few moments, taking in the angle, and realized I had two ways of answering; lie and oversell myself to a man that I didn't like for a job I didn't care about, or just be honest.

### THE CONFLICT BETWEEN SECURITY AND FREEDOM

Rather than giving him a reason to keep me on, I spoke candidly about the reasons why it was time for me to quit. My boss was taken aback and confessed he wasn't planning on firing me; he used that question as a tactic to motivate his sales guys to work harder. However, having listened to my rant, he knew I wasn't fulfilled. He offered me five weeks of paid leave with a company car and encouraged me to take time out to visualize my future progression within the company. When I returned from my break, I handed in my resignation. The time off had given me the space to reflect on what I wanted to do in the years ahead. While remaining employed with the company would have given me short-term financial security and good social connections, in reality, I was using employment as an excuse to avoid leaving my comfort zone and the uncertainty that accompanies starting up a business. So, for me, I could only fully commit to becoming a Life Coach on the same day that I was willing to stand by the courage of my convictions and follow my heart rather than listen to my head.

The conflict between security and freedom is an interesting one. Security, in many ways, is the easier path to take. It's expecting someone else to take care of you and knowing that you just need to show up and believe that it will all work out. Freedom, on the other hand, can be harder. It's believing that you can achieve anything you want because you know that you're in control of your life and you can create the life you want for yourself. Ultimately, the choice between security and freedom comes down to a question of trust. Do you trust yourself enough to build the lifestyle you want, or would you rather put your faith in someone else? There is no right or wrong answer, but when it comes to you or your future coachees making major lifestyle-changing decisions, it's important to be aware that both security and freedom are powerful motivational forces that will shape the choices that you make. For example, if you value security above all else, you may be more likely to choose a steady job with a predictable income over a more risky venture with the potential for greater rewards. Alternatively, if you prioritize freedom, you may be more likely to take a chance on a new business venture or move to a new city in search of new opportunities. Whichever side you fall on, it's important to be aware of the role that values play in your decision-making.

## STRAYING FROM THE COMFORT ZONE

When you establish your own coaching practice, it's highly beneficial to assist your clients in recognizing and questioning their values. Since values are typically deeply rooted in individuals' thinking and operate in their unconscious mentality, it can be a fascinating procedure. This refers to the reasoning and decision-making that people don't intentionally do. When people refuse to make positive changes in their lives, they often use excuses. However, every decision ultimately comes down to one's values. Fear of leaving their comfort zone is typically the reason people resist change. Despite being scary, change is necessary for personal growth and progress in life.

Understanding the connection between our values is crucial for making better choices, as it helps us identify what distinguishes those who struggle in life from those who succeed and find fulfillment. This is especially important considering the variety of decisions we face on a daily basis, ranging from small and insignificant to life-changing. Our values act as a compass, guiding us in life and shaping our decisions. When we have a clear understanding of our values, making choices becomes easier and more decisive. Yet, when our values are unclear or do not align with our actions, we may make choices that do not benefit us, leading us astray.

Sometimes people make decisions based on one value or priority without considering how it may affect other aspects of their life. This can lead to a values conflict where two important outcomes clash and result in less fulfillment in one or both areas. For instance, a man may opt for a medical career as he values helping others, but may not notice that the strenuous job hours have a negative impact on his marriage. Or, a young woman might decide to move to a new city to be closer to her family. While this might seem like a wise decision at first, she soon learns that the increased cost of living eats into her savings and costs her the financial comfort that she had prior to moving. The principle of opportunity cost states that we cannot have everything we want; having one thing must come at the cost of something else. Understanding this principle can help you make wise future decisions by taking time to reflect on all of the values that are potentially at stake. Only by doing this will you be able to help people make informed choices.

**RISK: THE ENABLER OF ALL HUMAN PROGRESSION**

Although it might not always seem like it, people are innately wired to take risks. Whether it is deciding to cross a busy street or trying a new food, taking risks is a core human value that is essential for making progress in life. Despite often being considered a vice, risk is a value that some people will prioritize more than others. I'm not talking about blowing your life savings on gambling or taking up extreme sports; I am talking about embracing the calculated risks necessary for making progress in life (and also for general human advancement). Every major breakthrough in history has been the result of someone taking a risk. From the Wright brothers taking to the skies in their homemade airplane to Neil Armstrong setting foot on the moon, humanity has always reached new heights by embracing risk.

Imagine a world without one of our three main food staples: corn. If you tested the carbon source in the average Westerner's body, nearly two-thirds would come from corn. Despite being a staple of the human diet today, 9,000 years ago, those large corn cobs were the size of wheat grains and had the consistency of a raw potato. If it were not for generations of farmers innovating and taking the risk of breeding the barely edible plant, we would not have corn as it is today.

A few years ago, I read a news article about a woman who witnessed a man kidnap a young child. To prevent the man from getting away, the woman jumped in front of the car and risked her own life to potentially save the life of a child she didn't even know. Risk sometimes involves doing what is "right" rather than apathetically accepting whatever will be. Life does not happen without the uncertainty of risk. Despite many people's best efforts to create a world of certainty, risk is the enabler of all human progression.

Some people learn from experience that taking risks precedes experiencing excitement. As Ralph Waldo Emerson wrote:

> There is a time in every man's education when he arrives at the conviction that envy is ignorance; that imitation is suicide; that he must take himself for better, for worse, as his portion; that though the wide universe is full of good, no kernel of nourishing corn can come to him but through his toil bestowed on that plot of ground which is given to him to till. The power which resides in him is new in nature, and none but he knows what that is which he can do, nor does he know until he has tried.

It is often said that the difference between high achievement and low achievement isn't due to a person's abilities or ideas but the courage to take a calculated risk. This is certainly true in many cases, but it is important to remember that a calculated risk is only as good as the calculation itself. Before taking any risks, it is essential to carefully consider all of the potential future outcomes. Only after doing this can you truly know whether or not a risk is worth taking. Of course, even with the best calculation, there is always some element of chance involved. But without taking risks, no one would ever accomplish anything great.

## THE CONNECTION VS. AUTHENTICITY CONUNDRUM

Almost fifteen years ago, I connected with an old military comrade called Dave. At the time, I wasn't connected with many of my old army friends. Some had died, and others had just moved on in life—this was before the dawn of people being globally connected via social media platforms. Dave and I would meet up every now and again for a coffee or a beer, and we would talk. Although we didn't talk about anything particularly meaningful in our time together, we respected each other to a degree and appreciated each other's company.

One day the two of us agreed to meet up for food close to where I lived. As we began talking, Dave proved himself to be distant and quite distracted by something that hadn't yet become apparent (as I'm usually good at reading people). As the conversation, which was more of a one-way monologue from Dave, progressed, I began to feel frustrated with how dishonoring the interaction was. Dave wasn't even remotely interested in listening to me and, instead, chose to complain about his financial challenges and suggest that as a former soldier, my responsibility should be to support him through the tough financial times he was facing. As I listened to Dave rant on, I could smell stale alcohol on his breath from the night before as he signaled to the waiter and ordered a $45.00 rib eye steak and chips.

Within fifteen minutes, I was tired of listening to Dave complain and behave like an entitled child. And this brought my thinking into a state of conflict. Should I stay silent or tell Dave to get a grip on himself and stop behaving like an infant? To do the latter might damage the connection between us—albeit it wasn't healthy anyway, and I also didn't have many other male relationships at the time. Or should I just keep listening to Dave complain and compromise my integrity by entertaining an utterly disrespectful conversation? I'd bought Dave meals in the past, which he never reciprocated. This current occasion was no exception. I wasn't happy, and Dave was attempting to manipulate me into giving him money.

I then remembered what I'd sacrificed to spend this time with Dave. I'd recently begun dating Karen (who is now my wife of nine years) and had passed off on an afternoon out in Edinburgh cafe-hopping with her. I subtly interjected, "Seriously, Dave, if you don't control the noise that's pouring from your mouth and start treating my time with more respect, I'm out of here." What happened next wasn't my decision. Dave threw a temper tantrum and told me that I should be more interested in my veteran brothers before storming out and allowing me to pick up the bill for the food he had ordered but not eaten. That day I ate rib eye steak and chips for lunch. I was also fully aware of the conscious decision I had made to prioritize being authentic with Dave (and risk his disapproval) rather than remain quiet, compromise my integrity and remain connected within a dishonoring exchange.

I tell you this story to highlight another values conflict that people face. The opportunity-cost of prioritizing authenticity instead of connection. You might be wondering why a story of this nature has worked its way into a Life Coaching handbook. Well, if you will remember back to section one, I did explain that for a Life Coaching relationship to be fruitful, a coachee must be open to interacting, receptive to perspectives that differ from their own, and appreciative of the input they receive. Dave failed in all three of these areas, and the decision I made that day was to act congruently and in alignment with my values. I'm certainly not saying that making values-based decisions are easy, but they do send a message. In 2017, Dave reconnected with me for relationship coaching, which he wanted to pay me for. He explained that I'd impressed him that day by being one of the only people he'd ever known to be "real" with him. I went on to help Dave make some major improvements in his marriage and also in the way that he connected with his two young sons.

**GROWTH AND COMFORT: TWO MUTUALLY EXCLUSIVE VALUES**

To most people, change is scary, and the unknown is a greater cause of stress in more people's lives than what the known is. You will find that some of your future coachee's natural inclination is to protect themselves from the unknown. Some people do this by erecting walls composed of defense mechanisms to ensure the longevity of their comfort and security. Defense mechanisms keep people secure in the "nice and cozy," where nothing ever changes. Defense mechanisms also keep people away from change, personal growth, development, learning, understanding, and insight. To put it bluntly, they prevent some people from living.

It's interesting to think about what motivates people to change. For some, the pain of staying the same is simply too great. They may be in a situation that is unhealthy, and the thought of remaining in that state is intolerable. Others may be motivated by the potential rewards of change. They see the possibility for growth and development, and they are willing to take risks to pursue those goals. Regardless of what drives them, those who are able to create lasting changes in their lives are usually those who are willing to step outside of their comfort zones to embrace uncertainty and risk. Personal growth and the comfort zone are mutually exclusive. Your future coachees can grow and achieve all of the goals they want for themselves, or they can stay safe and comfortable. Unfortunately, they just can't do both at the same time, and this is why it's important for a Life Coach to ensure that all coachee goal setting is values-aligned. The price of comfort is often stagnation and fruitlessness.

The price of pursuing your priorities is hard work. Those who prioritize safety and comfort play to not lose the game of life by hedging their bets, playing small, avoiding risk, and shying away from growth opportunities. But by avoiding hardship, people miss out on the positivity it brings—the satisfaction of achievement, the fulfillment that comes from growing in wisdom and courage. Those who prioritize growth are playing to win. It's a very different attitude. This is a proactive, conscious, and purpose-driven approach to a life that has the boldness to effortfully pursue or create what is valuable. Life is a package deal: the rough always comes with the smooth. Those who want the highs must be willing to experience the lows. That's just part of being alive. There is no easy, comfortable life—this is just an illusion.

**PRINCIPLES INTO PRACTICE QUESTIONS:**

1. What values discussed in this section have resonated the most with you?
2. What are you currently doing in your life that conflicts with your priority values?
3. What might happen if you were to only devote energy to pursuing your priorities?

# RESPONSIBILITY FIRST, FREEDOM SECOND

"The disappearance of a sense of responsibility is the most far-reaching consequence of submission to authority."

—STANLEY MILGRIM

Two chapters ago, I discussed Maslow's hierarchy of needs. Why do you think having this knowledge might be important to Life Coaching? Well, Maslow's hierarchy is important to Life Coaching because it offers a framework for understanding what motivates human behavior.

Life Coaches work with mentally healthy and goal-oriented individuals, so by knowing the factors that motivate people, a Life Coach can better support their coachees in moving toward goals that align with their values. The hierarchy of needs also shows us how all people have different needs and priorities at a given time. Finally, the hierarchy of needs reminds us that growth is an ongoing process. Just as people continue to grow and change throughout their lives, so too do coaches need to continually grow, develop and improve themselves. Maslow was the first psychologist to study healthy people and realized that people place themselves in risk-taking situations not because there is something "mentally" or "medically" wrong with them but because something motivates them. According to Maslow, all people have certain needs that they will spend their entire lifetime trying to fulfill. These needs range from self-esteem to being esteemed by others, as well as personal growth needs that people must prioritize if they are to grow in truth, goodness, creativity, responsibility, and wisdom. Maslow also discovered that when basic needs are fulfilled, individuals move up the hierarchy. In other words, people are constantly seeking to improve their lives and meet their needs in different ways. However, some people do this more effectively than others.

All of this means that as you start having Life Coaching conversations with people, they will tell you about their goals and aspirations, but the most important piece of detective work you can carry out is discovering the values that motivate people to do anything. Values are like the software programs that run in the background of our lives. If we want to change the way we operate, then we need to reprioritize our values. If you listen carefully to what people complain about, you can identify what hierarchy level they are functioning at. Our values guide our decisions, which is why it is so important to be aware of them. When we are not clear on our values, we can easily end up making choices that are not in alignment with what is truly important to us. As Life Coaches, one of our most important tasks is to help our coachees become aware of their values and how they are affecting their lives. Only then can they make conscious decisions about what goals they need to set and how they want to live.

Some people who think of responsibility view it as a burden that limits their freedom. However, another way of looking at responsibility is as something that empowers people to make wise decisions that allow them to create the lives they want. I will assume that this is what Maslow meant when he talked about "inner-direction." People with "inner-direction" rely on their intuition to make congruent decisions and view themselves as the authors of their choices and as being responsible for their own lives. People who become more responsible become more free and less controlled by their past experiences or other people's expectations.

Values aren't infallible; also, they aren't the same thing as your moral compass. Whilst some people wrongly assume that morality exists as an objective standard, morality, like your values, is fully subjective. This is because morals are influenced by your values. It would be nice to think that everyone regards certain things as immoral, such as murder, cruelty, abuse, violence, or prejudice, but the truth is that everyone defines the limitations and exemptions to morality differently. Some people believe all violence is wrong, whereas others believe some violence is wrong, but violence against animals is OK. There are then those who believe violence in self-defense is OK, but then everyone has different ideas of what self-defense is: some people might throw a punch if someone threw one first, whereas others would throw a punch to defend their honor if someone called them names. Your values determine what you deem as morally right, but unfortunately, your values aren't always inclined to be 100 percent moral.

Unmet values cause people to feel empty, dissatisfied, or unfulfilled, with a nagging feeling that something is missing. In contrast, people who learn effective strategies for meeting their needs develop the freedom to be themselves without needing approval or acceptance from anyone else. Values can be mistaken for wants. One way to distinguish a need from a want is to see if you can live optimally without it for a few weeks. If you can, it is probably just a want or a preference. Marketing causes many people to wrongly believe they need more than they do to be fulfilled in life. The first step you can take toward living a more fulfilling life is to identify what values are important to you, then start developing strategies for meeting those needs in ways that are beneficial to yourself and others. People who learn to meet their needs in healthy ways become more stable and grounded individuals who are better equipped to make well-considered choices and also relate to the world.

## ALL VALUES COMMONLY FALL INTO FOUR CATEGORIES:

1. **Security Values:** these typically include a need for safety, stability, information, clarity, certainty, honesty, financial security, order, authenticity, and meeting all obligations.
2. **Influence Values:** these typically include a need for control, dominance, wealth, authority, power, praise, morality, freedom, perfection, leadership, recognition, and influence.
3. **Achievement Values:** these typically include a need to create,

accomplish, achieve, strive, perform, excel, succeed, make a contribution, be valuable, and provide a great service to others.
4. **Intimacy Values:** these typically include a need for intimacy, relationships, and connection and to be listened to, needed, included, valued, appreciated, heard, and connected within a group—to collaborate, communicate, and be connected to something greater than just oneself.

As you create a balanced life for yourself, you become naturally qualified to support your coachees in making the decisions required to create balance in their own lives. Balance simply involves ensuring that all of our values are being met to some degree or another. It is important to take the time to examine your values. Our actions are usually auto-piloted by expectations based on what we think we want. However, there is usually a deeper, unexpressed value present at all times. By becoming more aware of your underlying values, you'll be able to make wiser lifestyle choices and cultivate more satisfying relationships. For example, you may seek attention when you just want better connections with people. You might prioritize making money when you really just need security. You might try to impress people when your need is for respect. You might stay safe instead of pursuing freedom. All of these choices would be different if you were aware of your underlying values. Therefore, it is wise to take the time to examine your values and become aware of what is important to you.

**EXERCISE 1: USE THIS SPACE TO WRITE YOUR TOP TEN VALUES**

..........................................................................................................................

..........................................................................................................................

..........................................................................................................................

..........................................................................................................................

..........................................................................................................................

..........................................................................................................................

..........................................................................................................................

..........................................................................................................................

..........................................................................................................................

..........................................................................................................................

EXAMINE THE VALUES IN YOUR TOP TEN LIST AND ASK YOURSELF:

1. How can I meet these needs easily and without unnecessary effort?
2. In what areas of my life have I already successfully met these needs?
3. What are two new ways you can meet each need in a more satisfying way?
4. How do your values influence your everyday actions and decision-making?
5. In what ways do you find that your values sometimes conflict with each other?
6. How might this knowledge of values inform your future practice of Life Coaching?

**EXERCISE 2: SET A GOAL THAT ALLOWS YOU TO DEMONSTRATE YOUR VALUES**

Set a meaningful goal for yourself that will allow you to measure how congruently you demonstrate one of your values by acting on it. Identify any necessary blocks that you must eliminate from your life in order to achieve this goal.

# SECTION FOUR SUMMARY

In today's complicated world, many people find it difficult to know what the "right decision" is to make; regarding their careers, finances, relationships, and social activities—all of which people will approach a Life Coach for assistance with. A common problem people have is a lack of personal vision regarding how they might improve and who they could grow to become. This lack of vision can result in people making sub-optimal choices that do not align with their deepest values and priorities. A Life Coach worth his or her salt will help a person get clear about such things before any big decisions are made. Simply put, the more clarity a person has about what their values are— the better equipped they'll be to make wise life choices, as opposed to being blown around by every wind of change that comes their way.

**IMPORTANT LESSONS TO REMEMBER:**
- A highly developed values system is like having an internally built GPS.
- Values are like software programs that run in the background of our lives.
- Balance involves all of your values being met to some degree or another.
- Values aren't infallible and aren't the same thing as your moral compass.

- Taking a well-calculated risk is only as sensible as what the calculation is.
- Inner strength is a matter of integrity, not toxic behavior or muscle mass.
- The decisions you make today shape the outcomes you produce tomorrow.
- Consistency involves living life without superficiality, hypocrisy, and deceit.

**SECTION FOUR NOTEWORTHY IDEAS**

Use this space to note down any ideas that have struck you as important throughout this section of the handbook. Also, write down any questions that might be beneficial for your future consideration and self-reflection.

## SECTION FIVE

# COMMUNICATION SKILLS AND PRINCIPLES

Being an effective communicator will help you develop stronger relationships and connections with everyone around you. Forming healthy connections with people is essential for your future coaching efforts to be fruitful. When you take the time to really listen to what other people are saying and make an effort to understand their point of view, you can build strong relationships based on mutual understanding and respect.

# ON BECOMING AN ARTICULATE COMMUNICATOR

*"The two words 'information' and 'communication' are often used interchangeably, but they signify very different things. Information is giving out; communication is getting through."*

—SYDNEY J. HARRIS

The ability to communicate well is one of the most important skills that you can possess. Communication is the act of conveying information from one person to another and involves being able to send and receive information in a way that is clear, concise, and understandable. In order for a communication to be successful, a message must be conveyed, received, and understood by all parties. This means that the sender and receiver of the message must be able to assign the same meaning to the information being communicated. When this doesn't happen, communication tends to break down and become ineffective. Mastering the ability to communicate effectively is something that all people who want to connect meaningfully with others need to make a priority. When we actively listen to what other people say and make a conscious effort to understand their point of view, we can start forging strong and cohesive relationships. Communication is the key to success in every area of your life.

Even if you've never seen the show, you've likely heard of the famous phrase: "We were on a break!" from *Friends*. "We were on a break!" is a recurring line by Ross Geller that has its roots in the fifteenth episode of the third season of *Friends* when Rachel, frustrated with Ross's possessiveness over her as her boyfriend, says they should take a break from their relationship. Depressed, Ross goes to a bar with his friends and sleeps with a girl.

When Rachel finds out what happens, she permanently ends their relationship because he cheated, whereas Ross defends his actions by claiming they were on a break, so it didn't constitute cheating. While this miscommunication is played off as a running gag for the remainder of the series—and has extended into the cultural vernacular for over twenty years since—it's a prime example of how miscommunication can destroy relationships.

History is rife with examples of poor communication resulting in disastrous consequences. On October 25, 1854, at the height of the Crimean War, Lord Cardigan, commander of the British Light Cavalry, received orders to attack the Russian army to prevent them from carrying off the guns from the British supply base near Balaclava. The actual order from Lord Raglan, the British commander-in-chief, was to cut off a small convoy that was carrying a portion of the guns, a much more manageable task for a brigade of 670 men. However, by the time the order was relayed to Cardigan, he believed that their mission was to retrieve all the guns from the entire Russian army, which vastly outnumbered them. Having no way of knowing about the convoy from his vantage point, Lord Cardigan carried out the orders without question. The tragedy was captured by Alfred Tennyson, who wrote:

> Forward, the Light Brigade! Was there a man dismayed? Not though the soldier knew someone had blundered. Theirs not to make reply, Theirs not to reason why, Theirs but to do and die. Into the valley of death rode the six hundred.

The Charge of the Light Brigade on October 25, 1854, was a disastrous mistake, the result of misinformation and miscommunication. Of the 673 men who charged across the valley that day, less than 200 returned home. While your miscommunication may not lead to such devastating consequences, it can still seriously damage your relationships. Being an effective communicator will help you develop stronger relationships and connections with everyone around you. Forming healthy connections with people is essential for your future coaching efforts to be fruitful. When you take the time to really listen to what other people are saying and make an effort to understand their point of view, you can build strong relationships based on mutual understanding and respect, and that can stand the test of turbulence.

**PRINCIPLES INTO PRACTICE QUESTIONS:**

1. How has miscommunication negatively affected your past relationships?
2. In what ways have you been on the receiving end of poor communications?
3. Historically, in what ways have you been the deliverer of poor communications?
4. Why do you think it's important to master your communications as a Life Coach?

# THE HEART OF WHOLESOME COMMUNICATION

*"Between what I think, what I want to say, what I believe I say, what I say, what you want to hear, what you believe to hear, what you hear, what you want to understand, what you think you understand, what you understand...they are ten possibilities that we might have some problem communicating."*

—BERNARD WERBER

What makes a good communicator? When people think of good communicators, they think of famous speakers, from politicians to leaders of global movements and famous podcasters or television presenters. But being a good speaker doesn't necessarily make a person a good communicator. The ability to choose just the right words or explain yourself succinctly can be beneficial when you need to make yourself understood, but speaking is just one facet of communication. The way we communicate with other people, and especially with ourselves, determines the mental and emotional quality of our lives.

We all know the saying, "It's not what you say; it's how you say it." And while there is truth to that, effective communication is about much more than just saying the right things. It's also about how well you listen to others and respond to what they're saying. All too often, we get caught up in our own thoughts and fail to really hear what others are trying to tell us. Or we might hear them but fail to respond in a way that takes their feelings and perspectives into account. As a result, miscommunication and conflict are all too common. But when we take the time to truly listen to others and respond thoughtfully and respectfully, we can build strong relationships, better understand each other and find common ground.

Communication has little to do with what you say or how eloquently you say it. Rather, it's about how articulately you express yourself, how attentively you listen to people, and how appropriately you respond. Healthy communication is different from delivering a charismatic "TED Talk" monologue. Communication should always be dialogue, a two-way street, and connect different people's perspectives to allow for enlightenment, growth, and understanding. Good communicators engage in dialogue, listen to hear other people's perspectives, are conscious of the intention behind what people say, and don't resort to reductive and over-simplistic analyses of the information they hear.

We all experience the world differently, and all people communicate in a way that seems normal to them. Problems arise when two people interact in two completely different ways, while both parties assume that their independent communication style is the only one that's "right." It can be easy to make assumptions or jump to an incorrect conclusion during communications. However, if your goal in communicating is to understand the person instead of jumping to assumptions or judgments, better trust-based communication will occur. When interferences are present, they can affect how a message is transmitted and received, causing it to become misunderstood or miscommunicated. We have all been there; a discussion takes an awkward turn, and we find ourselves feeling defensive and putting our guard up. When this happens, it's wise to carry out a "check up from the neck up" and see if we are assuming something that isn't true. Oftentimes, defensiveness is rooted in an assumption that we are making about the other person's motives or intentions. For example, we might assume that someone is judging us when they give us constructive criticism. Or, we might assume that someone is trying to start an argument when they express a different opinion than our own. If we can take a step back and examine our assumptions, we may be able to diffuse the situation and see the other person's perspective more clearly. As they say, assumptions are the mother of all screw-ups; by checking in with ourselves, we can avoid making them in the first place.

Good communicators understand that dialogue is the best way to facilitate the transmission and reception of information. They ask questions, share their thoughts honestly, and encourage other people to do the same. Accurate and unambiguous communication is tough to master, and it can take much practice for a new Life Coach to become an effective communicator. Sometimes, ironically, the most important aspect of communicating is hearing what isn't said by another person. In order to truly understand what another person is trying to communicate, we must be attuned to the words they are saying and how they are saying (or not saying) them. Is your coachee using nonverbal cues? Are they conveying emotion? By attending to both verbal and nonverbal communication, we can get a more accurate picture of what someone is authentically trying to say. Upon being able to do this well, we can then start building robust Life Coaching relationships on a foundation of trust and understanding.

Framing your communication within a Life Coaching context starts with understanding your coachee. In other words, who are you talking to? This may seem like a silly question, but it is important to consider things like age, gender, nationality, generation, and educational background when thinking about how best to communicate with someone new. Different types of people communicate in different ways, so it is important to be aware of this and adjust your way of communication accordingly. Catching confusion or misunderstandings early is vital for trust to be sustained, which is why this section of the handbook will now unpack some simple, yet profound communication skills that will help you ensure the messages you receive and send within your coaching relationships are precise and coherent.

**PRINCIPLES INTO PRACTICE QUESTIONS:**

1. How easy might other people find it to communicate authentically with you?
2. Is your default communication style monologue or dialogue? How does it serve you?
3. In what areas might you have room for improvement in your communication skills?

# CURIOSITY: THE ENABLER OF HEALTHY DISCUSSION

*"Listen with curiosity. Speak with honesty. Act with integrity. The greatest problem with communication is we don't listen to understand. We listen to reply. When we listen with curiosity, we don't listen with the intent to reply. We listen for what's behind the words."*

—ROY T. BENNETT

In order to have a great coaching conversation, you must engage with all of your senses. You need to be able to see your coachee, hear what they are saying, and feel their energy. If you can do all of these things, you will connect well with people and respond to what they say to you appropriately. Healthy discussion is about far more than just the words that get spoken between you and your coachees. It's about the connection and trust that gets forged—which happens as you are fully present, utilizing all of your main senses and **curious** about people.

It's essential to be fully present when Life Coaching—seeing, hearing, and sensing what your coachees are saying and how they're saying it. If you become aware that your focus has shifted away from the other person and onto yourself, it's time to quickly recalibrate. When you're not present, you're not listening to understand a person; rather, you're only listening to reply to them. And when you're not really listening, you risk not understanding what's said—or responding to what is said in an unhelpful, inappropriate, or trust-damaging way.

Being fully present with people requires you to be in "the moment," without judgment or distracted by your own "head-chatter." It's about giving people your full attention and discerning what they're saying, verbally and non-verbally. As you master this, you create a healthy space in which people will feel heard and valued. From this space, understanding and trust can grow.

One of the challenges new Life Coaches face is learning how to interact authentically with people they don't know very well. Prior to having years worth of coaching experience, it's quite normal to feel tongue-tied and unsure of what to say. When this inevitably happens, just prioritize remaining connected with the other person by (a) asking them thoughtful questions that you want to know the answer to, (b) paying attention to what they say, and (c) responding to what they say appropriately. By making a conscious effort to connect with people, you'll find that naturally flowing conversation happens with ease. When you prioritize remaining present and connected with your coachees, you give them permission to behave similarly. This is when a Life Coaching discussion can become a genuine and powerful one.

Sadly, the coaching industry is plagued with incompetence and superficiality. Today, many who call themselves a Life Coach are more interested in impressing their social media followings with pre-scripted questions and language patterns than they are in facilitating authentic dialogues that empower people to understand themselves and make wise decisions that will transform their lives. This top-down, prescriptive approach does a disservice to the coachee-coach relationship and also robs people of their autonomy. If we are to truly help people grow and change, we must let go of our need to be in control and just become curious.

As you prioritize remaining connected with people, you cannot fail to build powerful Life Coaching relationships. If you become tongue-tied or unsure of what to say (which will inevitably happen), instead of thinking about "what the best next thing to say" might be, get out of your head, redirect your focus away from yourself and back on connecting with the other person to LEARN about them. As you begin to notice the other person more, you may find yourself feeling **curious** about them. Curiosity stems from a desire to understand people, and it is the enabler of healthy dialogue because it creates questions that you'll genuinely be interested in asking. The act of focusing on others will immediately make you feel calmer and more present in the conversation, giving you a greater chance of building rapport and a relationship with the other person that is based on intrigue, understanding, and trust.

Too often in our social interactions, we focus on getting something from the other person—whether it's information, approval, or validation. As a result, we can come across as being pushy, self-righteous, self-centered, or even manipulative—which, unfortunately, is rife throughout the Life Coaching industry. But if we can shift our focus back toward simply being curious about people, we become able to create far healthier and more influential Life Coaching relationships. When we're genuinely curious about understanding others, we will naturally see them as complex human beings worthy of our full attention and respect. We're also more likely to ask probing questions that can help us to understand them better. In turn, they'll become more likely to trust us and feel comfortable confiding in us as their Life Coach.

So the next time you find yourself in a conversation, resist the urge to think about what you want to say next. Instead, really listen to what the other person is saying and let your curiosity guide you before all other things. You may be surprised at how much better your conversations go—and how much more intimately you connect with people as a result.

**PRINCIPLES INTO PRACTICE QUESTIONS:**

1. What is it like to spend time with people who are curious about you?
2. What state of mind prevents you from being curious about people?
3. What state of mind allows you to be curious about people?
4. What typically gets in the way of your being curious?

# THE PERSON-CENTERED COACHING APPROACH

*"The individual has vast resources for self-understanding, for altering his or her self-concept, attitudes and self-directed behavior—and these resources can be tapped into if only a definable climate of facilitative psychological attitudes can be provided."*

—CARL ROGERS

Carl Rogers (1902–1987) is the psychologist whose name is synonymous with the person-centered approach to counseling. Throughout his academic career, he also gained experience as a therapist and authored multiple books, including *Client-Centered Therapy* (1951) and *On Becoming a Person* (1961). The emphasis across Rogers's writing is on the importance of each person as the architect of their individual destiny. Rogers, who was born in Illinois, studied theology but switched to psychology in 1931 before pioneering person-centered therapy in the 1940s and becoming instrumental in laying the foundations and theory for the practice of counseling by non-medical laypeople. Rogers believed that every person had the ability to reach their potential in life when a person is given the right support. This was a radical idea at the time and has had a lasting impact on psychology. In order for a person to reach their potential, Rogers believed that a number of criteria must be met. First, there must be a strong desire or motivation to change. Second, the individual must have a clear picture of what they want to achieve. Finally, the individual must have the resources and support necessary to create change. Rogers's approach to psychology was aligned with Maslow's concept of the self-actualizing person, but he went further. Rogers sought to redefine the "skilled helping" relationship by arguing that positive behavioral change can only occur when the relationship between a coach and coachee is built on mutual trust and respect. In his book, *On Becoming a Person*, Rogers discussed the attitudes that must exist for one person to positively influence another to grow and take a greater degree of responsibility for themselves: these attitudes include empathy, congruence, and unconditional acceptance. Much like how an oak tree will not grow without sunlight and water, without these three conditions, healthy Life Coaching relationships might not develop as much as they otherwise could.

## THE THREE CORE CONDITIONS FOR INFLUENTIAL COACHING
### THE CONDITION OF EMPATHY

The ability to empathize is valuable in many contexts, but it is especially important for Life Coaches. When coaching, it is important to accurately understand what your coachees priorities are, without just agreeing with what they say. This is where the distinction between empathy and sympathy becomes key. Sympathy stems from a desire to be agreeable, while empathy stems from a desire to understand people. Empathy does not mean accepting all of a person's feelings but simply trying to understand where they are coming from. As a result, an empathic coach will ask open-ended questions to try to get a sense of what the coachee needs and what their priorities are. This allows them to provide more targeted coaching. In the words of Rogers (1959):

> The state of being empathic, is to perceive the internal frame of reference of another with accuracy and with the emotional components and meanings which pertain thereto as if one were the person, but without ever losing the "as if" condition. Thus it means to sense the experience of another as he senses it and to perceive the causes thereof as he perceives

them, but without ever losing the recognition that it is as if I were hurt or pleased and so forth. If this "as if" quality is lost, then the state is one of identification.

*Exercise 1. Listening to Your Mind*

To empathically relate to other people, you must first have management over your own mind, which can only happen to the degree that you are aware of what's happening in your mind. Take twenty minutes (use a stopwatch if you need to) to sit in silence and listen to yourself. In this time, don't think. Instead of thinking, just identify the thoughts and ideas that "pop" into your mind and then write them all down. It doesn't matter how mundane or irrelevant the thoughts may be. The point is just to practice becoming more aware of your mind's habits.

## THE CONDITION OF CONGRUENCE

There is little more off-putting than being in the presence of an incongruent person. But what exactly is congruence? Congruence (or genuineness) describes a core personal quality that every credible coach must possess. This quality is one that naturally laces sincerity, integrity, authenticity, and transparency throughout the coaching relationship. In order to be congruent with a coachee, you must first be without pretense or façade within yourself. This means that Life Coaches should know themselves from the "inside-out" before they even attempt to coach another person. In the absence of self-knowledge, it would be impossible to cultivate an open or honest relationship with a coachee. This means that, unlike a conventional therapist who might have been trained to hide their personality, a congruent coach has no façade and is keen to allow a coachee to experience them as they are.

Being "open" and "honest" certainly doesn't imply compassionless frankness; however, when empathy and unconditional acceptance are also active within a coaching relationship, frankness will be less of a problem. Congruence sets an example for those who may find it difficult to be open and genuine themselves. One of the greatest risks you can take in life is just being yourself, but by having the courage to be the fully unabridged version of yourself, you naturally encourage other people to do the same.

*Exercise 2. Identify Your Incongruences*

Take a few minutes to think about how you conduct yourself when in the company of people that you know and trust. Then compare this to how you might behave around people who you don't know or trust so well. In what ways might you behave incongruently at times? What might incongruence cost you within some of your more important relationships? Why?

## THE CONDITION OF ACCEPTANCE

The need for positive regard is present in all human beings, of whom many will do almost anything to acquire it. People need love, acceptance, respect, and warmth from others, but unfortunately, these attitudes are often only given to people conditionally. Too often, people are judged on their looks, possessions, accomplishments, or their failures. We are all guilty of doing this at one time or another. You might see someone who is wealthy or successful and assume they have it all together, or another person struggling and assume them to be a lost cause. A person is a continually changing constellation of potentialities, not a fixed quantity of personality traits. Unconditional acceptance lets you look beyond the surface-level traits that people often characterize themselves by to see the person underneath. When you accept people, what a person has done in the past or plans to do in the future becomes irrelevant: you are only concerned with helping them to understand the decisions they need to make in the "here and now." By adopting this attitude, you can create a healthy Life Coaching environment in which people feel safe to ask questions, be "real" with you, honest with themselves, and make the decisions that they need to make to grow and fulfill their goals.

*Exercise 3. Conveying Positive Regard*

Think about a time when you received unconditional acceptance from someone who helped you without wanting anything back in return. How did this person convey these positive attitudes to you? What did experiencing these positive attitudes teach you?

The quality of a Life Coaching relationship is one of the best predictors of its outcomes. A growing body of research from the American Psychological Association is beginning to show that "person-centered" relationships that incorporate empathy, congruence, and unconditional acceptance are a vehicle through which many positive behavioral changes take place. However, all people have different relationship needs, and no single set of relationship parameters will ever be necessary or sufficient for all people. But, if you want to practice Life Coaching in a way that stands to generate your coachees the best possible outcomes, then disciplining yourself to establish empathic, congruent, and unconditionally accepting relationships is one of the wisest investments you can make. All too often in our fast-paced lives, we sacrifice deep relationships for shallow ones, and the busyness of life prevents us from connecting with people meaningfully. Strong relationships are central to influential coaching. By taking time to understand your coachees' needs and offering them high-quality relationship support, you will inevitably help them to master their minds and mountains. Never belittle the value of relationships in coaching—focus on building strong, supportive relationships, and you'll be well on your way to making a real difference in people's lives.

**PRINCIPLES INTO PRACTICE QUESTIONS:**

If you've ever had an experience where you felt like someone fully understood where you were coming from or could truly relate to how you felt—that's empathic understanding. What role do you see empathy playing within a Life Coaching relationship?

# THE SEVEN STAGE COMMUNICATION CYCLE

*"Communication is one of the greatest sources of hope for people. Communication does more than keep families or businesses going; it's the essence of all human relationships. How we communicate with others ultimately determines the quality of our lives."*

—VIRGINIA SATIR

Ever since our ancestors uttered their first grunts, miscommunication has been a part of our everyday lives. A reader might misinterpret part of this book and take offense, a customer misreads an instruction manual; a colleague misinterprets a work request; a married couple clash over misunderstanding who was going to pick up the children from school. One would have thought that miscommunication would drop with the advancement of technology-based communication aids. Alas, this isn't the case. Today, humanity is more connected than ever before, yet so many people stray further from mutually understanding each other. Every time you misunderstand a coachee due to poorly communicating, you invite discord into the coaching relationship and lose credibility in their eyes.

Some people are old enough to remember watching TV on a stormy day, having to get up every ten minutes to wiggle around the antenna on top of the television to get the picture back into focus. Analog broadcasting was the norm from the dawn of the twentieth century until digital broadcasting was introduced in the early 2000s. There was nothing wrong with analog broadcasting; it wasn't broken, but it grew outdated. The low-resolution sound and picture quality that analog offered couldn't compete with digital broadcasting that broke down transmissions into eight-bit chunks. Once high-resolution picture and sound became the standard, no one looked back at analog that had served them for nearly a century.

Much like data transmission methods have evolved to allow for better TV viewing, a Life Coach can't rely on outdated methods of communicating, such as passively sitting whilst a coachee transmits information (which still happens in many traditional talking therapies). To produce a higher quality of exchange, a coach must break down a coachee's broadcast into smaller bite-sized chunks for processing and analysis. It's one thing for a coach to be skilled at communicating verbally and non-verbally, and then it's something else for a Life Coach to understand how human interactions are structured and, thus, the danger zone area in which many interactions break down. When a Life Coach understands how communication is structured, they can avoid the danger zone of miscommunication and create effective two-way interactions that are always grounded in fact and never in guesswork or assumptions.

It is not uncommon for miscommunication to happen. This is because when people interact, they each do so from their own individual perspectives, without access to what each other is hearing or assuming. Thus, each person filters what the other is saying through the lens of their perception and awareness. Emotional factors such as fear, attraction, or anger also play a crucial role in interpretation. A conversation breakdown can be defined as the point within an exchange where one party prioritizes listening more to their assumptions about the other person and less toward understanding what the other person is trying to communicate.

Disjointed communication occurs when there is a discrepancy between what is said by one person and what is heard by another. For example, an employee receives feedback from a manager regarding the caliber of his listening. The employee overthinks the feedback, assumes the worst about what his manager "may have meant," takes his assumption to heart, and then quits the following day after taking offense at his manager devaluing his communication style. In truth, his manager's intention was simply to foster an environment of personal growth and improvement within the workplace. But this example shows the cavity that often exists between one person's intentions and another person's interpretation.

With Life Coaching, all communication can be codified as a cycle and broken into seven stages. The communication cycle is a framework that describes the stages of every communication exchange you will have. Thinking about the communication cycle when you're planning or delivering a coaching session will help you understand the different stages that your conversation will go through and ensure that each session is as effective as possible.

**STAGE 1. THE SENDER**

The sender is the first link in the communication chain. This is the person who is expressing information, be it verbally or nonverbally. The message that the sender conveys (i.e., you) will be interpreted by the receiver (i.e., your coachee), so it is important that the sender takes care to communicate clearly. To do this, the sender must be aware of their own thoughts and feelings and how these may be conveyed to the other. A sender must also be attuned to the receiver's needs in order to ensure that the message is understood. Only when both sender and receiver are attuned to each other can communication be truly effective.

**STAGE 2. THE MESSAGE**

The message is the information that the sender expresses. The Greek philosopher Aristotle once said, "For rhetoric to be effective, it must be constantly accompanied by a psychology." In other words, in order for a message to be effectively communicated, it must be tailored to the psychological state of the receiver. This is because the way in which a message is received is just as important as the message itself. If the receiver is in a state of anxiety, for example, they may be more likely to misinterpret the message or fail to comprehend it entirely. Conversely, if the receiver is in a state of relaxation, they will be more likely to receive the message in the way that it was intended. Therefore, it is essential that the sender takes into account the psychological state of the receiver when crafting their message. By doing so, they can ensure that their message is received in the way that they intended it to be.

**STAGE 3. ENCODING**

This is how the sender conveys their message. How we say something is just as important as what we say. The way we deliver our message—through our tone of voice, body language, or other cues—can add meaning and context that words alone cannot convey. This is known as encoding, and it is an essential part of effective communication. When we are aware of how we are encoding our message, we can ensure that our intention is clear and that our message is received as intended. This is especially important in cross-cultural communication, where different ways of encoding can lead to misunderstanding. By being aware of the role of encoding in communication, we can make sure that our message is received loud and clear.

**STAGE 4. THE CHANNEL**

The channel through which communication takes place is just as important as the message itself. The right channel can make a message more effective, while the wrong channel can create confusion and misunderstanding. For example, a face-to-face conversation is usually more effective than an email exchange because it allows for immediate feedback and clarification. On the other hand, an email exchange can be preferable to a phone call because it allows for more thoughtful consideration of the message. Similarly, a video conference can be a good middle ground between face-to-face and email communication, allowing for both real-time interaction and the opportunity to review the conversation later. Ultimately, choosing the right channel is a matter of understanding what your coachee naturally prefers.

## STAGE 5. THE RECEIVER

In all human communication, the receiver is the person toward whom the message is directed. The sender encodes their message with the intention of having it decoded by the receiver. In order to do this, they must take into account the receiver's cognitive biases or ways that they tend to interpret information. These biases can distort the message and make it difficult for the receiver to understand. In order to avoid this, the sender must be aware of the biases and adjust their message accordingly. By taking into account the receiver's biases, the sender can increase the chances that their message will be received as intended.

## STAGE 6. DECODING

Decoding is the way the receiver interprets a sender's message by translating the sender's tone, pitch and words into their own thoughts. In other words, it is taking a sender's message and assigning their own meaning to it (because humans are meaning-making machines!). The problem with decoding is that people are often not aware of how they unconsciously interpret other people's messages. It's human tendency to assume that how we perceive a situation, or in this case, interpret a sender's message, is 100 percent accurate all of the time. But this is rarely true. Your coachees each have their own perspectives and biases that influence how they decode what you say. Thus, it is important to be aware of how your message might be interpreted by your coachee and be ready to correct them if or when they are wrong.

## STAGE 7. FEEDBACK

Feedback is the response of the receiver to the sender's message. Feedback is essential in communication because it helps you to know how well your message has been decoded by a coachee. There are two types of feedback: verbal and non-verbal. Verbal feedback is when the receiver responds with words, for example, by saying "yes" or "no" or by asking a question. Non-verbal feedback is when the receiver responds with their body language, for example, by nodding their head or crossing their arms. Both types of feedback are useful as they provide information that can help you to reframe your message or even invite your coachee to recommend how you might improve your future communication with them. This will certainly be an excellent way to solidify the trust in your coaching relationships.

You can probably sense when you are being talked at rather than talked with. And so can others. Coaches who genuinely want to understand their coachees can't go too far wrong. Once you're willing to see other people's perspectives and listen wholeheartedly to their feedback, you'll be considered an empathetic communicator and an excellent Life Coach. Listening is one of the most important skills a coach can have. It's the key to understanding your coachee's needs and helping them identify and achieve their goals. When you listen attentively, you show that you value what your coachee has to say. You also gain important information that will help you tailor your coaching to meet their individual needs. Active listening also demonstrates empathy, which is essential for building trust and rapport with your coachee. Trust is essential for effective coaching, as it allows the coach-coachee relationship to flourish and provides the foundation for a meaningful exchange to occur.

**PRINCIPLES INTO PRACTICE QUESTIONS:**

1. How might understanding these stages allow you to deliver highly-influential coaching?
2. How can you ensure that the message you send out is the same message that's received by the important people in your everyday life (i.e., family members or work colleagues)?

# CORE COACHING COMMUNICATION SKILLS

*"Usually, when you listen to someone make a statement, you hear it as a kind of echo of yourself. You are actually listening to your own opinion. If it agrees with your opinion, you may accept it. But if it does not, you will reject it, or you may not even really hear it."* He then went on to explain, *"When you listen to someone, give up all your preconceived ideas and subjective opinions; you should listen and observe what his way is. We put very little emphasis on right and wrong or good and bad. We see things as they are with him and just accept them. This is how we communicate with each other. If we have nothing to say, we say nothing."*

—ZEN MASTER SHUNRYŪ SUZUKI

Communication skills can be divided into two principal components: verbal and non-verbal. In this chapter, we will explore some of the core communication skills that you can draw upon in your Life Coaching. We shall discuss the significance of non-verbal aspects of communication in coaching, with special reference to the substantial influence that non-verbal behavior exerts within a coaching relationship. Non-verbal communication includes all the cues that we send out through our body language and tone of voice. It also includes our use of space and our choice of words. All of these factors contribute to the message that we communicate to others. When we are aware of the non-verbal cues that we are sending out, we can use them to our advantage in order to create a more fruitful coaching relationship.

### ACTIVE LISTENING *(NON-VERBAL)*

Active listening is a term commonly used in relation to coaching. There are several factors necessary for active listening to happen, which include the observation of a coachee's non-verbal behavior, as well as understanding verbal content and meaning. It goes without saying that the "way" something is said is just as important as the actual words spoken. This is especially relevant in a Life Coaching context as some coachees may have difficulty in finding the right words to accurately express themselves and their priorities. In these circumstances, accompanying non-verbal cues often speak much more eloquently than words. Listening and attending to people are skills that always go together in coaching. To listen entirely means to pay close attention to what is being said beneath a person's words. You listen not only for information and facts but also for the person's feelings, attitudes, and unspoken assumptions. One of the challenges for a new coach is developing their own style of attending, which suits them individually and also complements the person they are coaching at that moment in time.

### ATTENDING THE PERSON *(NON-VERBAL)*

There is a short story by Leo Tolstoy called *The Three Questions*. In the story, the king came to the conclusion that if he always knew the right time to begin everything; who the best people to listen to were, and who to avoid; and if he always knew what the most important thing to do was, he would never fail in anything. With this epiphany, the king offered a reward to anyone who would teach him the right time for every action, the best people to be around, and how to know what the best things to do were. Despite all the wise men who came forward, no one gave him the same answer, and they all seemed to contradict each other.

Still wishing to find answers to his questions, the king decided to consult a wise old hermit. The king had to leave his castle and venture into the woods to find the hermit, whom he found digging the ground in front of his hut. The king went up to him and said: "I have come to you, wise hermit, to ask you to answer three questions: How can I learn to do the right thing at the right time? Who are the people I should pay more attention to than to? And, what affairs are most important and should be my number one priority?"

The hermit listened to the king but didn't answer. Instead, he carried on digging. Believing the hermit was too exhausted from his work to answer his questions, the king offered to dig the hole for the hermit while the old man took a break to think about his response. After the king had dug two large holes, he repeated his questions to the hermit, but the hermit still said nothing. The hermit, however, extended his hand and told the king to take a rest while he carried on digging. The king, determined to get an answer from the exhausted hermit, refused to return the spade and instead carried on digging.

After a while, the sun began to set, and the hermit still hadn't answered the king's questions. "I came to you, wise man, for an answer to my questions," the king sighed, "If you can give me none, tell me so, and I will return home." Before the king could say another word, the hermit leaped up. "I can hear someone running. Let's go see who it is." The king turned around and saw a bearded man running out of the wood with blood pouring from his stomach. When he reached the hermit and the king, he collapsed, unconscious, but the hermit and king were ready to help. They undressed the man, attended to his wounds, carried him into the hermit's hut to lie him on the bed, and brought him fresh water when he awoke.

The king, exhausted from his day's work, fell asleep in the hermit's hut and only woke the following day at the sound of shuffling. Facing the king was the bearded man, now wide awake and in awe. Sheepishly, the bearded man admitted that he was an enemy of the king; the king had executed his brother, and he vowed to take his revenge. However, one of the king's bodyguards had intersected the bearded man's ambush and nearly killed him were it not for the care of the king and the hermit. The bearded man, now in debt, apologized, and swore allegiance to the king, who forgave him. However, the king was far more occupied with the three questions still pressing on his mind. So he left the bearded man and the hut to find the hermit outside sowing seeds in the holes that they'd dug the day before.

"For the last time," the king begged the hermit, "Please answer my questions."

"Why," the hermit replied, "You have already been answered!"

Confused, the king pressed the hermit to elaborate.

"Do you not see?" replied the hermit. "If you had not stopped me yesterday to dig these holes but had gone your way, that man would have attacked and possibly killed you. So the most important time was when you were digging, and I was the most important man, and to do me good was your best business. Afterward, when that man ran to us, the most important time was when you were helping him, for if you hadn't attended him, he may have died without having made peace with you. So he was the most important man, and attending him was your best business. Therefore, the most important time is now as it is the only time you have. The most important person is who you are, and the most important thing is to do your best for people all of the time."

Attending people in communication means giving our full undivided focus and attention to their verbal and non-verbal communication. It is a skill that involves remaining fully present and engaged while interacting with another person and being disciplined enough to resist the temptation to multitask or let your mind wander. It also means being interested in hearing what the other person has to say rather than just waiting for your turn to speak. Active listening is often the most effective form of non-verbal communication a coach can use. However, it is often underestimated by people. The truth is that our personal presence within a Life Coaching relationship is often more important than anything we could say. Our coachees must see that we are interested in them. Only then will they trust us enough to open up, be honest and discuss their deficits, discrepancies, and goals. Attending is often regarded as a passive process rather than an active life skill, but in truth, attending to people in your presence is possibly one of the most influential communication skills you might develop.

## COLLABORATIVE LISTENING *(NON-VERBAL)*

As a new Life Coach, your priority will be to either collaborate with your coachees or to control them. Collaborative coaching requires collaborative listening on your part, which is the process of reflectively listening to others with the intent to understand their perspective. This requires you to let go of your own preconceptions and biases and suspend judgment. When you listen to people in this way, you will create a space for acquiring understanding and building a deep connection with them. While you might not always like what your coachee is saying, through collaborative listening and understanding their perspective, you will develop a deeper respect for their views and an appreciation for their priorities. Additionally, by really hearing and understanding what someone is saying, you will be able to more effectively help them achieve their goals. So collaborative listening is not only respectful and appreciated by coachees, but it is also an essential skill for effective coaching.

## USING IMMEDIACY *(VERBAL)*

The term immediacy is used to describe the process of discussing what is actually taking place "right now" within a coaching situation. Practicing immediacy involves focusing attention on the immediate dynamics within a coaching relationship to facilitate reflection on the coachee's part. The timing of practicing immediacy is critical and, when judged right, can be used to subtly challenge closed-mindedness and defensiveness and heighten the coachee's self-awareness. The following is an example of immediacy in action:

COACHEE: *"I've spoken with many coaches, and no one's been able to help me yet."*

COACH: *"Let's talk this through and figure out exactly what hasn't worked for you. By doing this, can we prevent this relationship from just being another repeat of the past?"*

In the example given, immediacy was used by the coach to draw attention to the coachee's immediate concerns. Immediacy can feel "risky" for the coach and possibly "confrontational" to experience for the coachee, as it invites the coachee to explore the specific reasons for the response that are having toward a coach within the immediate moment.

## THE SOUND OF SILENCE *(NON-VERBAL)*

An old piece of Taoist wisdom asks the question, "How do you see through murky water?" The answer is to stop muddling it up through your actions. When you disturb the water, you kick up dirt and mud, causing the water to become murky. The water only becomes clear again when you stop, sit down, and allow the dirt to settle around you. But the real question is, can you find the patience to wait until your dust settles and the water becomes clear?

The value of silence should not be underestimated. In order to listen to someone, it is essential to be silent. This does not mean simply remaining quiet, but rather being present and paying attention to the person who is speaking. It can be difficult to remain silent, especially when there are pauses in a conversation. Those who are uncomfortable participating in silence often feel tempted to fill in conversational pauses with irrelevant noise, meaningless chatter, or finishing people's sentences for them. Silence allows you to reflect on what has been said, and when you are quiet, you send a message that you are invested in the conversation and that you value the person you're talking to. Often, within a goal-focused Life Coaching context, your coachees will need pauses of time, space, and silence to collect their thoughts and respond. If you don't give them this opportunity, they may see your intervention as being either intrusive or insensitive. All people communicate through silence at times, and this can help them to find clarity in aspects of their life, goals, or problems that may have been obscured to them in the past. By learning to embrace silence, we open ourselves up to closer relationships and deeper levels of communication. When we are silent, we are able to listen more deeply to people, which can lead to greater understanding and empathy.

## COACHING APPEARANCE *(NON-VERBAL)*

How a coach presents themselves can reveal much. Personal values, and even mood, are often discernible in a person's general appearance. A coach who dresses scruffy and unkempt might be less likely to retain the confidence of a coachee than a smart-dressing coach otherwise would. On the other hand, an excessively glamorous or suave appearance might be unappealing to some coachees who have body image or personal looks issues. However, no style of clothing or dress has the same meaning for everyone, which means that a coach should probably dress in whatever way is personally comfortable for them without attempting to make some form of a statement. Probably the only hard-and-fast rule pertaining to dress and appearance is respect for coachees. A coach must remain authentic but present themselves visually in a way that inspires confidence in their ability and coaching competence.

### REFLECTION/REFLECTING BACK *(VERBAL)*

Reflecting back is the process of restating and paraphrasing the words and feelings of the other person. By reflecting, the other person can, in turn, "hear" their thoughts, allowing them to focus with greater clarity on what they're saying and what they need to say next. In a sense, reflecting back is like holding up a mirror in front of people so that they can see themselves clearly and sense-check the accuracy of the words that exit their mouth. Reflection is also referred to as "reflecting back," and to be effective, must always be done unobtrusively so that a coachee is unaware that it's happening. The following is an example of reflection in action:

COACHEE: *"I'm frustrated and feel that I'm not progressing as much as I should."*

COACH: *"You're frustrated and not progressing as you should be."*

COACHEE: *"Yes, I'm just not certain about how I should be prioritizing my time."*

COACH: *"So you are uncertain about what your priorities need to be."*

COACHEE: *"Yes, that's totally accurate."*

Reflecting shows the other person that you're doing your best to understand what they're saying and attempting to comprehend the world from their perspective. Reflecting back does not require asking questions; its purpose is to help the coachee feel understood and give them the chance to explore or clarify their ideas further. *"You feel apprehensive about the changes. You seem excited, but I'm also beginning to sense that you're apprehensive at the same time,"* are examples of reflective statements. You might find you get responses such as, *"Did I really say that?"* or *"Hearing back what I've just said has made the problem clearer in my mind."*

### SUMMARIZING AND CLARIFYING *(VERBAL)*

The skill of summarizing is used when a coach wants to respond to a series of statements or even to an entire coaching session. As with reflecting, summarizing requires a coach to stay within a coachee's frame of reference (i.e., how a person summarizes their own experience). Some of your coachees might talk at random, unclear about what their priorities need to be, and get easily side-tracked into other related or unrelated issues. This can make it difficult to follow all that they say; therefore, formulating an accurate summary also requires active listening and an ability to draw all the coachee's random "thinking threads" together into one coherent narrative. The following is an example of summarizing in action:

COACHEE: "Somedays I get overwhelmed. I don't know what routine tasks I should prioritize first, and sometimes waste an entire day doing something completely irrelevant that takes me in a completely different direction from the one that I actually want to be going in. This is frustrating and can cost me between 50–75 percent of my working week."

COACH: "So, am I right in hearing that you need to clarify what your priorities are because, without clarity, you are wasting time and feeling overwhelmed?"

COACHEE: "Yes, that's right."

When summarizing, a coaches role is to recite the factual elements of the coachee's story and confirm that what the coachee said has been fully understood. Through summarizing, a coach checks his or her own understanding of what had been said. The coachee is then offered time, space, and silence to add any details that have been missed or to agree with the summary. Accurate summarizing should always show understanding of what the coachee has said, reflect the coachee's internal frame of reference, and be provisional to a coachee's agreement.

## THE ART OF REFRAMING *(VERBAL)*

Human beings are story-making and meaning-making machines with an ingrained habit of connecting different events to identify similarities (or differences) between them and create explanations for their daily experiences. Reframing is a useful coaching skill that will allow a coachee to consider alternative possibilities for their current assumptions. Reframing involves placing an old story into a new frame (a way of looking at things), which offers an entirely different perspective. The idea behind reframing is that the frame through which your coachee views a situation will determine their point of view. If that frame is shifted, their way of thinking will often change along with it. Some people get trapped in a narrow way of looking at things. Their way of thinking might carry a message that disempowers them in some way. Your ability to help people reframe their thinking can help to enlarge their perspective and sense of future possibility. Reframing is just looking at things differently; it involves taking challenges that your coachees face and redirecting any "downtrodden" perspectives in an alternative direction that presents new opportunities or alternative pathways that weren't apparent minutes earlier. Another way to understand reframing is to imagine looking through a camera lens. The picture seen through a lens can be changed to a view that is closer or farther away. By changing what is seen in the camera, the picture can be viewed differently.

Let's say that one of your coachees hopes to launch a new business and just learned that he can't get the bank loan he wanted. Naturally, your coachee might first focus on disappointment, so your opportunity is to help him brainstorm new ways that he might; (a) generate new alternative funding, or (b) build a business that doesn't require any major up-front funding at all. That is all reframing entails. Reframing, whether you practice it independently or with your coachees, can be a helpful way to turn problems into opportunities for change and personal growth. With practice, you can learn to ask yourself questions like, *"Is there another way to look at this situation?"* or, "What are some useful reasons why this could have happened?" remind yourself that the initial conclusion you arrive at in a given situation is only one possible way of looking at things.

### ASKING QUESTIONS *(VERBAL)*

One of the challenges of listening to people discuss their lives is that curiosity can get aroused, and when this happens, some people go on a fact-finding mission to clarify details in their head rather than seeking to understand the other person. When communicating, some people ask too many questions, which may be perceived as more of an inquisition than a discussion. As a consequence, active listening doesn't happen, and trust can get damaged. Asking too many questions can come across as being intrusive, interfere with the flow of a conversation and prevent a coach from hearing what a coachee wants to say. Instead, the coach should strive to create an open and supportive environment where the coachee feels free to discuss whatever is important to them.

### OPEN AND PROBING QUESTIONS *(VERBAL)*

Asking open and probing questions allows for a thoughtful exchange to happen between two people, and creating an environment where reflective dialogue can happen is essential for any Life Coaching relationship to sustain. For example, if you were to ask a coachee, *"How are you doing?"* You'll likely get a response such as, *"Ok, thanks."* Closed questions are those that can usually only be answered with a one-word answer and rarely qualify for a thoughtful response. Open and probing questions naturally encourage people to reflect, talk more reflectively about themselves and allow for more meaningful, reflective coaching exchanges to happen. By asking open and probing questions, you will create space for your coachees to dig deeper in their thinking and expand upon something they have already said. The following are examples:

COACH: "Can you tell me what's important to you here?"

COACH: "And what might happen once you've reached your goal?"

COACH: "Could you describe your goal to me in more specific detail?"

COACH: "What specifically makes this goal so important to you?"

## POSSIBILITY INCREASING QUESTIONS *(VERBAL)*

All too often, people find themselves stuck in a rut, wondering why they're not getting the results they want. Rather than taking responsibility for their own lives, they point to outside circumstances, making excuses and rationalizations that sound perfectly reasonable. But if you listen closely, you'll hear a tone of resignation that betrays what's possible for them. You will hear about difficult situations, uncontrollable circumstances, rigid timelines, and people who are inflexible or unwilling. It may not sound like irresponsibility, but that's all complaining ever is. It is human nature to believe that we know what is possible and what is not. We see the world through our own lens, and we filter out information that does not fit with our existing beliefs. This can be helpful in some ways, as it allows us to make quick decisions based on our past experiences. However, it can also limit our potential. If we believe that something is impossible, then we will never bother to try to achieve it. We may even give up before we have even started. This is why it is so important for coaches to help their clients explore their beliefs and assumptions about what is possible. Only then can the client begin to see the possibility of achieving what they may previously have perceived as being an impossible goal. The following are examples of possibility-increasing questions:

COACHEE: "I want to get married, but I'm past my best-before date."

#1 COACH: "Which age range of people will you still be more than appealing to?"

#2 COACH: Which exciting dating options haven't you committed to trying yet?

#3 COACH: In what ways can you change to become more appealing to more people?

Many people convince themselves that they can't do something before they've even attempted it. Why is this? It could be due to a variety of reasons, such as a fear of failure, having failed at learning when they were younger, or just a lack of confidence. However, usually, it's because people mistake their beliefs as facts. By asking possibility-increasing questions, you can encourage your coachees to consider their goals with the "opportunity for growth" they have in mind, rather than trying to "change their mind" about what is and isn't possible for them. For example, a man who assumes that he cannot learn new things might avoid setting goals that require him to learn something new. However, by reframing his goal as an opportunity to learn, he may be more likely to take action. In this way, possibility-increasing questions can help people to overcome their self-imposed "perceived" limitations, achieve their goals, and sometimes even surpass their own expectations.

### CHUNKING-UP QUESTIONS *(VERBAL)*

The next time you're seeking to help a coachee expand their view on a situation, try employing the chunking technique. Chunking is a pattern of questioning that allows the person being coached to shift from a more detailed perspective to a broader one and vice versa. When you ask questions that encourage your coachee to "chunk up," they will be able to see the situation from a more holistic view, like standing on top of a mountain and seeing the landscape below. This can be helpful in making wiser decisions by taking into account all of the relevant information. Asking questions that cause your coachee to "chunk down" will help them focus on smaller details within the larger picture. By chunking-up or chunking-down, you can assist your coachee in gaining a better understanding of their current situation.

Chunking-up questions will provoke a coachee to consider things from a purpose-orientated standpoint rather than from the perspective of specific details. Seeing things from a purpose-oriented perspective will allow your coachee to contemplate life's broader questions without being distracted by the details of their day-to-day lives. Chunking-up is great for those too focused on the specific details of their daily interactions and who have no clear vision for their life, as chunking-up helps them get a broader picture of their life and purpose. Here's an example of what a chunking-up line of questioning might look like:

COACHEE: I want to finish reading this Life Coaching handbook.

COACH: For what purpose do you want to finish reading this handbook?

COACHEE: Because I want to become a super-effective Life Coach.

COACH: For what purpose do you want to become a super-effective Life Coach?

COACHEE: Because I want to develop a highly credible reputation.

COACH: For what purpose do you want to develop a highly credible reputation?

COACHEE: Because I want to prove myself to my parents.

COACH: For what purpose do you want to prove yourself to your parents?

As you can probably see, asking chunking-up questions will allow your coachee to gain absolute clarity about the reason why they want to do or achieve anything. Once you know what your coachee's main source of motivation is, you can then question whether their goal-setting approach is likely, or unlikely to be one that enables them to get what they want. Chunking-up questions are a powerful tool for coaches, as they help to lead coachees into thinking existentially about the "ultimate reasons" why they even want to do anything. By asking these types of questions repeatedly, coaches can help their coachees to reflect on the deeper meaning and purpose behind their actions. This, in turn, can help them to clarify their goals, values, and motivation. Asking chunking-up questions can therefore be a helpful way to encourage your coachees to think more deeply about their life and their choices.

**CHUNKING-DOWN QUESTIONS *(VERBAL)***

If you notice that the person you're coaching is too focused on the big picture of things but has no actual means of realizing their vision, you may want to help them chunk down to examine their steps and hold them accountable. Chunking-down is about asking questions that help coachees zoom into their lives to gain a more myopic perspective of the world and better understand their circumstances. It allows them to reframe their thinking and develop a clearer sense of what they need to do in order to achieve their goals. In other words, it helps them to focus on the task at hand rather than getting overwhelmed by the larger goal. As a result, chunking-down can be an invaluable tool for coaches who want to help their clients move forward in a more practical and action-step-oriented way. Here's an example of what a chunking-down line of questioning might look like:

COACHEE: I want to become a super-effective Life Coach.

COACH: How specifically might you become a super-effective Life Coach?

COACHEE: I could start by completing this Life Coaching handbook.

COACH: And how specifically will you develop competent coaching skills?

COACHEE: I could start by participating in Achology skill development sessions.

COACH: And what specifically must you do in these skill development sessions?

COACHEE: I must practice the principles that are presented in this handbook.

COACH: And how specifically will you…

As you can probably see, asking chunking-down questions is the process of asking your coachee progressively more specific questions about what they must do to achieve a goal or realize a certain vision. The benefit of this approach is that it can help your coachee to gain absolute clarity about what they need to do in order to achieve their desired outcome, or even just to start making progress toward it. Asking chunking-down questions is therefore a valuable tool that every coach should make use of. Simply put, chunking-up involves asking simple questions to get a coachee thinking about the reasons WHY they wish to achieve something. On the other hand, chunking-down involves asking questions that get a coachee thinking about the actionable steps they must take to turn their goals into a reality.

## POSITIVE ORIENTATION (VERBAL AND NON-VERBAL)

Problems draw most people like magnets! Your interest in your coachee's life may tempt you to ask questions about the details of his past or current problems. But getting insight into the historical reasons and causes for problems isn't necessarily, (a) helpful for your coachee, and (b) the best use of your limited time together. A coachee telling you the history of their problems is not going to help your coachee move from where he is to where he wants to be.

If you were to think about problematic behavior, you might picture someone engaging in harmful activities like drug use or gambling. However, not all problematic behavior is physical. Just think about how damaging it is to keep on revisiting negative past events in your mind. Like a hand-held too close to a fire, problematic memories can keep on burning people who never cease focusing their attention on them. The effects of problematic thinking can creep up on people over time, sometimes decades. In this way, problematic thoughts and memories are similar to slow-growing diseases like cancer or heart disease. By the time people realize the damage that has been done, it can require a major effort to reverse.

Another reason people engage in destructive thinking is that, unlike burning their hand in a fire, people often struggle to identify when their thinking is detrimental to their goals. So, like problematic behavior, the first step toward breaking the cycle is being aware of the problem. Your opportunity as a coach is to use reflecting, silence, summarizing, and questioning to help your coachees reorient their problematic mindset toward

1. generating a positive life outcome that inspires them, and;
2. how they might progress toward this positive outcome.

Positive outcomes should be understood as the specific results that matter the most to your coachee. So the starting point of being positive outcome focused is to define what their priority is and plan your future coaching support from there. This ability to influence people's attention is key to your future Life Coaching success. And this is also what separates Life Coaching from disempowering forms of therapy, in which a talking therapist might make their client's negative thoughts and fears the central point of discussion for months or even years.

The following dialogue examples of a coach remaining positive outcome focused:

COACHEE: "I hate my career, and it makes my life feel so unworth living."

COACH: "What exciting new career path would make your life more fulfilling?"

COACHEE: "I don't know. I don't even know where to start looking."

COACH: "What potentially rewarding career paths could you start exploring?"

### TONE AND DEMEANOR *(VERBAL AND NON-VERBAL)*

It is important to keep your voice neutral and unconditionally accepting at all times when coaching people. Strive to avoid sounding "friend-like" in order to discourage your coachees from attempting to explain the specific details of their life story. This isn't to say that your coachee's history isn't important, because it is. But focusing on the past is the opposite of focusing on future-oriented goals and objectives—which is what Life Coaching should always serve to assist. Work hard to keep your voice rhythmically and tonally consistent in order to encourage your coachee to remain in an objective, reflective, and solution-oriented head-space. This will allow them to identify potential solutions more clearly and allow the Life Coaching process to be more effective overall.

### BOUNDARIES AND SPACIAL AWARENESS *(NON-VERBAL)*

You are most likely already familiar with the concept of personal space. Personal space is an important concept to be aware of in coaching sessions. You know when someone stands or gets too close to you; it may feel like they're "in your space" which can (a) feel uncomfortable, and (b) distract you from what you are focusing on. In a Life Coaching session, be careful not to "step into" or breach your coachee's personal space. This can be distracting for them at best, and completely invasive at worst. Make an intentional effort to create the personal space that your coachees need—this can vary from coachee to coachee and will be informed through discernment and your own social awareness. It is also important to be aware of the personal space that you need as a coach. Be careful not to overcrowd your own space and become uncomfortable or distracted. In sum, creating the right amount of personal space will show a deep respect for the individual and help create a productive, focused environment.

## COACH SELF-DISCLOSURE

Self-disclosure has a powerful impact on how your relationships with other people form, progress, and sustain. Think about it this way; how much are you willing to trust people that you barely know anything about? Self-disclosure involves sharing information about yourself with another, which can range from simple things like your current challenges to more intimate details such as your long-term hopes and fears. But, how you share, what you share, and when you share are just some of the factors that determine whether self-disclosure is effective and appropriate. The following dialogue examples of a coach self-disclosing:

COACHEE: *"The idea of starting a new business petrifies me!"*

COACH: *"I can relate to your fears. When I started out in business, I was also petrified and didn't have much experience. Over time, I made mistakes, learned valuable lessons, and this is what led me to where I am today. This means that you can grow in a very similar way."*

Self-disclosure can be a powerful tool for a coach that helps to build rapport with a coachee by indirectly conveying a valuable lesson or principle. Self-disclosure can also be a useful form of challenge, so long as it is suitably timed, and delivered with a coachee's best interest firmly in focus. However, before a coach self-discloses, a certain level of coach/coachee trust must first be in place. The depth of honesty that a Life Coach discloses should reflect the level of trust that has already been built within the Life Coaching relationship—this simply means that you will disclose less personal information to a new coachee than you would to someone that you already know well and have a rapport with. While self-disclosure is not always necessary to build trust, it can be a valuable way to deepen an existing relationship.

When you implement these communication skills into your Life Coaching process, you will foster deeper connections, create stronger bonds of trust, and maintain greater insight into your coachees' thoughts and priorities. Your coachees will become more motivated and better equipped to make necessary changes and bridge the gap between what they have and want. No other skill in coaching will bring so much benefit as learning to communicate effectively.

**PRINCIPLES INTO PRACTICE QUESTIONS:**

1. Which of these communication skills do you already use when communicating?
2. Which of these communication skills do you need to work on improving the most?
3. In what ways could you use questioning to facilitate meaningful dialogues with people?
4. Ask three people to give you feedback on your communication strengths and weaknesses.
5. In what ways might chunking-up and down increase the depth of your coaching sessions?

**SOCIAL LISTENING EXERCISE:**

One way of developing your listening skills is to practice in social situations. Pick a public venue to visit. Once there, focus on what people are saying, paying close attention to their non-verbals, tone of voice, facial expression, and periods of silence in the speaker's delivery. Pay attention to the speaker's effect on those who are listening. Do people appear interested, or do they seem bored, for example; and, if so, why might this be? How do you listen when others speak to you? How do other people seem to listen when you speak to them?

# THE ROADBLOCKS TO HEALTHY COMMUNICATING

*"It is one of those simple paradoxes of life: When a person feels that he is truly accepted by another, as he is, then he is freed to move from there and to begin to think about how he wants to change, how we wants to grow, how he can become different, how he might become more of what he is capable of being."*

—THOMAS GORDON

I always found maintaining a relationship with my father difficult. He wasn't a vindictive man by any means, but he was a very poor listener. My father knew I hated being interrupted, so he would actively interrupt and talk over me regularly. It was never malicious, but he found it funny to see his son get frustrated, and what my father saw as teasing, I experienced as totally dishonoring. By the time I was in my twenties, I was renowned for being a "talker" who could hold people's attention and the space at the heart of any party. I always hated being ignored and interrupted. This, as you can imagine, was a hurdle I had to overcome when I got into Life Coaching. As I've stressed, Life Coaching begins with listening to what people say or sometimes don't say. Back in 2010, this wasn't an easy task for a chatter-box who was eager to be the center of attention—like me. In my early days as a coach, I found it difficult to resist integrating my own thoughts, opinions, and life stories into a coaching session. And sometimes, I did this to the detriment of some of my coaching relationships.

There are many roadblocks to communication that can negatively impact a Life Coaching relationship. Being aware of these roadblocks can often mean the difference between relationship failure and success. When we are unaware of these roadblocks, we miss out on opportunities to connect with people and build influential relationships. We each have a communication style that is influenced by our former relationships, past life experiences, and current priorities. If we are unaware of our communication style, we may inadvertently create barriers to communication. To be fruitful communicators, we must be aware of our style. Only then can we adapt our communication to meet the needs of a situation and the people involved. With this level of self-awareness, we can remove the roadblocks to communication and build Life Coaching relationships that are wholesome and productive.

In his book *Parent Effectiveness Training*, Dr. Thomas Gordon presented twelve roadblocks to effective communication. While his book was more geared toward helping parents improve their communication with their children, the principles can be applied to all Life Coaching conversations. Following is Dr. Gordon's *(slightly modified)* list of the twelve roadblocks that prevent healthy communication from happening between people.

**ROADBLOCK 1. DEMANDING**

*("You have to...," "You must...," "You will...")*

The term "demanding" is often associated with an authoritative communication style. In certain business and political contexts, leaders may adopt a Machiavellian approach to leadership, where they prioritize being feared over being liked. While this tactic may be effective in certain situations, it can result in oppression and is not conducive to building long-term relationships that require open communication. A Life Coach cannot take this approach to communication without drastically hampering their effectiveness in connecting with a coachee. In order to build a strong coach-coachee relationship based on trust and respect, it's important for Life Coaches to communicate in a way that is congruent, supportive, and encouraging. The coach should be someone with whom the coachee feels comfortable being honest. If a coach's communication style is too demanding or autocratic, it will only serve to alienate the coachee and make it difficult to build rapport. In order to be an effective coach, it is essential to adopt a more democratic communication style that values dialogue and mutual understanding.

## ROADBLOCK 2. WARNINGS

*("If you don't, then…," "You'd better stop that, or…")*

When working with stubborn or change-resistant coachees, Life Coaching can be frustrating. For example, some coachees may be slower in their learning process and may take longer to reach the realizations they need; it can thus be tempting to resort to more manipulative tactics to gain the desired outcome faster. Whilst coercive language may achieve the outcomes you want, it won't be for the right reasons. Precautions need to be taken when using any form of language that may be perceived as threatening. Few coaches will openly threaten their coachees with the stereotypical "do this or X will happen" kind of way, but many unknowingly use subtle forms of threatening techniques without realizing it.

The purpose of the Life Coaching process is to help clients overcome the hurdles that stand between them and their goals so that they can be empowered to make necessary changes in their lives. If you employ fear tactics, such as "without devotion and hard work, you will not get what you want!" to motivate your coachees, you may see them achieve the desired outcomes; however, their motivation for change and progress will be based on fear and anxiety instead of congruence with their values. As a result, your coachee's situation might change, but not the coachee within him or herself.

## ROADBLOCK 3. MORALIZING

*("What you really should do is…," "You ought to…," "It's your responsibility…")*

The heart of coaching is about supporting coachees in their efforts to find their own answers and solutions. When we tell our coachees what they "should" or "ought to" do, we are not coaching. Instead, we are imposing our own beliefs on them. Such messages bring to bear on others the pressure of some form of duty or obligation. People frequently respond to such "shoulds," "oughts," and "musts" by defending their own postures even more strongly. These moralizing messages can communicate to your coachees that you do not respect their ability to decide wisely for themselves, so they should just accept and adhere to doing whatever you deem as being "right." Moralizing messages do not communicate empathic understanding and acceptance. In fact, they convey criticism ("You ought to know better."). Like other authority-based responses, these have a risk of blocking further communication and bruising the coaching relationship since they convey that you are wiser than your coachee. When we coach, we create space for our coachees to explore their values, find their own answers and decide accordingly. In this way, we respect their autonomy as human beings who are capable of growth.

**ROADBLOCK 4. ADVICE GIVING**

*("What I would do is...," "Why don't you...," "Let me suggest...")*

If you're like most people, you probably don't think twice before offering advice or suggestions to others. After all, it's only natural to want to help out when someone is facing a challenge or dealing with a difficult situation. However, it's important to be aware that giving advice can sometimes do more harm than good. When you offer your opinion without it being asked for, it can communicate a lack of faith in the other person's ability to solve their own problems. This can prevent them from thinking through their issue and considering alternative solutions. Additionally, offering unsolicited advice can create dependency-based relationships, which are not empowering for either party involved. So next time you're tempted to offer your two cents, take a step back and consider if it's really what the other person needs. You may just find that sometimes, the best thing you can do is simply listen.

## ROADBLOCK 5. OVER-INTELLECTUALIZING

*("Doesn't it make sense that...," "Here's where you're wrong...," "The facts are...")*

Some novice Life Coaches who have read many books might try to influence a coachee's situation with facts, logic or information. It is wise to remember that the purpose of Life Coaching is not to teach or persuade, but rather to create a healthy space for people to grow. When a coach excessively uses logic and facts, it creates a defensive atmosphere where the coachee might feel like they are being attacked. This not only deems the Life Coaching relationship ineffective, but it also discourages a coachee from wanting to keep on engaging in dialogue. All coaches will benefit from understanding applied psychology principles (many of which are shared throughout this handbook), but it is equally as important to impart this understanding in a person-centered and humane way. By doing so, you can create the most wholesome environment possible for your coachees to grow and mature in.

## ROADBLOCK 6. JUDGING AND ASSUMING

*("You aren't thinking clearly...," "That wasn't a particularly wise decision...")*

It is human nature to judge people. It's easy to do, especially upon hearing about people's problems or challenges. Some people think they know what's best for you, and likewise, you will also think that you know what's best for others. It's easy to make evaluations of people's circumstances without knowing all of the facts. But what most people don't realize is that doing this instantly destroys trust and rapport—which are key ingredients of a healthy coaching relationship. Negative evaluations will strongly influence your coachee to keep their feelings to themselves. They will quickly learn that you aren't the kind of person that it's OK to be honest with. So, no matter how skilled you are at predicting people's behaviors, you aren't a mind reader, and never try to be. If you start making assumptions about why a coachee behaves the way they do or judge them for their outcomes, you will kill any trust you may have already built with a coachee or kill any opportunity of initiating it.

### ROADBLOCK 7. PRAISING AND APPEASING

*("You did the right thing!" "I couldn't agree more...," "The same happened to me...")*

We often think that a positive agreement will help a coachee to keep on making decisions and taking action. Contrary to the common belief that such support is beneficial, it often has negative effects on people. A positive evaluation that does not fit another person's self-image may also evoke denial or distrust. Also, if praise is too frequent, its absence may be interpreted as criticism. Praise is often felt to be a subtle way of manipulating people to act in a certain way. A coach who praises a lot runs the risk of making a coachee so dependent on the praise that they cannot function without it. While there are certainly risks associated with praise-giving, there are also benefits. In some cases, people need to hear that they are doing "well" in order to feel motivated to keep on "keeping on." In other cases, offering sincere and well-timed praise can be an important way to build relationships and show appreciation for someone else's efforts. Ultimately, whether or not praise is helpful depends on the individual situation and the type of relationship between you and your coachee.

### ROADBLOCK 8. LABELING AND QUANTIFYING

*("You're a worry-wart...," "You are a unique person...," "It seems you have ADHD...")*

Labeling people is the opposite of what Life Coaching should be about. It is a sad fact that many people go through life feeling "not-good-enough," inferior, or just plain wrong. All too often, this is because they have been labeled by a "professional" before being given a chance to explain themselves and their circumstances. Whether it is a psychotherapist assigning them a diagnosis or a school teacher putting them into a "gifted and talented" or "remedial" class, the effect can be damaging to their self-image. It is no wonder that so many people feel defensive when they are labeled in this way. Life Coaching, however, should be about understanding people, not putting them into boxes. A Life Coach's top priority should always be to help their coachee see themselves clearly, develop a future vision for who they can grow to become, and break free from the negative or restrictive "self-quantifying" labels that have been holding them back—possibly for years. When you invest time into understanding your coachees, you will discover that even the labels they use to define themselves barely fit them at all.

**ROADBLOCK 9. OVER-ANALYSING**

*("You're just trying to...," "What your problem is...," "You feel that way because...")*

We have all engaged in attempts to psychoanalyze the people around us. It can be tempting to try and figure out what motivates others, especially when we feel like we have a good handle on our own motivations. However, this can often be a fruitless endeavor, and one that risks damaging our relationships with others. When we try to analyze people, we communicate that we think we have them all figured out. This can be threatening to them, and if our analysis is inaccurate, it can cause hurt or anger. Moreover, when we over-analyze people, we indirectly convey a message of superiority. This often blocks further communication from happening and damages relationship trust. It is important to remember that everyone is complex and unique. Rather than trying to figure out what makes others tick, it may be more productive just to ask them, shut your mouth, and listen attentively to what their response is.

**ROADBLOCK 10. SYMPATHIZING AND CONSOLING**

*("Don't worry...," "Look on the bright side..." "Everyone goes through this...")*

Coaches are not professional coddlers, and no one is helped to improve their life by being given emotional smothering or sympathy. Therapists that use reassurance in extreme forms of "alternative therapy" tend to do so to exploit people who want to believe that they will feel better if they talk themselves out of their problems, minimize their difficulties, and deny the gravity of their issues. Such messages are not as helpful, period. To sympathize with a coachee when they have a problem only demonstrates that you don't understand anything about them or their situation. Ineffective coaches misuse sympathy as a means to avoid providing wise counsel and, for a time, make a coachee feel better without actually resolving any issues, leaving the coachee just where they were before coaching. A coach's duty is to help a coachee develop self-understanding, find solutions to their problems and take decisive action that will lead to a more desirable future state. This requires the coach to ask powerful questions, provide honest feedback, and help the coachee develop insights and awareness about themselves. It does not require the coach to be sympathetic or reassuring; these things will typically only serve to hinder the Life Coaching process and a coachee's progression.

### ROADBLOCK 11. INTERROGATIVE QUESTIONING

*("Why did you do that?...," "And then what...," "Did you let your wife know?...")*

Freudian psychology emphasizes digging deep into a person's past to determine the origins of a belief or a behavior. While there may be some value in this approach, it ultimately emphasizes the coachee's problem more than the solution that they must put in place. Yes, questioning plays a crucial role in the coaching process, but this doesn't mean you should approach your coaching sessions with a list of pre-prepared questions to ask—and this is also the reason why I haven't loaded up this handbook with lists of pre-scripted questions. Overly formulated, pre-prepared questions will never encourage a coachee to open up to you because they're interrogative, not curious. As every experienced coach knows, the success of coaching depends heavily on the relationship between coach and coachee. With trust and rapport, the coachee will be more likely to open up and objectively explore the factors holding them back. Only ever ask questions that you are genuinely interested in discovering the answer to, and don't overwhelm people with impersonalized lists of pre-scripted, interrogative questions. If you don't care about the questions you ask, your coachees won't care about the answers they give—nor will they care to come back to you for further Life Coaching.

## ROADBLOCK 12. AVOIDING AND DIVERTING

*("Let's not talk about it...," "That's your problem...," "You think you've got problems...")*

Most people are generally quite serious and intent when they get the courage to talk about themselves. If they hear a response that ignores them, it can make them feel rejected and belittled. When a Life Coach fails to acknowledge something important that a coachee says and then proceeds to change the subject, this will unquestionably prevent the Life Coaching relationship from going any further. Not only does this type of response communicate a lack of interest on the part of the Life Coach, but it also conveys a lack of respect for the coachee's situation. In order to build a successful coaching relationship, it is not enough just to "show interest" in what your coachee has to say. It is only by genuinely "being interested" in what they say that you can hope to earn their trust and respect—and keep it.

We all have certain words and phrases that we use more often than others. This is especially true of Life Coaching professionals, who often develop their own jargon and groups of friends, who adopt common turns of phrase. When you begin coaching people, be prepared to lose all of your coaching jargon and tune into the characteristics of your coachee's language. By doing this, you can connect with them more effectively. The key is to be aware of the effect that your words have on people. Are you using language that is respectful and humble? Or are you using language that is arrogant or condescending? The choice of words you use will reflect your attitude and either build rapport or create barriers between you and your coachees. Choose your words wisely and prioritize maintaining the connection you have with people before a word even exits your mouth. Life Coaching (and communicating) doesn't have to be as hard as many "professional textbooks" make it out to be. By understanding these twelve barriers that prevent healthy communication from happening, you can treat your coachees in the way that you'd like to be treated and, in turn, prevent these roadblocks from taking you off-road onto dangerous or unhealthy relationship terrain.

**PRINCIPLES INTO PRACTICE QUESTIONS:**

1. Which of these twelve roadblocks do you identify with the most?
2. How have these roadblocks undermined your relationships with people in the past?
3. Which of these roadblocks must you work hard to cut out of your communications today?

# THREE LEVELS OF RELATING TO PEOPLE

*"Dispassionate objectivity is a passion for the real and for the truth."*
—ABRAHAM MASLOW

There is an Indian parable of three blind men who come across an elephant for the first time. The first man touched the elephant's trunk, the second touched its legs, and the third grabbed its tail. Each man stroked a different part of the elephant, then tried to describe what they felt based on their limited experience and knowledge. Even though all three men had a real experience of touching an elephant, they couldn't relate to what it was, nor could they collectively explain what they had been exposed to. A similar phenomenon also occurs for people who don't have the words to articulately explain what their needs, wants, and priorities are. Indirectly, this elephant story can illustrate how important "out-of-the-box" thinking and communicating can be throughout some Life Coaching sessions.

The more you can empathize with a person, the more rapport you will build with them. Being able to look through the eyes of another person's experience will let you see how they might be feeling, what is important to them, and also what questions your coachees will benefit most from being asked. Rapport happens naturally when you speak to people on their wavelength and use their language to connect and synchronize with them. Rapport is marked by alignment and similarity. With rapport in a relationship, all resistance will disappear.

Have you ever had the experience of "mentally dissociating" during a social exchange and sensing that you can see and hear yourself, as well as the other people you are interacting with? It's like watching events unfold on a cinema screen with you and your peers being characters in the scene. In coaching language, this experience is referred to as entering a "third person" perceptual position, which allows you to change your "mental camera angle," "switch radio stations," "distance yourself from a situation" and take an objective birds-eye view—rather than being caught in the heat of the moment. From this perceptual position, you can see what is occurring clearly, and also make a wise decision about how to best respond.

Using perceptual positions (and perceptually repositioning yourself) is the mental discipline of adopting multiple points of view, beyond just your own, in an organized way. It is often said that the ability to walk in another person's shoes is the key to understanding them. And indeed, the ability to see things from the point of view of another is a valuable social skill to develop. For example, in a Life Coaching relationship, it can help you understand your coachee's motivations, goals, and how they see their challenges. In Life Coaching, the ability to see things from different angles can allow you to find areas of common ground and set healthy relationship boundaries. Practically, perceptually repositioning yourself into another person's perspective will let you create a rich sense of another person's experience by using only your memory and imagination. Let's get an overview of what the three different perceptual positions are.

**POSITION 3**
Seeing, hearing and feeling the situation through filters of an observer

**POSITION 1**
Seeing, hearing and feeling the situation through own filters

**POSITION 2**
Seeing, hearing and feeling the situation through filters of the other person

There are three basic positions of perception that we can take in any situation: first position (our own shoes, seeing the world through our own eyes), second position (standing in other person's shoes) or third position (neutral observer).

## POSITION 1: YOURSELF (ASSOCIATED SELF)

In the first position, you look at the world through your own eyes; you are processing life through your own values, beliefs, emotions, and biases—with your own needs influencing your thinking. The first position is your first-hand and subjective experience of a situation. From this perspective, you can only perceive through the limitations of your comprehension. The following example shows what a coaching exchange might be from position 1:

COACHEE: "I hate my job and want to change my career."

COACH: "What new career path do you want to transition into?"

COACHEE: "I'm not sure. Just something that I find more fulfilling."

COACH: "OK, so should we explore what some good options might be?"

COACHEE: "Yes, let's do that."

There's nothing wrong with adopting this first position in your coaching conversations, and it will produce results. However, questioning a coachee from this position will; (a) give **you** no insight into what your coachee needs from a career, and (b) give your **coachee** no insight into why their current career path is not fulfilling them. So, you might help your coachee to change their career path, but the chances of them receiving a paradigm shift are minimal.

**POSITION 2: THE OTHER (EMPATHY POSITION)**

The second position is the empathy position in which you "place yourself in another person's shoes" and experience a situation from your coachee's position. When communicating, most people are generally more interested in voicing their own needs than in listening to the needs and perspectives of others. It is for this reason that marriages fail, and business partnerships continue to collapse. The second perceptual position is always the starting point with your coachees. The only way to understand how your coachees think is to experience things from their perspective. This will give you the knowledge needed to ask them questions that help them figure out the reason "why" they want to make changes and improvements in their lives. The following example shows what a coaching exchange might be from position 2:

COACHEE: "I hate my job and want to change my career."

COACH: "OK, can you help me to understand what your current job is like?"

COACHEE: "Sure, I don't have any opportunity to get really creative."

COACH: "OK, so doing something creative would really tick your boxes?"

COACHEE: "Yes, I'd love to do something much more creative."

Coaching from this second position will let you understand the reasons why your coachee is dissatisfied and wants to change. From this position, your coachee will be more likely to discuss which of their values aren't being met and their motivation for wanting change to happen. Once you know what the personal values are that your coachee needs to fulfill, you will then have a target for directing your goal-setting and action-planning efforts toward.

**POSITION 3: NEUTRAL OBSERVER (OBJECTIVE POSITION)**

From position three, you detach yourself from both parties' perspectives within an exchange (i.e., both yours and theirs), and develop a "fly on the wall" stance—which always tends to be an objective one. From this stance, you can objectively consider an entire coaching scenario and encourage your coachee to also evaluate how their situation might appear to an outsider or onlooking third parties. This level of detachment from your coaching relationship will allow you to be more present in the moment, hear what is said, and also identify new or more helpful perspectives that, until now, may have been overlooked by either you or your coachee. The following example shows what a coaching exchange might be from position 3:

COACHEE: "I hate my job and want to change my career."

COACH: "OK, so what is it about your working environment that you dislike so much"

COACHEE: "I don't have the time or space I need to creatively express myself."

COACH: "OK, what changes could be made that might improve this for you?"

COACHEE: "I guess, I could apply for a new role or speak to my boss?."

From this position, you dissociate yourself from any inclination you might have to solve your coachee's problems and also distance yourself from the dissatisfaction of your coachee. Also, from this position, you can invite your coachee to dissociate from their immediate situation to evaluate what potential opportunities for change might exist immediately at hand. You will find that even if this third perceptual position doesn't equate to your coachee identifying a solution, they will be more likely to have some form of paradigm shift in their thinking.

The overriding purpose of perceptual repositioning is to remain as unbiased in your coaching as possible. Some people refer to it as compassionless, but it's only by emotionally detaching yourself from people's subjectivity that you can position yourself into fully objective support. By considering the viewpoints of yourself, the other, and an objective third party, you will see the questions you can ask that will allow your coachees to evaluate their circumstances from new and objective perspectives—which is essential for a paradigm shift to happen in your coachees, while allowing you to provide significantly more level-headed coaching support.

**PRINCIPLES INTO PRACTICE EXERCISE:**

Next time you feel stuck in a situation, ask yourself how the smartest person you know might tackle it. Or if you need more objectivity in a given situation, step to an analytical third position (like being a fly on the wall). Play with shifting the perceptual positions—and especially try to explore the positions that come less naturally to you.

# THE FOUR PHASES OF THE LIFE COACHING RELATIONSHIP

*"I never cease to be amazed at the power of the coaching process to draw out the talent that was previously hidden within an individual, and which invariably finds a way to solve a problem previously thought unsolvable."*

—JOHN RUSSELL, HARLEY-DAVIDSON LTD.

From the offset, Life Coaching centers around the priorities that your coachees want to pursue. People come to coaching in the hopes of change. They are searching for a new life direction or have goals to reach. People come to coaching for many reasons. They are motivated to achieve something great: to start a business, make more money, write a book, or become more satisfied in their career. They hire a Life Coach because they want to create more balance in their lives. Sometimes people just want peace of mind, to de-clutter their lives, or because they want a better quality of life. Whatever the reason for coaching, it starts with the coachee.

Many years ago, a woman approached me for coaching. In the first conversation I had with her, she claimed to want to work with a Life Coach because she was tired of speaking with her counselor after twelve years of ineffective therapeutic discussion. When I asked the lady what she wanted to achieve through our time together, she replied, "I just want someone who will listen to me." I declined this lady's request. A coaching relationship must begin with a specific purpose, and end with that specific purpose being met. Open-ended, purposeless, and dependency-based relationships do not create an effective coaching environment.

When I began coaching in 2009, some of my earlier coaching relationships didn't work out well. Some of my coachees expected that I would somehow "fix their life" without effort on their part. While I was always integral from the outset, I sometimes failed to set clear expectations concerning the structure of the coaching relationship and set boundaries.

Effective Life Coaching centers around inquiry and discovery. A good coach will ask probing questions, listen deeply, and help individuals find their own answers. This process of self-discovery allows people not just to set purposeful goals for their futures but also gain a deeper understanding of themselves throughout the process. Understanding the four natural phases of a coaching cycle will prepare you to guide your coachees from their current state of affairs to a future state of affairs that they deem more meaningful. As a rule, all Life Coaching relationships are characterized by four consecutive phases, which usually overlap to a degree.

**PHASE 1: PREPARING A COACHEE FOR COACHING**

The first phase of coaching is all about preparation. In order to sustain a healthy and goal-oriented Life Coaching relationship, you must establish what boundaries must exist within the relationship and manage your prospective coachee's expectations. At this early stage of the relationship, a failure to set boundaries is a failure to manage your coachee's expectations. Your coachee must understand what you expect of them and what they can expect of you.

Prospective coachees may want to achieve a certain professional, relationship, or economic aim. They might expect you to accomplish this goal on their behalf. While setting achievable goals is crucial, new coachees must understand that coaching is a collaborative working partnership. You will accompany coachees on their journey toward their goals and explore alternative options along the way—it's critical that they know this from the start.

CLARIFY WITH YOUR PROSPECTIVE COACHEES THAT THEY WILL:
1. Turn up on time and focus during coaching sessions
2. Take responsibility for driving their own progression
3. Attend coaching sessions ready to make decisions
4. Take relevant action in between coaching sessions
5. Be open, honest, and unguarded during coaching

CONFIRM WITH PROSPECTIVE COACHEES WHAT THEY CAN EXPECT:
1. Your full undivided attention during coaching sessions
2. Accountability to ensure their action-taking is congruent
3. Genuineness, transparency, and integrity on your behalf
4. Complete confidentiality and unconditional positive regard
5. A brief follow-up (by email or phone) between sessions

Before you can develop a plan of action to help your coachee achieve their goals, you must first manage their expectations. One of the first elements in coachee orientation is getting agreement on ground rules and administrative procedures. Mutually agreeing on details such as session times, cancellation policy, and payment arrangements are key to creating trust in the early stages of a relationship. Coachees will begin to establish expectations of the caliber of coaching you will deliver based on your handling of these basic administrative details.

Every coaching interaction must also begin with a clearly defined purpose, and it is your responsibility to collect all the relevant information about the prospective coachee's goals, challenges, and what they expect to gain from spending time with you. This is important to prevent unrealistic expectations from being formed in your coachee's mind and reduce the risk of your coachee becoming disappointed due to their expectations not being met.

**PHASE 2: THE COACHEE DEEP DISCOVERY PHASE**

People invest in coaching in order to solve problems and achieve things. As a coach, it's your job to help them get there by spending as much time as needed provoking exploration, deep discovery and self-reflection until your coachee can describe their priorities clearly in simple, measurable, actionable, realistic, and time-oriented terms. Once you have clarity around what your coachee needs to achieve via coaching, you can then establish the steps that your coachee must take to start making progress. Without a clearly defined goal in mind, it would be difficult to measure progress and gauge whether or not your Life Coaching is effective.

The deep discovery phase of the coaching relationship is a key time for both coach and coachee to get to know each other, and for the coachee to self-disclose openly about their current situation. This stage of the relationship is about exploration, and it's important that both parties feel comfortable enough to really dig deep. In this phase, you begin the process of getting to know your coachee from the inside out. Being genuinely curious and willing to work with whatever shows up is central to the effectiveness of the deep discovery phase of a Life Coaching relationship. Your curiosity allows a coachee to explore and discover.

THE DEEP DISCOVERY PHASE SERVES TO ANSWER THESE QUESTIONS:
1. Where do you want to make a positive difference in your life?
2. What is most important to you in your relationships with others?
3. What makes you successful when trying to change something?
4. What values and principles are non-negotiable in your life?
5. What might hinder your progress or cause you to get stuck?
6. What are your primary motivations for wanting to change?
7. How would you like me to support you when you're stuck?

In this exchange, you and your coachee will contribute to shaping the purpose of the coaching alliance. The conversations during this phase will touch on many different topics, including life purpose, personal mission, current priorities, or unmet values. By exploring all of these areas, you will gain a better understanding of what's really important to your coachee and also what might be holding them back from making positive changes. Ultimately, the goal of this phase is to help a coachee identify their motivations for wanting to change something about their life and create a practical plan of action that will enable them to make change happen. *(We will explore how this is carried out in the next section of the handbook.).*

**PHASE 3: THE ACCOUNTABILITY AND ACTION PHASE**

The third phase of Life Coaching is built around accountability and action. Accountability is one of the most important aspects of a coaching relationship and is typically what gives a coachee the confidence to keep on taking risks, working hard, and progressing. If a coachee knows you are holding them to account for their actions, they are more likely to take positive steps forward. Accountability also helps to deepen trust within the relationship. It is important to remember that you are not responsible for your coachees' action-taking or learning. It is up to your coachees to make decisions and take action. Accountability simply creates a space for reflection and growth in between coaching sessions and comes with no judgment, blame, or scolding. Accountability allows for reflection and leads to greater clarity around goals, and it invites your coachees to give an account of what they have committed to and delivered upon.

ACCOUNTABILITY WITHIN A LIFE COACHING
RELATIONSHIP ASKS QUESTIONS SUCH AS:
1. What specifically will you do?
2. When specifically will you do it?
3. What are the specific results of your actions?
4. Which of your actions have worked out well?
5. Which of your actions didn't work out so well?
6. What would you do differently next time?
7. What specifically have you learned?

Ultimately, the coachee is responsible for taking steps outside of the coaching relationship. They choose to be held accountable by the coaching relationship so long as the coach adds value by providing enlightening insights and asking appropriate questions. When the coaching relationship moves to the accountability phase, your responsibility is to uncover any honest reasons for inaction, ensuring that the coachee's goals are congruent and remain aligned with what they claim are their foremost priorities.

The questions you ask will naturally be intuitive if you retain an interest in your coachee's continual progress and maintain an attitude of curiosity. Accountability is equated with answerability, liability, and account-giving. In other words, one who is accountable must perform an action. For a coaching relationship to sustain, there must be accountability laced throughout it. There are times when even positive intentions can be stalled by a simple shortage of ideas for action. Yes, it is your coachee's responsibility to decide on their goals, priorities, and action steps, but accountability gives structure to the ongoing coaching process and is the infrastructure that keeps a coaching conversation alive. Without it, progress may stall or even stop altogether as some coachees wait for further clarity or permission that may never come. When both parties are clear on what accountability within the relationship must be and how it will occur, trust can further develop, and the coaching conversation will only continue to strengthen.

## PHASE 4: THE CLOSURE (OR SECOND AGREEMENT) PHASE

A major purpose of coaching is to help people become more independent, responsible, and effective in their decision-making. This means, in effect, that the Life Coaching relationship, unlike many other relationships, will inevitably end. Endings can be difficult for all of us, and both parties within a coaching relationship are no exception in this respect. But the end of a coaching relationship should only happen after its purpose has been achieved. Sometimes, during the accountability and action phase, a coachee will identify new goals that they want to pursue also. If this happens, a secondary coaching agreement can be negotiated, but in most cases, it is good practice to document the new goal and wait until the first goal has been achieved before moving on to the next. This allows both coach and coachee to focus on one goal at a time and allows for a better evaluation of the coaching process and its effectiveness.

Some people struggle with endings, and this is especially true of those people who have been impacted by hurtful separations or relationship breakdowns in the past. It's wise to be aware of your attachment style and how it may impact the way that you end relationships. If you tend to avoid loss, you may inadvertently lead your coachee to become dependent on you, which goes against the principle of autonomy. It's important to be conscious of any avoidance tendencies you have and counter them when necessary. This will allow you to end Life Coaching relationships in a way that honors both yourself and your coachee.

**PRINCIPLES INTO PRACTICE QUESTIONS:**

1. What boundaries do you have in place that are non-negotiable in your relationships?
2. How might you establish non-negotiable boundaries in a Life Coaching relationship?
3. How do you typically respond to people who do not honor their commitments?
4. What impact does your attachment style have on how you end relationships?

# SECTION FIVE SUMMARY

It is safe to say that communication is the glue that holds Life Coaching relationships together. Communication is the act of expressing ideas, knowledge, and thoughts and understanding what is said by others. The communication process involves sending and receiving messages and can take many forms. Verbal communication is the spoken word, and non-verbal involves actions, body language, and gestures. The most important judgment you need to make is whether a message ever needs to be sent. Some coaches talk too much, and others talk too little. A coach must be able to understand a coachee's needs and create space for them to express what they are thinking or feeling. Only through attentive communication can you help people to articulate the goals that will allow them to positively transform their lives.

**IMPORTANT LESSONS TO REMEMBER:**

- Information is about giving out; communication is about getting through.
- The most important thing in communication is hearing what isn't said.
- No communication has taken place until the other person has felt heard.
- Two people participating in two monologues do not create a dialogue.

- Prioritize understanding people's motivations and values before all things.
- There is only one principle for becoming an effective talker—learn to listen.
- Sometimes, remaining silent can be more powerful than speaking 1000 words.
- When the trust in a relationship is high, communication is instant and effective.

### SECTION FIVE NOTEWORTHY IDEAS

Use this space to note down any ideas that have struck you as important throughout this section of the handbook. Also, write down any questions that might be beneficial for your future consideration and self-reflection.

# SECTION SIX

# COACHING SKILLS AND GOAL SETTING

Setting clear and achievable goals is an essential aspect of Life Coaching, where individuals are assisted in determining their priority goals and the steps needed to accomplish them. A well-defined goal serves as a driving force that motivates a person to progress, and improve, and it is the epicenter of all coaching—be it personal or business-oriented. Nonetheless, deciding on the "right" goals to pursue can be challenging, and will impede coaching progress if handled poorly. This section of the handbook discusses different aspects of the goal-setting process.

# QUANTIFYING PRESENT AND DESIRED STATES

*"Setting goals is important, but how goals are reached matters equally as much. The destination is only the end of a journey. The route to a destination might be long and arduous, so every step along the way must become part of the plan."*

—MICHEAL HYATT

You can't set goals until you identify a problem that exists due to not having certain goals met. Problem recognition naturally occurs when people realize that there is a significant difference between their "desired state of affairs" and their "actual state of affairs." Simply put, most human suffering arises from unfulfilled desires. Though some scholars may have made the human experience seem more complex, the reality is that those who are successful in obtaining what they want are typically happy or content, while those who are unsuccessful tend to be unhappy or depressed. This is just how human beings respond to their life circumstances.

The process of problem recognition integrates many of the concepts that have been discussed in earlier chapters of the handbook. For example, your coachee's values, priorities, self-esteem, and source of motivation are relevant here. To put it simply, a person who is experiencing loneliness, lack of fulfillment, insecurity, inefficiency, or boredom must first recognize and acknowledge these issues before setting goals to overcome them, and calling upon the support of a Life Coach.

The motivation a person has to resolve their problems will depend on two factors: the scale of the discrepancy between what they have and what they want and the importance they place on the problem being resolved. Some people spend years focusing on the discrepancies between what they have and what they want but never make it their priority to work hard or invest in addressing the voids. You will typically hear those people voicing an opinion on social media or protesting on the streets while waiting for a politician or "superior human being" to come along who will somehow make their discrepancies disappear.

Problem recognition must result in a problem being accurately defined so that a person can set appropriate goals and then take suitable action steps toward resolving it. And this is where Life Coaching comes into play—you cannot coach a person who has no clearly quantified deficits, discrepancies, "positively-framed" goals, or general dissatisfactions. So this brings us to section six of the handbook, in which we will now cast our focus toward goal setting and the principles you must understand if you are to support your coachees in addressing their discrepancies and scaling-up their outputs or general satisfaction in life.

Recognizing problems and defining them can be a challenging part of the coaching process. It's interesting that we can so readily identify what we don't want in our lives but have more trouble defining what we do want. Defining what we want will often require much reflection and soul-searching. This can be a complex process, but recognizing and defining problems is an essential step that must be taken before Life Coaching can even begin.

Recognizing problems, goal setting, and action planning are central to successful coaching. If you dive into a Life Coaching relationship without first defining your coachee's deficits, discrepancies, goals, or dissatisfactions, you have no basis against which to gauge the efficiency of your coaching. Before Life Coaching commences, your coachee must have an ideal outcome that they are motivated to pursue. It's only with this outcome in mind that you can create a vision, mission, and sense of purpose to plan your coaching efforts around.

Present state, desired state, and contract state are the three essential ideas that you need to understand if you want to deliver purposeful Life Coaching conversations. These three states become the unique reference point for all of your goal setting and Life Coaching efforts.

The term present state refers to your coachee's current situation and the circumstances that they want to either change, improve or resolve. This state is where they "currently are" in life and includes the discrepancies, deficits, or dissatisfactions they have in one or more of their life areas. It is important for a coach to understand the term "present state," because this is the starting point for all of the coachee's future self-reflection, goal setting, and personal growth.

The term "desired state" refers to the moment after a discrepancy has been addressed, a deficit has been fulfilled, a dissatisfaction has been satisfied, or a goal has been reached. The desired state is often an idealized version of reality that may or may not be achievable—it is what your coachees want and is also what motivates them to take action. It is the light at the end of the tunnel that they hope to reach. It's useful to note that desired states can be fleeting and will often change as a person's present state changes. To understand this, just think about the last time you started pursuing a goal that you were passionate about, to begin with, but over time, your passion dissolved, and your priorities reoriented themselves. Also, many of your coachees will have different desired states for different purposes and situations.

Within a Life Coaching context, once you have quantified your coachee's present and desired states, you can then move to the contract state. The contract state is a crucial step in the Life Coaching process. It is within the contract state that you will discuss and agree upon the action steps that are to be taken, the obstacles that must be overcome, and the progress that must be made between what your coachee currently has (i.e., their present state) and what they want to have (i.e., their ideal state) achieved before termination of their relationship with you. This agreement will act as a guidepost for subsequent Life Coaching sessions that enable a dissatisfaction to be satisfied or a goal to be achieved. Through the contract state comes the goals and purpose of the Life Coaching agreement and contract. Then with this agreement in place, you have a basis for integrating accountability into the coaching relationship and can begin the rewarding process of helping your coachee create changes in their life.

Throughout the rest of this section in the handbook, we will explore some of the coaching models and principles that you can draw upon to help your coachee decide which goals and future outcomes are most worthy of their time, effort, and investment. As you grow in coaching experience, you will see that many people set uninspiring goals (that are more like "nice ideas" than goals) which don't internally motivate or compel them to take decisive action. Doing this is a big waste of time. In the next few chapters, we will explore an existential approach and also a visionary approach to goal setting. These tend to be the most purposeful types of goals that people can devote their lives to pursuing.

**PRINCIPLES INTO PRACTICE QUESTIONS:**

1. What is currently the greatest source of dissatisfaction in your life?
2. What outcomes must be in place for you to become satisfied in this area?
3. What are three steps you can take toward improving this area in your life?
4. When would Life Coaching ever need to be more than the last three questions?

# AN EXISTENTIAL APPROACH TO LIFE COACHING

*"Knowing where you're going is far more important than getting there quickly. Honor your priorities. Don't confuse activity with progress. Decide what you want, decide what you're willing to exchange it for, and then go to work."*

—H. L. HUNT

It is often said that there are two certainties in life: death and taxes. While this may be true, there are other things that all human beings can also be certain of. We are all going to die one day. We are all free to make our own decisions. We are all isolated and separate from each other. We all experience moments of purposelessness and meaninglessness.

### THE FOUR MAIN EXISTENTIAL CONCERNS

According to psychologist Irvin Yalom back in the 1980s, there are four main concerns that underlie all forms of human mental, emotional, behavioral, and existential crisis: death, freedom, isolation, and meaninglessness. Death, of course, is the great equalizer; it is the one thing that every human being will experience at some point in life. Freedom is another universal experience; we are all free to make our own choices, even if those choices are constrained by our circumstances. Isolation is a feeling that we all have at times; we can be physically alone or emotionally isolated from others. And meaninglessness is a sense of purposelessness or emptiness; many people feel that their lives lack meaning or purpose. While some people spend an entire lifetime avoiding these main concerns, they are also one of the unconscious reasons why many people make first contact with a Life Coach.

Until the 1950s, psychology had been dominated by two ideological forces; behaviorism and Freudian psychoanalysis. In the 1950s, a new tradition began to emerge because behaviorism and psychoanalysis did not, as far as Abraham Maslow and Carl Rogers were concerned, acknowledge core human capacities such as choice, creativity, personal growth, self-actualization, motivation, self-awareness, love, and subjectivity. The new tradition was called humanistic psychology; this later became known as the third force.

The existential approach to Life Coaching is based on a philosophical tradition that has historically been associated with the works of Kierkegaard, Nietzsche, Heidegger, and Sartre, who were all concerned with the purpose and meaning of life. These philosophers were interested in the ideas of free will and how people relate to death, freedom, isolation, and meaninglessness. This coaching approach seeks to promote self-awareness and personal growth by equipping people to explore what might make their lives become more meaningful and purpose-driven. You can probably see; therefore, that humanistic psychology and philosophical existentialism are very closely aligned.

COACHEE: *"Can you help me? I don't know what I want in life."*

COACH: *"OK, let's explore what your goals and priorities are in relation to death, freedom, isolation, and meaninglessness. How helpful does this sound to you?"*

COACHEE: *"Great, I could really do with getting some focus and clarity."*

The example I have just shared might seem extremely broad and ambiguous, and it is, but as you will discover when you start practicing Life Coaching, some of the goals that people will come to you with will also be extremely broad and ambiguous. Using the four main concerns as the starting point of a coaching conversation can help you to establish what your coachee's main priority life area is, which in turn, all subsequent goal setting can flow out of.

When we are not authentic, we are not true to ourselves. We allow others to dictate how we should think, feel and behave. We conform to what is expected of us, without question. This can lead to a sense of alienation from our true identity. We grow detached from the reality of who we are and what we need. A central goal of the approach is to help coachees become more self-aware and authentic by defining who they are and what they need. The person who is not authentic has a tendency to assume that it is other people, family members, and society who are responsible for defining who they are. This coaching approach encourages people to question what their primary concern (or objective) in life is.

## FOUR DIMENSIONS OF PERSONAL EXPERIENCE

As discussed, there are four main concerns that motivate a person to act or not act, and there are also four different dimensions of personal experience that make up a person's life: physical, social, psychological, and spiritual. Each of these dimensions is equally important in shaping how people characterize their identity, define what is important to them and set goals that will allow them to;

1. Approach their death with less anxiety and apprehension,
2. Pursue freedom in a way that doesn't compromise their freedom,
3. Address isolation through social and authentic interaction, and
4. Decide on a life purpose that defies any sense of meaninglessness.

The physical dimension of personal experience covers our basic human needs (food, water, clothing, shelter, warmth) and how we interact with the world. It also encompasses our representational systems (sight, touch, hearing, smell, and taste). Physical experience is essential to all human survival but can also play a role in how people define themselves.

The social dimension refers to our relationships. This includes family, friends, and colleagues. Our social experiences have a positive or negative effect on our mental and emotional well-being. For example, if we are accepted by our peers, we might feel socially confident and fulfilled. However, if we are judged, we may feel self-conscious or anxious.

The psychological dimension is concerned with how we feel about ourselves (self-esteem) and how we identify (self-concept and self-worth). Our psychological experience can be affected by our physical or social experiences. For example, a young man who identifies with his sexual orientation will experience confidence and boldness to the degree that he places value on all sexual orientations in general. Another example could be a woman who serves as a soldier in the military. The woman soldier will feel confidence in accordance with the degree of value and significance that she associates with "being in the military."

Finally, the spiritual dimension describes the individual's relationship with the transcendent, the ambiguous or the unknown. This can include a belief in a deity, God, or a higher power, but it does not necessarily have to be religious in nature. Someone who has a strong spiritual "faith" infrastructure may find that it helps them to cope with difficult life experiences. It can also offer a sense of purpose that transcends "beyond" science.

We all experience the world in our own unique way. Our individual perspectives are shaped by a variety of factors, including our culture, our values, and our personal history. These factors come together to form our "lenses of perception." When we encounter new people or situations, we filter our experiences through these lenses, and this can impact how we think and behave. For example, someone who has experienced much bereavement may approach death with more fear and sadness than someone who has had less exposure to death. Or, someone who comes from a culture that values independence may have a strong need for freedom, while someone from a collectivist culture may be more comfortable with interdependence. By understanding these four different dimensions of personal experience, you can gain insights into why people think and behave in certain ways toward death, freedom, isolation, and meaninglessness. You can also use this knowledge to empathically interact with your coachees, even when you don't share the same worldview.

An important point to make about existential coaching is that those who use it should be interested in its concepts and the philosophical tradition from which it stems. Existential coaching can be helpful for people who are struggling with life transitions or who feel stuck in a rut. Existential coaching can be beneficial for people who are interested in philosophy and who want to gain a better understanding of themselves and their place in the world. However, it is important to note that not everyone will find existential coaching helpful. Some people may not be interested in the concepts or find the ideas too challenging. Additionally, people who are experiencing poverty, political oppression, or homelessness may not be able to relate to the existential focus on freedom of choice. But for those who are open to it, existential coaching can help your coachees to generate a balanced outlook on life and also find a true source of motivation that will inspire their future goal-setting endeavors.

**PRINCIPLES INTO PRACTICE QUESTIONS:**

Many people live their lives without ever taking the time to think about the bigger picture. They focus on their day-to-day concerns and goals and never stop to question the nature of their existence. When thinking existentially, we must ask ourselves what we hope to achieve before our time is up. Such reflection can be daunting, but it can also be incredibly liberating. It allows us to see our lives in a new light and to appreciate the time we have been given.

1. What existential outcomes do you hope to achieve before your time is up?
2. How do these existential outcomes relate to your short-term goals and priorities?
3. In what ways might thinking existentially influence your future Life Coaching?

# UNCOVERING DEFICITS, PASSIONS, AND PURPOSE

*"The purpose of life is not to be happy. It is to be useful, honorable, and compassionate, to have it make some difference that you have lived and lived well."*

—RALPH WALDO EMERSON

It is a common saying that the two most important days in life are the day we are born, and the day we figure out why. This is because, without understanding our role in the world, we cannot design a purpose-oriented future that is (a) purposeful, and (b) fulfilling. No one is born with a pre-scripted life purpose; instead, it is up to each of us to commit to a life path.

The average human lifespan is just 25,550 days. That's it. Once those days are gone, they're gone forever. Sadly, some people never take the time to reflect upon what their purpose in life might be. Many people leave school, stop learning, and stagnate in an ideology or career path that doesn't add value to their lives—or to anyone else, for that matter. As a result, people end up living in quiet desperation, chasing after empty goals that don't even resonate with them.

The question of what makes life purposeful has haunted thinkers for centuries, and there is no easy answer, although the process of searching for one's purpose is an insightful one. And even if you never find a definitive answer, the process of asking the question,

"What could the greatest purpose of my life be?" will help you to gain clarity over the things that you cannot commit any more of your time to. Greek philosopher Aristotle once said, "The purpose of life is to be happy." But if you look at the state of the world today, happiness is evidently not enough. The truth is that a life lived only for itself is meaningless. To truly live, we must dedicate ourselves to a positive "world-improving" purpose that reaches beyond mere gratification. If you want to know why you are here, begin with choosing a life path that's greater than serving your own pleasure.

The great industrialist, Andrew Carnegie, was born in a small weaver's cottage in Dunfermline, Fife, Scotland (incidentally, also my hometown). As a child, Carnegie was gifted books from his uncle, which inspired him to a lifetime of reading, learning, and entrepreneurial innovation. After immigrating to the US in 1848, Carnegie took a job as a messenger boy for the Pittsburgh telegraph office. By the 1880s, Carnegie had built an empire of steel and was the richest man in his era who accumulated $400M+ in his lifetime. Despite his excessive wealth, Carnegie never forgot his humble upbringing. By his death, he had donated over 90 percent of his wealth to foundations, universities, and other philanthropic organizations. His most notable achievement was his funding of a worldwide network of libraries, including his own homeland of Scotland. He built what is now the oldest library in Washington, DC, which bears the dedication, "To the Diffusion of Knowledge." While accumulating great wealth was one of Andrew Carnegie's most noted accomplishments, his real purpose was to use his means to benefit the lives of as many other people as his wealth would allow. Carnegie made it his purpose to ensure that all children would have the opportunity to access books in exactly the same way that he was able to as a child.

We all look for fulfillment in different ways. The following forty questions can help you explore what pursuits will allow you to carve out a purposeful future for yourself. Consider what is true as you answer, as it's your honesty that will prepare you to coach other people through the process of answering the same questions within one of your future Life Coaching sessions.

1. What would be your best possible outcome after reading this handbook?
2. What of your everyday activities do you find most satisfying or meaningful?
3. What path could you commit your future to that might be interesting or fun?
4. What work activities leave you feeling stressed, anxious or energy drained?
5. How would you invest your time or energy if you had no financial restrictions?
6. What interests did you have as a child that you were encouraged not to pursue?
7. How much more rewarding may your life be if you pursued these interests now?
8. After you die, how would you like to be remembered by people you care about?
9. If you died today, how will you be remembered by the people you care about?
10. Name two people who inspire you. What is it about them that inspires you?
11. Name two people who disgust you. What is it about them that disgusts you?
12. What skills do you have that you are naturally good at and passionate about?
13. What skills do you have that you are not naturally passionate about pursuing?
14. What good causes, initiatives, or charities do you believe in or identify with?
15. What career roles have you occupied in the past that felt purposeful to you?
16. What career roles have you occupied in the past that felt disinteresting to you?
17. How much time do you spend doing things that are disinteresting to you?
18. What would happen if you stopped doing things that are disinteresting to you?

19. In what ways does your current career path or studies reflect your priorities?
20. In what areas of your life does your decision conflict with your top priorities?
21. Describe the caliber of people that you enjoy spending time with the most.
22. What excuses do you make for not pursuing your primary interests in life?
23. What specifically is preventing you from committing to your primary interests?
24. What career opportunities make you feel most optimistic about the future?
25. What study opportunities make you feel most excited about the future?
26. What relationship opportunities make you feel most confident about the future?
27. What is the greatest act of kindness that you have ever experienced?
28. In what ways do other people experience this act of kindness from you?
29. If other people's opinions didn't matter, what would you commit your life to?
30. What groups of people could benefit the most from your support or assistance?
31. What part of society could be improved through your hard work and investment?
32. What product could you create that people might find valuable and pay money for?
33. What service could you deliver that people might find valuable and pay money for?
34. What problems have you solved that you could help other people to also solve?
35. What hard life lessons have you learned that others would benefit from learning?
36. What frustrates you the most about the society/community that you're living in?

37. What could you do that might stop other people from having the same frustration?
38. How would you approach your life differently if you had an opportunity to start over?
39. If you could share an important message with 1,000,000 people, what would it be?
40. What steps can you take to start sharing this important message with people today?

**PRINCIPLES INTO PRACTICE QUESTIONS:**

1. Use these forty questions as the basis of a conversation with a close friend or relative.
2. Use these forty questions as the basis of a conversation with a colleague or co-worker.
3. Invite someone you know for a "practice" coaching session and ask them these questions.

# PURPOSE FIRST, VISION SECOND, GOALS THIRD

*"Real confidence has no bluster or bombast. Real confidence settles in when you have a clear vision of exactly what you need to do and blooms as you wield the skills you have built through your hard work and discipline."*

—ROB BREZSNY

Are you now clearer in what your life purpose could be? Some people spend years seeking an answer to this question. A personal vision is the deepest expression of what we want in life. It is a description of our "ideal" future and not a prediction of what it "might" be. With a sense of purpose and a clear vision of the future, it's easier to take the first step toward it.

Each journey begins with a single step, but not every journey ends with a final destination in mind. When we start a project or journey with our end destination visualized inside of our mind's eye, we become less likely to get sidetracked along the way. "Start with the end goal in mind." This proverbial wisdom can be applied to all areas of our lives, from personal goal-setting to relationships or financial management to professional planning. Essentially, it means that we are wise to visualize what we hope to achieve before taking action. This might seem like a simple concept to some people, but it's unquestionably a wise one. With a clear vision of what we hope to achieve, we are less likely to be distracted by irrelevant details or make choices that would otherwise lead us astray. By beginning with the end in mind, we can stay focused on our goal and make better progress toward achieving it.

Over the last few chapters, we have explored the difference between "current state of affairs," "desired state of affairs," and now understand that all Life Coaching should enable a coachee to bridge the gap between what they have and what they hope to achieve. As you begin your journey as a coach, you will quickly learn that one of the most important things you can do for your coachees is to help them define an inspiring vision for their future. This "desired state of affairs" will become the driving force that motivates them to work hard and make change happen. Without it, they may just go through the "goal setting" motions without any real sense of purpose or clarity. People without a clear future vision are often easily distracted, have a tendency to drift from one idea to the next, and make unwise decisions.

Having a life vision gives you clarity around your future and what you want to get out of it—whether that's in the next month, year, or ten years. The dictionary defines vision as the act of anticipating what may eventually come to be. Vision is always future-oriented and creates context for all goal-setting efforts. So, as you start coaching people, take time to help them first clarify their vision; What do they hope to achieve? What kind of person do they want to become? Without a compelling vision, your coachee's decisions will be scattered all over the place. With a clear future vision, it will become significantly easier for them to prioritize investing time, resources, and energy into things that will enable them to progress.

One of my former coachees was Craig, an American actor who was financially affluent and professionally successful but who had sacrificed his romantic life for career progression and acting success. While Craig had a series of blockbuster hits to his name, he was left in his forties, single, socially isolated, and uncertain about what his future goals should be. I asked Craig what his future vision was, and he explained how ready he was for a change of lifestyle and also how much he longed to settle down, get married to the "right person," and start a family. When he started acting, his ambition was to become a famous actor and own prestigious Hollywood real estate. He wanted to star in a number of box-office hits and have his face on Broadway, all of which he'd accomplished. However, Craig's success had cost him getting married, starting a family, and settling down.

After a handful of coaching sessions, Craig became clear that his vision was to leave stardom behind and retire into full-time parenting—perhaps with one or two lifestyle businesses on the side—because he certainly didn't need to make any more money. This vision created the bedrock upon which all of our subsequent goal setting was carried out. Like a great athlete, we must have a clear vision of what we want to accomplish before we make a move. Vision, in preparation for taking action, is as important as taking action itself. In the same way that your future vision will determine your direction in life, it will also influence the companions you keep and how you spend your time. Your habits will also align to the scale of your vision. For example, if you want to launch a Life Coaching business, you might benefit from building relationships with people who also want to enter the coaching profession and spend time practicing to develop your understanding and competencies. The same is true for any profession or interest.

To help your coachees improve their lives, you must first help them develop a concise vision for what they hope to achieve. Deciding on this vision doesn't have to be complicated—and it may or may not be existential by nature. A future vision can be as simple as wanting to be married, building a business, or wanting to make a positive social difference—it just needs to be compelling and meaningful for whoever is defining it. This vision will serve as a guide that helps your coachees overcome any challenges and distractions that stand to hinder their journey of development and growth. When you can help people see beyond their current reality, you'll open them up to new growth opportunities. Future vision is what gives people the power to transcend their circumstances and create the life conditions that they want.

**PRINCIPLES INTO PRACTICE QUESTIONS:**

One of the most important aspects of coaching is helping your coachee to establish a clear and meaningful vision and think deeply about who they are, what they want, and what they are willing to sacrifice to achieve their goals. It is essential to do this work upfront, as it will lay the foundation for all future goal-setting and coaching sessions. Answer the following four questions for yourself to evaluate how useful they might be in your future Life Coaching.

1. THE EULOGY QUESTIONS:

1. What would you want to be said about you at your funeral service?
2. What would you want to be written about you on your tombstone?
3. Does how you live today reflect how you want to be remembered?

2. THE IDEAL DAY QUESTION:

Write a few paragraphs about what your "Ideal Day" would look like. Start your "Ideal Day" from the moment you wake up—and write out what you'd like the day to be like. What would you do? Who are you with? What goals or tasks are you working on? And so on.

3. MEET YOUR FUTURE SELF QUESTION:

Write a few paragraphs about the kind of person your "ideal" life partner would be. For example, are they kind, generous, sincere, creative, strong, decisive, responsible, etc.? Once you have defined this person, evaluate how many of the characteristics you have room for improving upon in YOUR life (so you don't end up being hypocritical in your relationships).

4. THE MAGIC WAND QUESTION:

If you had a magic wand and could create the life that you wanted within minutes, what life would you create for yourself? What would you do in the next three months, six months, one year, five years, ten years, and so on? Introducing "magic" frees you up to visualize without limitations!

# FIVE QUESTIONS FOR VISIONARY GOAL SETTING

*"Vision reaches beyond what is, into the conception of what can be. Imagination gives you the picture. Vision gives you the impulse to make the picture your own."*

—ROBERT COLLIER

It is important to remain aware of your frame of reference and how it shapes how you perceive everything around you. This includes your coachees and their perspectives. Your frame of reference is shaped by the life experiences you have had and the values you uphold. In the same way, your coaching clients also come with their own frames of reference shaped by their unique experiences, education, culture, religion, etc. Understanding how your frame of reference might potentially pollute your coaching efforts is essential in order to coach people toward articulately defining their visions and achieving their desired goals.

A useful tip when questioning is to keep in mind that you and your coachees will have different frames of reference. Due to this, the questions you ask should serve the purpose of gaining a clearer understanding of your coachee's frame of reference, focusing on their unique perspective and avoiding erroneous assumptions about what "might be" on your coachee's mind. By doing this, you will sustain a healthy rapport with your coachee and also better understand their needs. Ultimately, this will lead to more successful coaching sessions.

When working with a coachee to help them achieve their "desired state of affairs," encourage them to articulate their vision as clearly as possible. By taking time to explore their future vision in detail, you can help your coachees to better understand what they want and increase their chances of achieving success. The following questions illustrate some of the ways in which you can prompt your future coachees to unpack and explore their vision.

### 1. WHAT'S AN EXAMPLE OF THE OUTCOME YOU WANT?

As your coachee begins to explain their future vision, you can ask them to offer you an example of what their vision is really like for them. For example, if your coachee's vision is to progress in their chosen career path, you can ask them to give an example of what progress specifically means and will look like once it's been made. Once you have asked this simple question, all that's left for you to do is be silent, listen actively, feedback on whatever you hear, and wait for clarity. By asking your coachee to give you a practical example of what their vision is, you gain clarity around WHY the outcome is important to them and, therefore, will become naturally better placed to coach the coachee toward turning the vision into a reality.

### 2. WHAT DOES YOUR "DESIRED STATE OF AFFAIRS" LOOK LIKE?

What does your "desired state of affairs" look like? This is another thought-provoking question that you can use to tease out specific details of the coachee's future vision. This question will prompt your coachee to reflect on (and try to concisely articulate) what their vision is. Don't be surprised if some people are unable to answer this question, to begin with. Some people approach a Life Coach with only a vague idea of what they want, so asking them to talk about what their "desired state of affairs" actually looks like can steer their thinking toward developing a vivid mental image of what their future vision looks like, and also might entail.

### 3. SPECIFICATION PROVOKERS: "LIKE WHAT?" AND "SUCH AS?"

COACHEE: "I need to get some increased results in my business."

COACH: "Such as…?"

COACHEE: "I need to get some increased results in my relationships."

COACH: "Like what exactly…?"

Learning how to ask short and concise questions is like a Life Coaching superpower. Asking short and concise questions is easy for a coachee to understand and also serves the added bonus of keeping the coaching session "person-centered" and the coachee doing most of the talking. As you begin to draw out your coachee's vision, subtly ask unloaded questions, such as "Such as?" and "Like what?" By asking simple questions like this, you will demonstrate to your coachee that you are following what they're saying and that you want to understand them more. Upon earning your coachee's trust, they will find it easier to be completely honest about what their vision is for what they ultimately hope to achieve. This information will help you to steer your future coaching conversations toward attaining that vision.

### 4. WHAT WOULD A SUCCESSFUL OUTCOME LOOK LIKE TO YOU?

By definition, success is the outcome of an action within a specified period of time or within a specified parameter. Whether personal or professional, all of your future coachees will want to become more successful in one way or another. Asking, "What would a successful outcome look like to you?" can create context for an entire coaching conversation. You will have your own frame of reference regarding what success means, but what's more important is how your coachee defines success. With this definition comes specific and deliverable results that will give you grounds for setting specific action steps and future Life Coaching accountability.

### 5. WHAT WOULD FAILING TO ACHIEVE THIS VISION LOOK LIKE?

It is equally important for you to ask your coachee to describe what failing to achieve their vision might mean to them. More often than not, inviting people to talk openly about what they don't want to happen can help them to get a far more vivid picture of what they do want to happen. For example, your coachee may see failure as bankruptcy or getting divorced. In the same way that there are endless ways to define success, there are also many ways to define failure. How your coachee defines failure will give you insight into what their primary concerns are at that moment in time. If your coachee deems it to be important, you could host a coaching discussion around putting in place a "worst case scenario" prevention plan to put your coachee's mind at better ease.

**SUMMING THINGS UP**

As you may have noticed, "what" and "how" questions can strategically invite your coachees to concisely discuss their vision. The questions discussed in this chapter are non-intrusive, neutral, and create space in a coaching conversation for your coachees to fully reflect and express themselves honestly. All of these qualities are vital prerequisites for deepening the trust in a coaching relationship, and furthermore, by modeling this type of question yourself, you invite your coachees to do the same, which then becomes a useful tool that they can take away with them and use in other areas of their life. Ultimately, the goal is not to get your coachee to simply regurgitate what they think you want to hear but rather to help them connect with their values so that they can move forward in alignment with their true priorities.

**PRINCIPLES INTO PRACTICE QUESTION:**

The questions previously discussed are just five of many different questions you could ask a coachee with regard to their future vision or sense of purpose. What other questions do you think might be useful to ask a coachee at this stage of the Life Coaching relationship?

# CATEGORIES AND APPROACHES TO GOAL SETTING

*"The reason most people never reach their goals is that they don't define them, or ever seriously consider them as believable or achievable things to be pursued."*

—DENIS WAITLEY

A goal is a result or achievement that calls for action steps to be taken. At least, that's how the dictionary defines it. Anyone who has ever set a goal knows that setting goals is far easier than fulfilling them. Some people find goal setting difficult due to setting goals that are either too vague or unrealistic. By understanding the different categories and approaches to goal setting, you can help set your future coachees up for goal-setting success. There are four different categories of goals, which include short-term goals, medium-term goals, long-term goals, and visionary lifetime achievement goals. Alongside this, there are also two directional goal-setting approaches that include approach-oriented goals and avoidance-oriented goals.

When people talk about being "busy," they're usually referring to the volume of short and medium-term goals that bulk up their to-do lists and overwhelm them with pressure. People with many short and medium-term goals can easily get lost in the details of a bigger picture and ironically lose sight of the bigger picture. This is just one typical reason why accountability is such an important aspect of the Life Coaching process. People without a compelling future vision will find it tough to sustain the motivation and energy needed to turn that vision into a reality. Long-term and lifetime goals should always provide the source of inspiration for hard work in the short and medium-term—hence the reason we have talked about purpose, existentialism, and future vision in the opening chapters of this section.

Some people see goals as a generic set of outcomes that an individual or business might aim for, but it's generally more helpful to think about goals in categories. While there are many goal-setting models you could use in your coaching, the following offers you a straightforward framework to help your coachees consider their "big picture" first before deciding upon what their shorter-term action steps and priorities must be.

### CATEGORY 1. VISIONARY LIFETIME ACHIEVEMENT GOALS

It is said that the mind can only visualize what it reflects upon. In the same way, the human mind can recall past events, it can also visualize what the future might behold. This is what we call a vision. Visionary future forecasting serves as a mental guide for people who need to define what action steps must be taken to fulfill a visualized result. Often, people have trouble articulating their vision, and this is where you have the opportunity to help them deconstruct their vision into manageable short-, medium-, and long-term goals and take decisive action. Generally, visionary goals involve people being motivated by fulfilling a meaningful purpose that's greater than their own gratification. Visionary goals often involve solving a society-wide problem—which could be social, business, service-based, economic, technical, scientific or process-based by nature. For example, your coachee might want to launch a world-changing charity. Vision is where your coachee wants to get to, but the path they must take might still remain unclear. This is where your accountability, goal setting, and coaching will help to define the pathway they can take and the milestones that must be met along the way.

## CATEGORY 2. LONG-TERM GOAL SETTING

Have you ever wondered what your life will be like in five or ten years? Will you be on the same career path as you are today, or will you be doing something different? These are the questions you may be asking your coachees when the time comes to start setting long-term goals. Long-term goals require time and planning and won't be achievable overnight or within a few weeks. Instead, long-term goals are usually achieved over years or decades and require effort, hard work, and investment to fulfill. Long-term goals can be applied to any area of your coachee's life. Do they want a better relationship? Set a long-term goal. Do they want better health? Set a long-term goal. Do they want financial freedom? Set a long-term goal. Each long-term goal that your coachees set should be different, but must all contribute to the fulfillment of their visionary lifetime achievement goal. Long-term goals are typically connected to how your coachee defines "success" within their career, finances, relationships, or personal life, and completing them will take several years but shouldn't ever take a lifetime.

## CATEGORY 3. MEDIUM-TERM GOAL SETTING

Have you ever wondered what your life will be like in twelve or eighteen months' time? Will you be on the same career path as you are today, or will you be ready to start doing something different? These are the questions to ask your coachees when the time comes to set medium-term goals. Medium-term goal setting simply involves breaking down each of your coachee's long-term goals into achievable milestones. It can seem overwhelming to say, "In ten years' time, I'll have a business that is generating over $1 million annually." But it isn't so overwhelming to say, "In eighteen months' time, I'll be generating enough money from my own business that I can quit my day job." It can be useful to think about medium-term goals as the "milestone" goals that must be completed on-route to fulfilling a long-term goal and that also align with a main future vision. Medium-term "milestone" goals are the ones that can then get broken down into short-term goals (or action steps). For example, if your goal is to get promoted at work, a medium-term goal might be to earn some new relevant certifications in your field. Medium-term goals will keep your coachees motivated and also on track to something greater.

**CATEGORY 4. SHORT-TERM GOAL SETTING**

Short-term goals are typically those that can be achieved within twelve months or less. Short-term goals bridge the divide between where your coachee is and where they want to be in an action-oriented and achievable way. Short-term goals are the "to-do" list of items that must be achieved to enable the progression of a medium or long-term goal. For example, if your coachee's goal is to be self-employed, a short-term goal might be to open a business bank account or conduct research on any startup business funding that might be available. Other examples of short-term goals could involve reading a new business book each month, listening to an educational podcast, exercising two to three times a week, developing a healthy morning routine, or enrolling in an online course and upskilling in a relevant area. With similarity to medium-term goals, short-term goals create a reason for accountability in the coaching relationship and enable daily progress to be made on your coachee's larger and more visionary long-term objectives.

**APPROACH-ORIENTED AND AVOIDANCE-ORIENTED GOALS**

Approach-oriented goals are the meaningful life outcomes that people want to achieve and are highly motivated to pursue. In other words, they are the outcomes people want to achieve instead of avoiding. In 2020, Swedish research conducted on a group of participants found that over 55 percent of 1,066 people surveyed about their New Year's resolutions successfully kept them for one full year. One key finding in the study was that out of the participants who were evaluated for adherence to their resolutions, those who set approach-oriented goals (rather than set avoidance-oriented goals) proved to be more likely to keep their resolution (58.9 percent versus 47.1 percent). Approach-oriented goals focus on achieving positive outcomes (e.g., *"If I work hard for the next twelve months, I could build a financially sustainable business."*) versus avoidance-oriented goals that people create to avoid negative outcomes (e.g., *"If I don't work hard for the next twelve months I might end up broke."*) Avoidance-Oriented Goals are the goals people set to avoid an outcome that they don't want to see happen. When delivering approach-oriented goal setting as a coach, be specific about the positive outcomes they want to achieve and also why these outcomes are important to them. Approach-oriented goals must be actionable and come with defined action steps that will allow them to be fulfilled.

## COACHING TOWARD DESIRED OUTCOMES AND GOALS

People always approach a Life Coach with a desire to change something about their life. This desired change becomes the foundation on which all goals are set. As a Life Coach, one of the most important things you can do is to help your coachees to set congruent goals. This means taking time to understand what they want to achieve and helping them plan to get there. It is important to remember that people have different kinds of goals—long-term goals that align with their vision and values, short-term goals that are the steps they must take to achieve long-term goals and medium-term goals that are like a roadmap, holding everything together. As a coach, it is your job to help your coachee keep all of these goals in mind and work toward them simultaneously. Only by doing this will they be able to achieve what they may previously not have imagined possible.

## PRINCIPLES INTO PRACTICE QUESTIONS:

To define some of the practical short, medium, and long-term goals that might help you attain a significant life result that is important to you, consider the following four questions. *(Naturally, the more efficient you are at creating personal goals for yourself, the more competent you will become in coaching others in goal setting and achievement.)*

1. What positive and non-negotiable outcome must you achieve before you die?
2. What long-term goals must you achieve in order to produce this outcome?

3. What medium-term goals will allow you to achieve these long-term goals?
4. What short-term goals will allow you to achieve these medium-term goals?

# THE S.M.A.R.T. GOAL SETTING FRAMEWORK

*"You must set goals that are almost out of reach. If you set a goal that is attainable without much work or thought, you are stuck with something below your true talent and potential."*

—STEVE GARVEY

Any goal that's worthy of attention will require sustained effort, usually over several weeks or months. You can't complete an Italian language course in a day, nor can you thoroughly train for a triathlon in only a few weeks. It's significantly easier to succeed with clearly defined goals that are based in reality. Setting S.M.A.R.T. goals is one way to set specific, measurable, actionable, realistic, and time-related goals. S.M.A.R.T. goals were created in 1981 by George T. Doran. In his paper, "There's a S.M.A.R.T. way to write management's goals," he discussed the challenges of defining goals within established organizations. As a Life Coach, you might be interested to know that George believed it was the goal-setting combined with action planning that inspired most people to take action. S.M.A.R.T. goal setting is a useful tool to employ as a coach. To make sure that your coachee's short-, medium-, and long-term goals are realistic, clear, and reachable, each one should be:

    S—SPECIFIC (simple, sensible, significant)
    M—MEASURABLE (meaningful, motivating)
    A—ACHIEVABLE (actionable, attainable)

R—RELEVANT (realistic and results-based)
T—TIME-BOUND (time-based/time-sensitive)

Defining these parameters as they pertain to your goals will help ensure that your objectives are attainable within a given time frame. This approach eliminates generalities and guesswork, sets a clear timeline, and makes it easier to track progress and identify missed milestones.

## LET ME INTRODUCE YOU TO FRANK

Frank is the manager of a recruitment company called RecruitYou Ltd. Frank has been tasked with increasing morale throughout the company's staff by implementing a new culture of coaching and accountability. He knows he'll have to enroll many people to make this happen, but there's a problem. When Frank has set major goals that have involved enrolling people in the past, they've failed. Nobody seemed to understand the specific details of what needed to be achieved. Progression wasn't monitored closely, and, inevitably, didn't generate the specific results that he needed. That's why, this time around, Frank intends to leverage S.M.A.R.T. goals for setting an action plan and delivering this new culture of coaching efficiently. Let's use Frank's goal to implement a new culture of coaching and accountability throughout RecruitYou Ltd' to work through each step of the S.M.A.R.T. goal-setting process.

## STEP 1. S STANDS FOR SPECIFIC

A wish is an abstract concept like "getting healthy" or "making more money." A goal, on the other hand, is a specific, actionable intention. It's something that you can actually do. In order for a goal to be effective, it must be specifically defined, articulated, and answer essential questions such as: What specifically needs to be accomplished? Who specifically is responsible for delivering what? What specific action steps (or short-term goals must be taken to achieve it? Answering these questions helps get to the heart of what you're aiming for. Here's an example of a specific goal that Frank might come up with: "I must grow the number of trained coaches throughout the company to 100 people and create an online portal that will allow staff members to apply for coaching and accountability support."

## STEP 2. M STANDS FOR MEASURABLE

Specificity is a solid start, but quantifying a goal (that is, making sure it's measurable) makes it easier to gauge progress and know when it has been successfully achieved. Frank wants to grow the number of trained coaches throughout the RecruitYou company to 100 people. If RecruitYou achieves this number, that's technically a success, but does this mean that Frank can cease work? No, because to make this S.M.A.R.T. objective more impactful, he must define measurable and trackable benchmarks that his coaches must adhere to. Here's an example of a measurable goal that Frank might come up with: "I must ensure that all of the RecruitYou coaches undergo fifty hours of continuous professional development each year to ensure that all beneficiaries receive the highest possible caliber of coaching."

## STEP 3. A STANDS FOR ACHIEVABLE

Goals that aren't realistically achievable within a time frame aren't goals; they're just wishes. This is the point in the S.M.A.R.T. goal-setting process where a reality check is required to evaluate the sensibleness, feasibility, and possibility of a goal actually being delivered upon. Goals should always be realistic and never a pedestal from which people will fall. So the question must be asked: is this objective something that can reasonably be accomplished? Here's an example of an achievable goal that Frank might come up with: "I must set up an accessible online application process for volunteers to apply to become coaches and send this out in the staff newsletter before the end of this month. On the newsletter, I must also request that all volunteers reply within seventy-two hours of receiving the newsletter."

## STEP 4. R STANDS FOR RELEVANT

To achieve any goal, especially one that requires sustained effort, you must get crystal clear on your motivation. Relevant goals get relevant results, so for effective S.M.A.R.T. goal setting to happen, any action steps that get planned or taken must be relevant to the big-picture goal and align with whatever the initial objectives were. Here's where you need to think about the big picture. You've got to know what you're trying to achieve, why you're trying to do it, and what appropriate action steps must be taken in order to achieve the desired result. Here's an example of a relevant goal that Frank might come up with: "I must set up a survey monkey to evaluate exactly how many people throughout the RecruitYou company would like to volunteer to train as a coach, and also how many people will benefit from this new level of support. This way, I can feed back to senior management before getting started."

### STEP 5. T STANDS FOR TIME-BOUND

Every goal needs a completion date; therefore, the final step in the S.M.A.R.T. goal-setting process is establishing a reasonable time frame in which a goal must be achieved. Having a clear time frame is essential for checking progress and productivity along the way to reaching the goal. If, for example, a goal isn't met within the time frame, then it's time to reassess if the goal was achievable and realistic to begin with. Here's an example of a relevant goal that Frank might come up with: "I must invite my senior managers to state what their desired time frame is, and also establish the duration of training that all volunteer coaches must go through before the coaching initiative can begin. this way, I can set a time-bound goal that is also realistic and achievable."

To summarize, setting S.M.A.R.T. goals will help you establish specific, measurable, actionable, realistic, and time-related goals with your coachees that will provide them with the motivation and clarity they need to define and take the action steps to turn their priorities into tangible outcomes they can see. Coaching involves encouraging learning and action in the service of a longer-term goal or aspiration. As coaches, we want to ensure that our coachees do not just define a goal or reach it but that they also sustain it. S.M.A.R.T. goals involve finding the balance between "too complicated" and "too easy" so that you grow without becoming discouraged through a lack of progression. Knowing how to set goals using the S.M.A.R.T. framework can help you support your coachees to successfully set and attain goals, no matter how visionary, long-term, medium-term, or short-term they might be. This S.M.A.R.T. goal-setting process can be used in all aspects of your coachee's life. From starting up a new business to increased productivity; or from finding a future partner to strengthening a marriage. It brings clarity to the process of planning and achieving goals.

**PRINCIPLES INTO PRACTICE QUESTIONS:**

For this exercise, answer the following questions and draft out a S.M.A.R.T. goal for yourself, or invite someone that you know to try to answer them:

1. What specific goal do you want to accomplish right now?
2. For what reasons is this goal so important to you?
3. Who must be involved to turn this goal into a reality?
4. What resources will be required to achieve this goal?
5. How long will this goal realistically take to achieve?

# THE EIGHT AREAS FOR LIFE COACHING FOCUS

*"The best thing is to keep a balance in your life, acknowledge the great powers around us and in us. If you can do that, and live that way, you are really a wise man."*

—EURIPIDES

People come to a Life Coach for a myriad of reasons, but one common goal is finding balance. And when I say "balance," I don't just mean between work and the rest of your life—though that's important, too. Our lives are made up of many different aspects, so it wouldn't be accurate to clump everything together under "life" and assume achieving balance there would cover everything. Neglecting any part of our lives can lead to disastrous consequences.

To help explain the concept of life balance, let's use an analogy. Imagine going into a shop to purchase paints for an art project. When you get to the shop, you realize that the paints are more expensive than anticipated; in fact, you only have enough money to purchase one paint container. You have to ask: Which paint should I buy? You look at the green, which you'll need for the landscape. But then there is the blue; what kind of sky could you paint without blue? You could probably make do without the white, but how do you make the other colors lighter? How do you make them darker without the black? Where is Bob Ross when you need him? Obviously, trying to create a painting with only one color is absurd, and so is dedicating all your time to one area of your life at the expense of others. To lead a fulfilling life, you must pay attention to all aspects of your life. You can't work if you neglect your health, and you can't maintain strong mental composure if you neglect your relationships for the sake of finances and work.

Some new Life Coaches assume that they don't need to have personal experience within certain life areas in order to effectively coach others. Respectfully, I disagree. Life Coaching is mostly practical and rarely intellectually based, which means the most valuable coaches are generally those who have the most varied and balanced range of life experiences. Would you ask for business coaching from someone who's never built a sustainable business? Would you ask for marriage counseling from someone with a track record of seven divorces? Would you hire a painter and decorator who'd only ever taken an online course? Would you ask someone who has never done any woodwork to advise you on building a staircase? You have hopefully just answered no to these questions. Before you can help a coachee to achieve life balance, you must first have balance within your own life.

In consumer-driven societies, many people feel the need to achieve more results and acquire more stuff rather than strive to lead a balanced or satisfying existence. This consumer-driven outlook seldom leads people to consider asking the question, "How much would ever be enough for me?" Asking this question often helps people to develop a less self-occupied mindset and focus on what is truly important to them rather than just acquiring more money or materialist belongings. It could also help people to find ways to reduce their consumption without compromising their quality of life. Asking the question, "How much is enough?" is a crucial first step in moving toward a more balanced way of living.

There is so much more to life than wealth and achievement. Sometimes, the most valuable aspect of a coaching interaction comes when a coachee realizes the cost that their current pursuits are bearing and how they might change their priorities to source a greater depth of balance and inner peace. In our fast-paced, materialistic world, it's easy to get caught up in the rat race and pursue things that don't really matter. We can lose sight of what's important and end up sacrificing our health, our relationships, and our happiness in the process. A good Life Coach can help people to take a step back, reassess their priorities, and make adjustments in their goals setting that will lead to a more perceptive and balanced way of living.

We each have different areas in our lives that are important to us. When these areas are working well together, we generally feel a sense of satisfaction and well-being. However, when one or more of these areas is out of sync, it can have a negative impact on our inner well-being and overall sense of fulfillment. Let's take a look at the following key areas of life and explore how they each work together to create a balanced and sustainable lifestyle:

## LIFE AREA 1. PHYSICAL HEALTH

Obviously, our physical health is important to our overall sense of well-being. When we are physically healthy, we have more energy and feel better both mentally and emotionally. Taking care of the body is central to living a healthy, meaningful life. As the saying goes, if you don't have your health, you don't have anything. The condition of your health determines the kind of activities that you can partake in. If we take our health for granted, we suffer in other areas of our life, including work, relationships, leisure, and financial security. There's no use in working sixty hours a week to earn a small fortune if you suffer from a stroke or die of a heart attack due to stress or poor nutrition. Living a healthy lifestyle requires a balanced diet and regular exercise. Taking part in recreational activities can improve your relationships and provide mental well-being, positively impacting everything you do.

## LIFE AREA 2. WORK AND CAREER

Our work is often a major source of satisfaction in our lives. When we enjoy our work and feel like we are making a contribution, it can add greatly to our sense of fulfillment. Work is the simplest way in which you contribute to the world. Everyone has a unique talent and a creative spark to share. How you share these things will profoundly affect the level of fulfillment you experience in your life. When a person is not successful in developing and sharing their talents, they may grow to lack confidence in themselves and lose any sense of purpose for their future. A negative self-image can result from this. In career development, many people become unbalanced and end up selling their soul, living to work instead of using work as a means to generate the income required to build a rewarding home life.

**LIFE AREA 3. LOVE AND RELATIONSHIPS**

Relationships are arguably the most important component of our lives. The strength of our relationships determines the quality of our lives. Time spent together in a relationship is as vital as water is to a plant; investing time in people is the only way to stay connected and maintain and nurture relationships. Good relationships provide us with a sense of belonging and support, improve our mental well-being, and enable us to thrive both personally and professionally. In contrast, bad or nonexistent relationships can have a negative impact on every aspect of our lives. It is, therefore, essential that we invest time into maintaining and strengthening our relationships. Only by investing time in people can we create the strong, supportive relationships that are essential to a rewarding and satisfying life.

**LIFE AREA 4. PERSONAL GROWTH**

Many people seek fulfillment in life through personal growth in areas such as education, mind development, creative pursuits, or spirituality. Each person's path to inner fulfillment is unique, but there are many commonalities. Setting and achieving goals is often a key part of the process. Without the capacity to grow beyond your current self, you have no basis for expecting anything beyond what you currently have in your future. Setting and achieving goals is the key to increasing your faith and experiencing greater hope for the future. Personal growth is bound to your life vision. Without it, you cannot expect to become the person you envision. Establishing life balance is not a one-time activity for either yourself or your future coachees but rather a cycle of continuous re-evaluation and improvement. In my experience of Life Coaching people, I've found that those who enjoy sustained improvements in life continuously remember to pause, connect with their priorities, rethink their options, evaluate alternatives, and implement direction changes as a matter of routine habit.

**LIFE AREA 5. FINANCIAL SECURITY**

Although I'm unsure whether money makes the world go round, having financial security certainly reduces stress and frees us to focus on other areas of life or work that are important to us. While most people are frightened of being too poor, too much money can result in difficulties of a different kind. In addition to providing you with peace of mind, wise personal financial management can give you the freedom and opportunities to support others, invest in good causes or projects you care about, or even create opportunities for other people. Money can buy many things, but not fulfillment. Often, integrity and healthy intimate relationships can suffer due to a person prioritizing making money over all other aspects of life.

**LIFE AREA 6. FUN AND RECREATION**

It's important to make time for fun and recreation in our lives. It's easy to get caught up in the busyness of life and forget to make time for ourselves or our families. Some people believe they don't have time to relax or that taking a break will compromise their productivity, but the opposite is actually true. Making time for recreation is vital for maintaining our mental composure. When we do things we enjoy, we release endorphins, which have mood-boosting effects. In addition, recreation can help us to reduce stress and improve our overall sense of well-being. So next time you're feeling overwhelmed, step back and consider how you can make some time for yourself. You may be surprised at how much better you'll feel as a result!

**LIFE AREA 7. CONTRIBUTION TO SOCIETY**

A sense of fulfillment that can be hard to come by in today's fast-paced world. The highest purpose of a person's life is to share themselves with others, and one way of doing this is by being of service and contributing to society through volunteer work or philanthropic activity. Regardless of your circumstances, a social contribution can have a profound impact on your overall outlook on life. Volunteer work, philanthropy, and other forms of social contribution help us feel connected to something larger and more purposeful than just ourselves. When we give, we receive much back in return—a sense of purpose, satisfaction, and even connection with other like-minded people. So, the next time you're feeling directionless, instead of reaching for your to-do list or possessions, try making a contribution to the world around you. You may find that it's the best thing you ever did for yourself.

**LIFE AREA 8. ROUTINE RESPONSIBILITIES**

It's easy to get caught up in the big picture and forget about the little things that keep life ticking along nicely. But without paying attention to the mundane tasks that keep our homes and families running smoothly, we can quickly find ourselves in hot water. Whether it's making sure the bills are paid on time, maintaining a clean home, ironing your clothes, emptying the washing machine, sweeping up the back yard, having neat and tidy cupboards, visiting family members, taking the kids to the park, or keeping the fridge stocked with groceries, these routine responsibilities are essential for keeping our lives on track. And while they may not seem particularly exciting or inspiring, they play an important role in helping us maintain a sense of order and control in our lives. So next time you're feeling overwhelmed by life's big challenges, take a moment to appreciate the simple things that help keep your world running smoothly. They may not be glamorous, but they're essential nonetheless.

To lead a contented life, you must strike a balance between your different life areas. When your life areas are in harmony, you will function at your best. However, when one or more areas are out of sync, it can lead to stress and discontentment. As a Life Coach, one of your many roles is to help people find balance in their lives. This involves identifying areas that may be out of alignment and helping them to correct the imbalance. In order to do this, you must first have balance in your own life. By modeling and maintaining a balanced lifestyle, you will be best equipped to help others find balance in their lives also.

**PRINCIPLES INTO PRACTICE QUESTIONS:**

1. Which of the above eight areas are you currently unbalanced in?
2. What goals must you set to become more balanced in those areas?
3. To achieve a healthier life balance, what action steps can you take today?

# THE FOUR SEASONS OF HUMAN PROGRESSION

*"Spring passes and one remembers one's innocence. Summer passes and one remembers one's exuberance. Autumn passes and one remembers one's reverence. Winter passes and one remembers one's perseverance."*

—YOKO ONO

Before we define an actionable process for setting goals within a Life Coaching context, let us first understand the four seasons of human progression that all people have the opportunity to go through in life (although not all people do). Understanding these seasons will give you a mental framework that you can use to influence the decisions that either you or your future coachees make with regard to investing your time, energy, and resources each day. The four seasons of human progression can be understood through the following story.

An old man, who had four sons, wanted them to become more analytical and take more time processing their life experiences. To test their analytical skills, he sent them on a quest to look at an old apple tree situated over five miles away. He sent his first son in the winter, his second son in the spring, his third son in the summer, and his youngest son in the autumn. After they had gone and returned, he called them together and invited them to each describe what they had seen. What unfolded was that each son had seen something different.

According to the first son, who went in winter, the tree was ugly, bent, and twisted. The second son disagreed, saying the plant was covered with green buds and full of promise. The third son disagreed, stating that the tree was laden with blossoms that smelled sweet and looked beautiful; it was the most graceful thing he had ever seen. In contrast to all the others, the last son said it was full of fruit and ripe with life. The old man explained to his sons that they were all correct; they'd all seen the same tree, but each had witnessed the tree in different seasons of its growth and development. The moral of this story was that he wanted his sons to realize how unwise it is to judge a tree, or a person, according to one season of their life, for a life can only be measured accurately at its end when all seasons are complete.

There is a saying that we are creatures of habit. Though this may be partially true, it is also true that we are creatures of change. All living beings go through seasons of change and transformation, both physically and psychologically. Seasons of change can be gradual or sudden, but they are always happening. Those who refuse to acknowledge the seasons of life will struggle with emotional and mental turmoil, whilst those who embrace and lean into them will find it easier to find their footing in life.

Nature provides us with many examples of how to flow with the seasons. For instance, we can see the leaves on the trees change color in Autumn and eventually fall off in winter. In spring, new leaves sprout, and the cycle begins anew. Similarly, we experience physical changes throughout our lives—puberty, pregnancy, menopause—and psychological changes too—growing up, changing jobs, moving house. All of these transitions are natural processes that we go through, just like the changing seasons. When we fight or try to resist them, that's when we struggle. But when we flow with them and let them happen, they can be immensely rewarding experiences that help us to grow and evolve as people. The four seasons of human progression fall into four distinct categories:

## SEASON 1. THE LEARNING YEARS

The learning years of life is the season that all people are born into. Learning doesn't just begin or end with conventional schooling.

Every day is a school day that presents us with endless opportunities to grow, mature, and evolve. If you are reading this, you are even learning right now! The human mind soaks up information, ideas, and experiences before organizing them into patterns and learnings—this is how beliefs and ideologies are formed. As time passes, beliefs and ideologies become more complex and begin incorporating relationships with other people and future goals or ambitions. For better or worse, children learn most from family interactions. The learning years teach us how to function within society so that we can be autonomous and self-sufficient adults. The idea is that the adults in the community around us help us to reach this point by supporting our ability to make wise decisions and take action for ourselves.

In an ideal world, all people would be raised in a healthy family environment by mature, balanced, heterosexual, and connected parents who demonstrate love, consistency, congruence, authenticity, responsibility, and unconditional acceptance through their everyday parent-to-child interactions. In reality, however, families like this are few and far between. So, unfortunately, children learn ineffective life strategies, warped worldviews, and damaging ideologies from childlike adults who aged but who sadly never matured in their thinking or learned a fruitful way of living life for themselves. The greatest outcome of the learning years is understanding what makes us different from everyone else. The learning years are often messy, and it's only those who commit to the process of self-actualizing, mastering a craft, becoming truly autonomous, growing in responsibility, and prioritizing personal growth over gratification and emotional appeasement that qualify to evolve up to a higher season of life.

You might be wondering what purpose this chapter serves within a Life Coaching/goal-setting framework. And if so, you are wise to do so. Today more than ever, people have an idea inside of their minds that they want to become financially free millionaires. We can thank great books such as *Rich Dad, Poor Dad* by Robert Kiyosaki, or *Think and Grow Rich* by Napoleon Hill for planting these seeds. Having an aspiration to become financially wealthy is fine. But unless this aspiration is preceded by a desire to build something valuable that can continue to generate income after retiring from an active work life, the aspiration is both naive and unrealistic.

## SEASON 2. THE EARNING YEARS

One day, a man wanted to give his friend, an architect, a gift. He didn't know what to buy his friend because he had everything he wanted, so he decided to design and build him a house. He cunningly asked his architect friend to design and build a house for him, which he did. The architect chose the best plot of land, the best building materials, and tradesmen to turn his plan into a reality, motivated by respect for his friend. When the house was complete, the friend thanked the architect, gave him the keys, and said, "Enjoy your new home, my friend."

My Grandmother told me a version of that story as a child, which has stayed with me for over thirty-five years. In the early years of life, we must prove our worth if we hope to survive. We must prove that we have a skill that's worth someone hiring, promoting, and paying us for. People who fail to do this can spend years in mundane employment earning a low minimum wage. This is the price of failing to master a skill and develop competency throughout the learning years. So the earning years involve using our skills and knowledge to create new products, services, and processes that create the kind of value that people will exchange their money for, time and time again. Some people have an unhealthy relationship with money and either love it too much or respect it too little. The truth is that money is just an enabler, and wise people pursue financial independence as a goal throughout their earning years.

For the majority of people, earning a good salary is the primary goal of their working years (which for some people can be fifty-plus years). And while a high income can certainly bring greater financial security, it doesn't guarantee financial independence. Financial independence is the status of generating enough wealth to cover one's living expenses for a lifetime without having to rely on employment income. This means that even if you lose your job or retire, you would still be generating enough money to cover your costs and sustain the lifestyle that you want—which might even involve buying your friends' or loved ones' houses! To achieve financial independence, you must ensure that your investments generate enough passive income to cover your living expenses. This can be a challenge, but it's possible with wise entrepreneurial thinking, innovative planning, and disciplined budgeting. And once you reach this point, you'll enjoy a level of personal liberation that few people ever experience. The earning years require hard work, discipline, and wisdom, and it's only those who build something valuable and generate income apart from paid employment who qualify to evolve up to a higher season of life.

## SEASON 3. THE LEGACY YEARS

I once knew a man in his early thirties, Chris, who was a writer with great aspirations for pioneering a meaningful life legacy for himself. His goal was to write a series of books and before his thirty-fifth birthday, launch a writing collaborative charity that would support young writers in the early years of getting started and finding paid work. Within itself, the goal was unquestionably specific, meaningful, achievable, relevant, and time-bound. While Chris had mastered his craft and developed highly valuable writing skills, he had failed to build his life in a balanced way. He was a single workaholic who worked twelve-hour days, six to seven days each week. An opportunity arose for Chris to have his writing charity funded by a philanthropic investor on exactly the same day that he was accepted onto a six-year, part-time degree course that had been on his bucket list for over a decade. To cut the story short, Chris chose to reenter the learning years at the cost of entering his legacy years at age thirty. His justification for doing so was the opportunity he had to study alongside like-minded others and potentially meet a suitable life partner in the process. An unbalanced life can be the thief of all progression.

Leaving a legacy means that you will continue to keep on making an impact in people's lives once you are gone. This might include helping future generations to implement the life lessons you've learned or leave behind a product range that allows people to live more fruitful or effective lifestyles. People want to know that their lives have meaning. A legacy is more than money or material objects. While inheritance can be a part of a legacy, the most valued forms of legacy are typically memories, friendships, and the principles that get passed down from older generations to the emerging ones. These intangible things make up the essence of each individual and are what we typically think about when we reflect on our lives. Legacy consists of things that cannot be measured in monetary terms and live on long after we are gone. It's impossible to "leave a legacy" without first investing years of study, skill development, and hard work into it. Though a Life Coach might offer wisdom and structure to those in their legacy years, the groundwork for success must be first done by the person. In the legacy years, people get to see how their hard work has positively impacted others. This is a satisfying time, as well as an opportunity to look back on one's life and choices. The legacy years are the stage of a person's life in which they might think about how to pass on their wisdom and insight to the next generation. For many people, the legacy years are when they begin to reassess their lives and think about slowing down. A coach can help people navigate this process, but only those who've already built something of significance.

**SEASON 4. THE GOLDEN YEARS**

The golden years are less of a "season of life" and are more of a "quality of life." After you amass wealth and build a life's work that can support you without ongoing hard labor or management, you can enter the golden years. When you reach this point in life, you will find that your priorities have shifted away from work and toward making the best use of the time that you have left. The golden years hold a certain serenity for those who approach them with reverence, as if they are taking the final step into life's temple. Observing life from this vantage point means seeing it as a tapestry rather than a patchwork. Life has given you the gifts of experience, wisdom, and knowledge, so at this stage, you can enjoy the last blooms of life while imparting everything that you've learned to those who are humble enough to listen.

This is the season of life where goal setting, action planning, stressing, striving and trying to figure out what the "best next thing" to do is become irrelevant. Not all people enter into the golden years.

Sadly, many aging people enter the latter stages of their life realizing the extent of their poor decision-making and unwise action-taking. For those people, the latter years of life can center around loneliness, financial destitution, and emotional despair—not because they were just unlucky or unloved, but because they failed to understand that life is a process that all people have the opportunity to either progress in, or stagnate in. Those who prioritize work before family, getting rich quick, closed-mindedness and apathy before hard work and proactive innovation get to walk in the consequences of their decision-making.

The golden years bring with them space to reflect, life lessons to write about, and a genuine passion to mentor those who can be identified as also working hard to progress through their learning, earning and legacy years. Think about the autobiography books that people tend to want to read the most. *Long Walk to Freedom* by Nelson Mandela, *The Autobiography of Benjamin Franklin* by Benjamin Franklin, *The Story of My Experiments with Truth* by Mahatma Gandhi, *The Diary of a Young Girl* by Anne Frank, *Chronicles,* Vol 1 by Bob Dylan, *I Know Why the Caged Bird Sings* by Maya Angelou, *The Autobiography of Malcolm X* by Malcolm X, *Agatha Christie: An Autobiography* by Agatha Christie, *On Writing: A Memoir of the Craft* by Stephen King, or *A Moveable Feast* by Ernest Hemingway. The books that have influenced my thinking more than any others, aren't academic textbooks written by scholars but are reflections on life, written by those men and women who built something great before entering their golden years.

I write about these four seasons, not from merely having a desire to fill up this handbook with more words, but from having an understanding of how life can be best navigated. I have arrived at this understanding after spending fifteen-plus years reflecting upon the wise decisions I have made, the poor ones I have made, the relationships I have found the most value from, and the relationships that I invest the most into. I have learned these lessons from having coached thousands of people through their achievements, failures, wins, losses, highs, and lows. In this time, I have simply identified a pattern in terms of the direction in which people tend to want to direct their lives, and it is these four seasons of human progression that I have just shared. There is no research behind these ideas, nor is there a science. Just life experience, which in essence, is the most valuable thing you can possess to coach and guide other people in life.

**PRINCIPLES INTO PRACTICE EXERCISE:**

Identify someone that you know who has already entered into their legacy or golden years. Make contact with this person and ask if you could interview them about the highlights of their life story and the main lessons they learned from progressing through these four seasons of human progression and growth.

# OVERVIEW OF THE GOAL-SETTING PROCESS

According to legend, Sisyphus was a Greek King who cheated Death (Thanatos) by chaining Death up so Death couldn't come and claim his life. Eventually, Death was freed, and Zeus punished Sisyphus by forcing him to strain under the weight of a boulder as he rolled it up a mountain, only to have it roll back down just before reaching the top. His story has been highlighted many times throughout literature as a metaphor for the torture of meaningless work. As absurd as Sisyphus's story may seem, many of us go through life in the same way.

Despite many people's best efforts, they grow old and tired by doing the same thing, day in and day out, letting life pass by because they become complacent with the monotony of it all. Hard work is a virtue that, if not appropriately applied, ends up being nothing more than wasted energy. Without a goal or a strategy for obtaining that goal, hard work is just as meaningless. Even when a person's goals are simple in nature, they afford a sense of direction that will, in time, lead to a better destination than if they had no goal at all. Because of this, each new Life Coaching relationship must begin with a specific end goal in mind. Throughout the following five steps, I want to give you a complete overview of a time-proven five-step goal-setting process that you can either apply to your own circumstances or integrate within a new Life Coaching relationship right away.

## STEP 1: DECIDE ON A VISIONARY PURPOSE

A vision provides a framework on which you can weigh up the relevance and significance of any long-term, medium-term or short-term goals you set for yourself and ensures that all action steps taken are directed toward a purposeful end. Too many people spend their lives climbing the career and social ladders of ambition only to find that reaching the top does not bring them lasting satisfaction. A clear vision will prevent you from getting stuck on paths that do not reflect your true priorities. To support a new coachee in the process of creating their visionary purpose, you might invite them to answer the forty questions that were shared in the "Purpose First, Vision Second, Goals Third" chapter of this section in the handbook. The questions posed will give you a basis for one or two full coaching sessions to surface what is important to your coachee and what visionary purpose they must achieve in life.

## STEP 2: DEFINE A POSITIVE "DESIRED STATE"

There are many disempowered coaches who deliver a disempowered variant of coaching that prioritizes trying to help people achieve avoidance-oriented goals. For example, a coachee wants you to coach them toward "feeling better" about the unfulfilling career they've been devoted to for the last ten years. This would be like a person who keeps putting their hand in a fire, asking a nurse to blow on it every week. Defining a "desired state" with your coachee will inspire them to redirect their attention away from the deficit that's currently in their life and toward the ideal outcome that they want instead. This alone is what will give you a basis for setting long-term, medium-term, short-term, or S.M.A.R.T. goals. For example, your coachee might want to become fitter, healthier, more balanced, generous, or creative rather than spending their days feeling sorry for themselves and their current undesired state of affairs. Positively framed goals allow you to focus on what will be beneficial, thus creating positive energy and momentum instead of feelings of self-pity or remorse.

## STEP 3: SET LONG- AND MEDIUM-TERM GOALS

Having specific, measurable, attainable, relevant, and time-bound goals are essential for Life Coaching success. Without these criteria, it can be difficult to gauge coachee progression. Additionally, goals can be fixed or flexible. Short-term goals tend to attract specific target dates, while medium or long-term goals can be more flexible. When goal setting, it can be helpful to consider all eight areas of life (as discussed in The Eight Areas for Life Coaching Focus chapter) and to set goals that will create a greater sense of life balance. Oftentimes, people get so caught up in achieving one particular goal that they neglect other areas of their life, which can lead to feelings of imbalance and dissatisfaction. However, by taking a more holistic approach to goal setting and focusing on creating balance in all areas of life, a person is more likely to end up feeling more fulfilled and content with their ongoing achievements.

## STEP 4: PREPARING AN ACTION PLAN

Action planning is the process of defining the steps that must be taken to create an ideal future reality. Depending on the scope of a goal, an action plan may be complex or extremely simple. Some people draft every detail of their plan with precision, while others prefer to take one step at a time and figure out what their next steps must be as they go. How people approach action planning is a matter of preference, and this is the part of the Life Coaching process where flexibility is key. By drafting an action plan, you will integrate accountability into your Life Coaching—possibly for the first time. A well-drafted action plan will help you to monitor progress toward the desired goal and make adjustments as or where necessary.

An action plan for achieving a goal doesn't need to be any more complex than the following;

F—Define the ideal **FUTURE** situation
I—**IDENTIFY** the tasks to be achieved
R—Define the **RESULTS** to be achieved
E—**EXPLAIN** the action steps to be taken

There are countless online software programs you can use for action planning, ranging from the simple to the complex, but after many years of coaching people, I've found that simple plans are generally the ones that people remain loyal to. Some people shy away from action planning because they see it as restrictive, but without a plan, it can be easy to get sidetracked or give up when things get tough. By taking the time to create an achievable plan, you can set yourself and your coachees up for success from the start. And if you ever feel like you're veering off course, simply refer back to your action plan to help you get back on track.

### STEP 5: REVIEW, ADAPT, AND ADJUST

As we have already mentioned, maintaining accountability is one of the most important functions of a good coach. The action-taking of Life Coaching doesn't ever happen within a coaching session; this fact alone bursts the bubble of those "guru-like" coaches who market themselves as being perfect or transformative. The real action of coaching takes place in your coachee's life between coaching sessions. As your coachee takes the action steps documented within the action plan, your role is simply to review ongoing progress to determine whether any adjustments to the plan must be made. This may involve extending a goal deadline, breaking action steps down to make them more manageable, or even modifying a goal entirely. By doing this, you can ensure that your coachee stays on track and does not abandon their goals due to a lack of progress. In addition, by frequently reviewing goals and offering feedback, you can help your coachee to monitor their own progress and remain motivated to keep on "keeping on." The future belongs to the flexible—those who are adaptable and ready to meet life challenges head-on. Those who are naturally adaptable tend to be the type of people who thrive on the unexpected and often alter their routines as frequently as possible. On the other hand, there are those who prefer to keep rigid "to do" lists and "air-tight" schedules. For them, it can be frustrating when circumstances that are out of their control require them to adapt and adjust.

In practice, it is crucial to remember that the purpose of Life Coaching is not to build long-term relationships but to empower the people you coach with the wisdom, self-knowledge, and tools that they need to achieve their future desired goals without your ongoing involvement. Without a doubt, having goals is the first step on the road to progression. Just as importantly, however, is having a plan to reach those goals. Having a goal without a plan of action to get there is like attempting to drive hundreds of miles between two rural towns without a GPS or a roadmap to keep you heading in the right direction. So, in the natural order of things, we will now discuss action planning throughout the next chapter.

**PRINCIPLES INTO PRACTICE QUESTIONS:**

Don't view goal setting as a complicated process that you need to remember and robotically lead other people through. Remember that Life Coaching is just a conversation that only ever needs to center around the following seven questions. See how well you can coach yourself by answering these questions in a way that is appropriate to your current circumstances.

1. What goal do you want to achieve?
2. Why do you want to achieve this goal?
3. Where are you in relation to that goal now?
4. What must you overcome to achieve this goal?
5. What action steps could you start taking?
6. What resources are available to help you?
7. What action steps will you take right away?

# HOW TO CREATE AN EFFECTIVE ACTION PLAN

*"Don't be a time manager, be a priority manager. Cut your major goals into bite-sized pieces. Each small priority or requirement on the way to the ultimate goal becomes a mini goal in itself."*

—DENIS WAITLEY

Anyone who has ever set a goal knows that it is not enough to simply state what you want to achieve. Without a plan of action, your goals are nothing more than daydreams. This is where action planning comes in. Action planning is the process of creating a roadmap for achieving your goals by defining a set of clearly-defined action steps and assigning a realistic timeframe for each step. While this may sound like a lot of work, the truth is that action planning can save you a tremendous amount of time and effort in the long run. By taking the time to figure out what steps need to be taken and when they need to be taken, you can avoid the frustration of spinning your wheels and making little or no progress. In addition, action planning can help to keep you accountable and on track by providing tangible evidence of your progress (or lack thereof). So, if you're serious about achieving your goals, or serious about coaching other people through the process of achieving theirs, don't forget the importance of action planning.

Creating an action plan is as simple as making a to-do list of action tasks that relate to any particular goal. By breaking a goal down into a series of actionable to-do tasks, the chance of them getting completed remains higher. And because action plans are flexible, they can be adjusted as a coachee's circumstances change. Perhaps most importantly, action planning creates a visible pathway to progression. As you help your coachee create their plan of action, just keep the following seven stages in mind to ensure its success:

### STAGE 1. A DETAILED DESCRIPTION OF THE GOAL TO BE ACHIEVED

Writing down a detailed description of the specific goal that needs to be achieved is the first stage of the action planning process. Specific goals are more likely to be achieved than general goals because they are measurable and have a deadline. When writing down a specific goal, it is important to be as clear and concise as possible. The goal should be realistic and achievable, and it should be something that can be completed within a reasonable timeframe. Additionally, the goal should be relevant to the individual or group's overall objectives. By setting specific goals, individuals and groups can increase their chances of achieving their desired results.

### STAGE 2. THE STEPS THAT MUST BE TAKEN TO ACHIEVE THE GOAL

When it comes to accomplishing goals, the first few steps are always the hardest. It can be difficult to know where to start—or even what steps need to be taken. This is where breaking down goals into specific, actionable steps can be helpful. By taking the time to break down each goal into small pieces, you can make the overall task feel more manageable and increase your chances of success. In addition, specific steps help to make the goal more concrete and increase your motivation to continue working toward it. When it comes to taking action, remember that every journey begins with a single step. So don't be afraid to get started today.

### STAGE 3. THE PERSON/S RESPONSIBLE FOR COMPLETING EACH TASK

As a coach, you play an important role in supporting your coachee as they work to achieve their goals. However, it is important to remember that your coachee is ultimately responsible for taking action and achieving results. This is because they are the ones who need to achieve their goals and determine what steps must be taken. There may be cases where your coachee needs to share responsibility with, or involve, another person (such as a partner when it comes to parenting, a freelancer or some form of service provider, or a co-founder of a company), but in general, your coachee should always be responsible for fulfilling their action steps.

### STAGE 4. WHEN THE TASKS MUST BE COMPLETED BY (DEADLINES)

One of the most common questions I have been asked throughout my years of coaching people is, "When should I complete this action step by?" The answer to this question depends on two factors that include; the magnitude of the action step and whether other third parties will be involved in the action steps fulfillment. For example, how much time did I need to write this handbook? Back in 2020, I initially thought that one year would suffice. However, as with all creative projects, you can't put a time frame round raw creativity—that's just a law of life. Secondarily, I gave no consideration to how long and arduous the editorial and publishing process might be—which took a full twelve months longer than first expected. So, to reiterate, it is important to consider the complexity of the action step. If the task is simple and can be easily completed in a short period of time, then it may not be necessary to set a deadline. However, if the action step is more complex or time-consuming, it may be helpful to set a "rough" deadline to ensure that any procrastination or indecisiveness is kept to a minimum. If a goal is urgent or time-sensitive, then it may be necessary to set a shorter timeline for the completion of an action step. Ultimately, the decision of when to complete an action step should always be made based on what is realistically achievable for the person setting it.

### STAGE 5. WHAT RESOURCES ARE REQUIRED TO ACCOMPLISH TASKS?

When making an action plan, you must carefully consider what resources are required in order for each action step to be fulfilled. This may include money, stationery, new equipment, or even employees with specific skills. Do you need a new computer or a reliable SUV? Failing to count the potential costs of what you might need can lead to frustration and setbacks further down the line. In some cases, failing to plan in this way may require that an entire plan gets scrapped, and in a practical business sense, is one very common reason why many businesses file for bankruptcy. So take time to identify all of the resources you will need before taking effective action. Once you have done this, you can then begin to look for ways to obtain the necessary resources. This may involve seeking financial assistance, sourcing suppliers or looking into equipment rental options. By taking the time to identify and acquire the resources that you need, you can help to ensure that your action plans have a much greater chance of success.

### STAGE 6. QUANTIFY ALL OF THE POTENTIAL RISKS AND CHALLENGES

When preparing a plan for a coachee, it is important to think about possible challenges and risks that may obstruct their progress. Recognizing potential obstacles helps to provide a basis for further coaching if these challenges do occur. Some common challenges and risks coachees face include poor time management, unrealistic goals, negative self-talk, and lack of motivation. However, by acknowledging these risks and challenges, it is possible to provide guidance that can help the coachee overcome them. Through open communication and a willingness to address potential risks and challenges head-on, it is possible to help your coachees create a carefully considered action plan that is more than ready to execute.

### STAGE 7. WHAT MEASURES WILL BE USED TO EVALUATE PROGRESS?

When setting goals, it is important to have a clear and measurable way to track progress. This will help to ensure that you are on track to achieve your goals and make necessary adjustments along the way.

Was an action step completed? When you set your coachee a challenge, how did they do? There are a few different measures you can use to evaluate progress throughout the goal-setting and action-planning processes. First, you must know the initial starting point. This will become a baseline against which you measure all progress. Next, you will need to identify the milestones or benchmarks to be reached along the way. These can be either short-term or long-term goals. Finally, the time frame creates a basis for ongoing coaching accountability.

Your coachees will expect more from you than a to-do list. They'll need evaluative feedback, including information on what they can improve, what you think would improve their efficiency next time, their strengths, and where they excel. Give your coachee constructive and objective feedback to encourage them. Were any new action steps identified in the process? Sometimes, even the best-laid plans may not yield the best results. There may be unexpected hurdles that crop up or oversights you and your coachee make that mean their plan isn't fit for them. The failure of one action plan doesn't mean a goal can't be achieved; it merely means a new action plan must be formulated. Revisions to action plans should never be viewed as failures but as a necessary part of the ongoing goal-setting process. By giving your coachee evaluative feedback, you help them to understand their areas of weakness and give them targeted information on how they can improve. Ultimately, this will help your coachee to be more efficient and successful in achieving all of their future goals.

In your role as a coach, you can motivate your coachees to set goals and look for balance in all aspects of their lives. Using this action planning process, you can ensure that each task in your (or your coachees') plan is completed on time, efficiently, and without undue delay. The result is that you'll be able to monitor progress made toward a goal, which reflects the discipline of your coachee and also the quality of your coaching. Following the successful creation of an action plan, update it at each session with further steps until your coachee achieves their goal. Over time, your coachee will become less dependent upon you and able to create action plans independently with a heightened level of autonomy.

## HOW TO CREATE AN EFFECTIVE ACTION PLAN

| Action Step<br>What needs to be done? | Responsible Person<br>Who should take action to complete this step? | Deadline<br>When should this step be completed? | Necessary Resources<br>What do you need to complete this step? | Potential Challenges<br>Are there any potential challenges that may impede completion? How will you overcome them? | Result<br>Was this step successfully completed? Were any new steps identified in the process? |
|---|---|---|---|---|---|
| | | | | | |
| | | | | | |
| | | | | | |
| | | | | | |
| | | | | | |

Action planning is the process of turning your strategy and goals into action. Use this simple action planning template as a model for quantifying your own goals, taking your ideas and mapping out the steps that will bring them to fruition.

**PRINCIPLES INTO PRACTICE EXERCISE:**

1. Do a google search and source an action plan template that resonates with you.
2. Choose a goal you have identified in this section and write out an action plan.
3. Once you have created an action plan for one of your own goals, ask someone you know if they would allow you to guide them through the same process.

# THE EISENHOWER DECISION-MAKING MATRIX

*"Who can define for us with accuracy the difference between the long and short term! Especially whenever our affairs seem to be in crisis, we are almost compelled to give our first attention to the urgent present rather than to the important future."*

—DWIGHT D. EISENHOWER

"Slow is smooth. Smooth is fast" is an old US Navy SEAL's saying. Navy SEALs move with great urgency, but they do not rush. Rushing creates an inconsistent pace, creating an environment prone to making mistakes and causing unnecessary problems. Tackling goals is much easier when one has clarity of thought and control over their immediate action, as such a mindset ensures fewer mistakes are made and the process, ultimately, runs more smoothly.

During his two terms as president of the United States, Dwight D. Eisenhower led the development of an Interstate Highway System, he pioneered NASA, integrated the first major piece of civil rights legislation into law since the Civil War, brought an end to the Korean War, welcomed Alaska and Hawaii into the union, and managed to keep the Cold War with Russia "cold" throughout his presidential term. And he did it all with elegance. Why were Eisenhower's accomplishments so impressive, and how is his impact still felt today? He understood the fundamental difference between urgency and importance. In a

1954 speech, Eisenhower cited an unnamed university president who claimed, "I have two kinds of problems, the urgent and the important. The urgent are not important, and the important are never urgent."

As a Life Coach, one of the most important skills you can develop is the ability to help people make sound decisions (which we've already discussed in depth in an earlier chapter). To help simplify the decision-making process, Dwight Eisenhower (who has been referred to as one of history's most "efficient" US Presidents) developed a matrix that categorizes the choices that can be made in a given situation based on their urgency and importance. Over three decades later, the Eisenhower Matrix became popularized in Stephen Covey's best-selling book, *The 7 Habits of Highly Effective People*. It is a simple decision-making tool that helps to distinguish between tasks that are important, not important, urgent, and not urgent, eliminating time-wasters and creating more mental space to achieve important goals. The matrix can be used within a Life Coaching relationship to define the criteria affecting the decision-making process with regard to all "to-do" items within an action plan. With the Eisenhower matrix as your guide, you and your coachees can become more efficient by prioritizing which action steps you must focus on delivering upon first and which ones you can delegate as "unimportant" or possibly even delete.

Within the context of a coaching relationship, the distinction between urgent/non-urgent and important/not important can sometimes be challenging to discern. Here's how Stephen Covey defined the two "chalk and cheese" terms in *The 7 Habits of Highly Effective People*:

> **Urgent** matters are those that require immediate action. These are the visible issues that pop up and demand your attention NOW. Often, urgent matters come with clear consequences for not completing these tasks. Urgent tasks are unavoidable, but spending too much time putting out fires can produce a great deal of stress and could result in burnout.

> **Important** matters, on the other hand, are those that contribute to long-term goals and life values. These items require planning and thoughtful action. When you focus on important matters you manage your time, energy, and attention rather than mindlessly expending these resources.

What is important is subjective and depends on your own values and personal goals. No one else can define what is important for you.

**THE DECISION-MAKING MATRIX IS DIVIDED INTO FOUR QUADRANTS:**

*IMPORTANT*

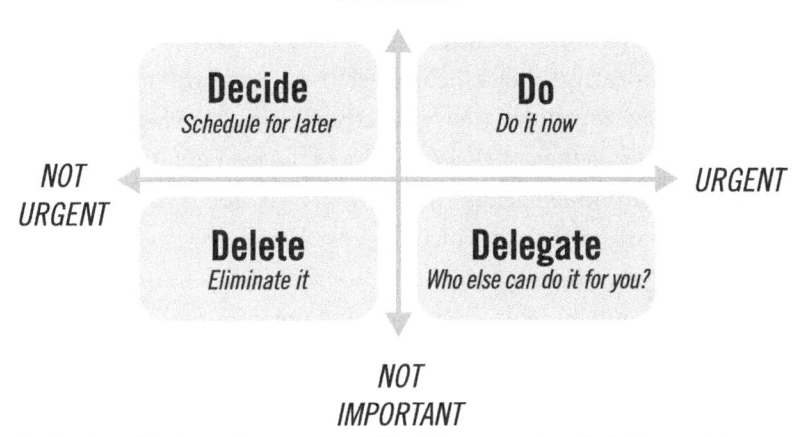

|  | **Decide**<br>Schedule for later | **Do**<br>Do it now |  |
|---|---|---|---|
| *NOT URGENT* |  |  | *URGENT* |
|  | **Delete**<br>Eliminate it | **Delegate**<br>Who else can do it for you? |  |

*NOT IMPORTANT*

The Eisenhower Matrix is a task management tool that helps you organize and prioritize your tasks by urgency and importance. Embodying this model as a habit will enable you to make wise decisions regarding how you use your time.

QUADRANT 1: URGENT AND IMPORTANT TASKS *(DO THEM ASAP)*

Urgent and Important tasks demand that you take action now. Choices that fall into this quadrant are referred to as "crises" that must be addressed right away. These are the tasks, action steps, or situations that require your full attention and cannot be put off. The majority of these task items have deadlines and will incur negative effects for failing to take action. Most often, these are either targets that were sprung on you from an external source or things that you put off until faced with a looming deadline. Either way, they require an immediate response. It's wise to note that spending too much time on urgent and important tasks can lead to an increased stress level, burnout, and the sense that time is spiraling out of control. Spending all day every day on urgent and important tasks will quickly rob you or your coachee of the energy and passion required to fulfill any meaningful goal with true justice.

## QUADRANT 2: NOT URGENT BUT IMPORTANT TASKS *(NEED A DEADLINE)*

Not urgent but important tasks are what Eisenhower referred to as projects, action steps, or situations that must be fulfilled but that aren't pressing as one of today's dire emergencies—they can wait until tomorrow if absolutely necessary. This category of action task will allow you to progress toward a long-term goal or priority. These tasks may not have a deadline or due date, so it is easy to put them off in favor of more urgent tasks. However, these items will likely have a greater impact on your long-term effectiveness in achieving long-term objectives. This is the sweet spot of time management and creates a basis for optimum efficiency. This is where you focus solely on new creative opportunities and growth. Focusing only on important tasks means that you can prioritize activities that reflect your skills and energy and contribute to accomplishing meaningful goals—while leaving you largely freed of pressing distractions.

## QUADRANT 3: URGENT BUT NOT IMPORTANT TASKS *(DELEGATE THEM)*

Think about times when you have been drawn into an urgent situation. Was this pressure self-inflicted, or was it imposed upon you by someone else who insisted that you help them meet their important goals but not your own? Urgent but not important tasks can be best described as interruptions, nuisances, or busy work. These are unexpected distractions that can disrupt your work and are rarely worth your time and energy. Urgent tasks are typically based on other people's expectations of you and will rarely get you closer to your meaningful long-term goals. Being driven to complete urgent but not important tasks means you will spend your days doing things that are typically related to someone else's priorities. It's generally wise to delegate as many urgent but not important tasks as possible. Can you hire a PA to manage your emails? Can you get your groceries home delivered rather than going to the store? What items on your to-do list could you find a really innovative way to automate?

## QUADRANT 4: NOT URGENT AND NOT IMPORTANT TASKS *(TIME WASTERS)*

Not urgent and not important tasks are time-wasting activities that should be ruthlessly cut out at all costs. These activities don't contribute to any meaningful progress on goals and can end up unnecessarily consuming up large chunks of time. According to Gerard Egan, author of The Skilled Helper book, people should never waste their time getting caught up doing things that are neither important nor urgent. Distraction is the enemy of progression. Tasks that are neither important or urgent are just "nice ideas" and result in some people wasting their entire lives. If you know someone who is visibly ineffective and unproductive in life, take some time to look at how they spend their days. Time is the most valuable commodity that we have access to as human beings, and people who waste the best years of their life partaking in non-urgent, non-important, and irrelevant tasks tend to also be those who spend the latter years of life speaking to therapists about their general state or sadness, boredom, and unfulfillment. You now know how not to be one of those people, and also steer your coachees in a similar direction.

The Eisenhower Matrix is particularly effective when a coachee is overwhelmed or unable to prioritize their tasks and responsibilities. This matrix allows you to help your coachees remain focused on what's important to them and avoid falling into the "urgency trap" when goal setting and determining their priorities for making wise action-orientated decisions. According to Stephen Covey, non-urgent but important tasks are the "Quadrant of Efficiency" where time spent engaging in these tasks will allow either you or your coachees to increase effectiveness and take practical steps toward delivering upon important long-term goals. This is where personal growth meets planning, distraction prevention, and action-taking.

**PRINCIPLES INTO PRACTICE EXERCISE:**

When you're faced with a set of action steps to complete, how do you decide which to tackle first? Do you select the task that's going to bring you closer to your long-term goals? Or do you give your attention to the most urgent item on your list that's screaming out to you the loudest?

Try using the Eisenhower decision-making matrix to avoid getting trapped in a state of general "busyness" and start achieving more of what's important to you today.

# THE "TWO LIST" TIME MANAGEMENT STRATEGY

*"The primary distinction between successful people and highly successful people is that highly successful people say no to just about everything."*
—WARREN BUFFETT

Some people assume that Warren Buffett's business success stemmed from his ability to make business acquisitions and purchase stocks at bargain prices. However, in reality, Buffett learned how to be an excellent time manager early in his entrepreneurial journey by learning to reduce his time on non-income producing activities and devote the best of his time only to profitable activities and his passions. This wisdom elevated him as one of the most successful investors in history. By learning to focus his time only on productive tasks, Buffett achieved a level of success that few could even dream of. One of the key lessons you can learn here is that once you have mastered yourself and a skill set, you can then master your time.

Time freedom involves choosing how to spend your time and who you spend it with. It's about appreciating the importance of your time and using it in ways that are important. Time freedom is about being intentional with your time and only allocating it to the things that are most important to you. Most people want to spend their time as they please (but instead work diligently at a job that doesn't reflect their expectations) before retiring at an age when their best years are behind them. Without time and freedom, people get stressed, overwhelmed, and overburdened and will often miss out on the important moments of life. Many people miss out on time freedom as they devote the best years of their lives to unimportant and time-wasting activities at the opportunity cost of productivity and efficiency.

In order to achieve time freedom, it is important to simplify your life and focus only on the important activities that generate the most fulfillment and financial rewards. To gain more time freedom, you must eliminate all unnecessary distractions that prevent you from being effective and achieving your most important priorities. There's no surefire method to gain time freedom, but the Principles into Practice exercise below can help you plan both the activities you must continue and those you should stop. Doing this will create more space in your life for designing a life that your future coachees might feel inspired to emulate.

Understanding how you spend the bulk of your time will enable you to identify areas where your coachees may be wasting theirs. In order to assess your own time use, keep a time log for a week or two and take note of how you spend your time each day, including work activities, commuting, exercise, or leisure pursuits. At the end of the week, review your time log and reflect on any patterns that emerge. Do you have difficulty sticking to a schedule? Do you tend to procrastinate on certain tasks? Answering these questions will give you valuable insights into your own time usage and can also help you to identify areas in which your coachees might improve their time management in view of becoming more efficient.

It may be helpful to use the following exercise when coaching an exceptionally busy person who complains about being unproductive or ineffective in their everyday action-taking. Alternatively, you might just find value in working through the exercise for yourself.

**PRINCIPLES INTO PRACTICE EXERCISE:**

1. Create a **Top Twenty** list of everything that you want to achieve in life.
2. Examine this list and decide what your **Top Five** priority items are.
3. Place the fifteen items you didn't choose on an **"Avoid at all Costs"** list.

**Note:** You will have observed that this activity is simple. By making two basic lists, a Top Twenty list of everything you want to accomplish in life and a secondary list of everything you must avoid at all costs, you've now established a set of standards for what you should commit the majority of your time to, and what must be forever removed from your attention and focus.

# A TOP TEN OF PROBLEM-SOLVING QUESTIONS

*"If I had only one hour to save the world, I would spend fifty-five minutes defining the problem, and only five minutes finding the solution."*

—ALBERT EINSTEIN

Armed with the information you've acquired thus far in the handbook, you can now help people to recognize their life deficits, set positive goals, and develop action plans geared toward attaining them. As a coach, one of your aims should be to guide your coachees from their current state of affairs to their desired state of affairs in the most optimal way possible. It can be tempting to want to solve your coachees' problems for them. However, this goal-setting process is designed to encourage them to use their own judgment, think strategically, and solve their own problems. This not only empowers them, it also helps them to develop skills they can use in the future. It is important to remember that, as a coach, you are there to guide and support your coachees—not to do the work or problem-solving for them.

Here, I'd like to share a series of creative problem-solving questions you can use within any coaching conversation to guide your coachees through the process of exploring and resolving abstract issues or challenges that they perceive themselves to have. Within themselves, these questions can even provide a conversational framework for an entire Life Coaching session. To begin with, you might simply ask your coachee to describe the issue or challenge they're facing in as much detail as possible. Once they've done so, you could then ask them to brainstorm all the possible causes of this issue or challenge. Once you have a good understanding of the situation, it's often useful to explore all the possible options for resolving the issue at hand. This can help your coachee gain clarity on what they might want to do next. By asking questions like the ones that follow, you can encourage your coachee to think creatively and openly about their challenges and ultimately help them to decide upon the most practical and appropriate solution that will best suit their immediate needs.

Coachee: "Help, I've got a huge problem that I don't know how to handle!"

You: (Option 1) "What is the simplest and most obvious solution to this issue?"

You: (Option 2) "If all limits were removed, how do you best resolve this issue?"

You: (Option 3) "If you knew you couldn't fail, what crazy ideas could you try?"

You: (Option 4) "What's the single most important factor to focus on here?"

You: (Option 5) "What are some radically unusual ways to tackle this challenge?"

You: (Option 6) "What new possibilities have you missed or not considered yet?"

You: (Option 7) "If you dug deeper, what could you learn about yourself here?"

You: (Option 8) "How would a five-year-old solve this challenge you are facing?"

You: (Option 9) "How would you resolve this challenge ten years from now?"

You: (Option 10) "What are some of the most ridiculous ideas you can think of?"

Challenges, we are often told, inspire us to think outside of the box and conjure up creative solutions that we might not have considered before. This is certainly true when it comes to asking problem-solving questions within a Life Coaching conversation. By taking time to reflect on an issue, we can often gain a new perspective and find the best way forward. In addition, questions that are curious in nature lend themselves to promoting creative thinking.

**PRINCIPLES INTO PRACTICE EXERCISE:**

Think about a problem that you are currently facing then ask yourself the ten questions and answer them objectively. Document your answers in a journal and reflect on what the best solution might be. If you are looking for a way to boost your Life Coaching problem-solving prowess, why not give these questions a try with someone that you know right away?

# PREPARING TO LEAVE A COACHING LEGACY

*"A good coach can change a game, a great coach can change a life."*
—COACH JOHN WOODEN

Prior to reading this handbook, you may have read many books on psychology and personal development written by some of the world's top experts in their field, you may have taken a dozen online training courses, and listened to hours of podcasts run by some of the world's leading figures in the personal development space, and to this, I ask: so what? So what? What does it mean to the world that you've read books and studied courses? What does it mean to your family, relationships, career, ambitions, and society that you know a little more about personal development and success?

As I stated earlier, knowledge isn't valuable until it gets applied. Knowledge is of no use to you or anyone around you if you consume it and sit on it; knowledge needs to be applied and shared in order to bring about change in the world. So, if I were to inquire about your personal Life Coaching "mission statement," how might you answer? Would you get anxious, start talking about the "personal transformations" that you're going to create in people's lives, or begin spewing "psycho-babble" like what many other new Life Coaches do? It can be easy to get wrapped up in the big ideas or the smaller details of Life Coaching and forget the main reasons why you started looking into coaching in the first place. Always think of a mission statement in terms of what you want to accomplish rather than what other people might want from you. Your mission statement should reflect your values, it should excite you, and also be something that you can easily articulate to others.

If you Google search "best coach in the world," you'll find hundreds of results of people claiming to be just that. You'll also find websites containing groups of "expert Life Coaches" who, according to their testimony, have coached presidents and world leaders and have built multi-million dollar coaching empires that afforded luxury mansions in the Hollywood hills, private jets, and Lamborghini cars, etc. If you were to then search "how to build a coaching business" you will discover that there are more people trying to sell overpriced Life Coaching business training courses than there are who offer the practical insights you must know in order to actually coach people. I know this from over fifteen years in the industry, and, like all industries, there are always some people who are more interested in making money or elevating their name than delivering a style of coaching that makes people's lives better.

The Life Coaching industry can be competitive, and those who call themselves coaches are typically judged by their "perceived" ability to produce "transformative coaching results." This can lead some less-scrupulous digital business people to pad out their resumes or make false promises in order to land high-paying clients or speaking gigs. I have seen with my own eyes, many coaching "superstars" take advantage of people's insecurities by claiming they can "cure" speech impediments, heal deep emotional trauma, give people visions of the future, and most ambiguously—"turn people's lives around." Please, please don't ever be fooled into believing that you have the physical, spiritual, or mystical ability to transform anyone's life. Because you don't. Your best chance of helping people involves remaining humble, just being yourself, and continuously striving to improve yourself personally and professionally. People don't need any more seven-figure coaching superstars or magicians; they just need wise, mature, decisive, and positive role models. And here lies your best chance to effect positive change.

Your legacy will be the contributions you make to other people's lives. The honey bee provides a great example of leaving a legacy. Honey bees have one simple task: collecting nectar and transporting it to the hive to make honey. As the bee gathers nectar, it indirectly serves its purpose by pollinating plants and flowers that you, I, and other animals rely on for food. While the honey bee goes about his work, the purpose he serves is significantly greater than the job he is tasked to do. Although most people enjoy eating honey, most human beings are indirectly impacted more by the honey bee's unintentional legacy, which is pollinating our plants and gardens. The legacy that you leave behind will be measured by the good works that you do and, sometimes, by the indirect impact that you make through the process.

I was once told by a wise man, "Don't do life to make money. Do life to make an impact." The greatest opportunity that you have as a new coach is to influence people's lives for the better. You can help people find their purpose, set goals, and even overcome challenges—but you certainly cannot "give" people these outcomes. The best that you can do is introduce people to new ideas, help people enlarge their perspective, and see things in a new light. In short, this is the only ability you have to influence positive changes within the lives of those you coach. The impact you make is more valuable than any success or professional recognition you may receive. It's your ability to positively influence people in their thinking and decision-making that will elevate you as a truly remarkable Life Coach, and increase your capacity to indirectly become a conduit for positive change in the world.

I believe that everyone has a contribution to make in the world and that it is our collective responsibility to share our wisdom and knowledge with the next generation. When we do so, we make the world a better place, and also inspire the emerging generations to do the same. This is possibly the most pertinent point of this handbook to share with you what my own personal mission is—not just through my coaching efforts, but through every conversation that I get to have with people who have the patience and ears to hear me.

> I will strive for excellence in everything that I do and do my best to become a living example of how to live for a purpose that's greater than

just myself. In doing so, I hope to inspire other people to grow in qualities such as responsibility, consistency in character, decisiveness, and inner strength. While I will do my best, I cannot determine the outcomes that I produce.

So that is my sole mission in life, and I invite you to join me in it.

In the final and upcoming chapter of this ultimate Life Coaching handbook, I want to share with you my first-ever experience with a Life Coach—even though this man didn't refer to himself as one. Peter Hope, a New Zealand-based builder, showed me a way to live life that transformatively impacted my thinking, relationships, finances, and character—more so than any other theoretical framework, accrediting authority, or attendance-based training course ever has done since. Peter Hope (Pete) was the conduit and turning point in my life, and I can only hope that part of what I have shared in this handbook will impact you. If even a portion of what I learned from Pete can influence your thinking, this handbook has achieved its goal.

**PRINCIPLES INTO PRACTICE EXERCISE:**

"I will strive for excellence in everything I do and do my best to become a living example of how to live for a purpose that's greater than just myself. In doing so I hope to inspire other people to grow in qualities such as responsibility, consistency in character, decisiveness and inner strength. While I will do my best, I cannot determine the outcomes that I produce."

Take some time to think about the mission statement I have just shared and invited you to join me in. See how it resonates with you, and then write a version that is congruent and reflects what your future intentions might be for your future Life Coaching endeavors.

# THE OPERATION PETE: COACHING INITIATIVE

*"When people are ready to, they change. They never do it before then, and sometimes they die before they get around to it. You can't make them change if they don't want to, just like when they do want to, you can't stop them."*

—ANDY WARHOL

The final chapter in a handbook of this nature is usually where people hope to find the answer which finally reveals the ten steps that the reader must take to achieve X or the twelve rules to be the best Life Coach in the world. Instead, I am going to use this last chapter to tell you a story. No guru, Life Coach, or handbook will give you the magical formula to Life Coaching success. There aren't twelve secret steps you can take, and there aren't certain rules or rituals to follow which will give you the amazing results you want. Life Coaching isn't that clear-cut.

Most people want to improve their lives, but not all people are ready to. Some people resist driving change in their lives by making excuses such as *"I don't know how to change"* or *"I tried to change but it didn't work"*. "Trying" is nothing more than wanting credit for something that you never intended to do (as highlighted by Master Yoda: "Do, or do not. There is no try"). In truth, many people only commit to making positive mindset and lifestyle improvements once they've hit "rock bottom" hard enough, and once their desire to change has become greater than their desire to remain exactly the same as they currently are.

We all reach a low point in life that we know we mustn't return to. This was true for me in 2006 upon realizing that my lifestyle habits (daily alcohol consumption, gambling, and drug usage) had cost me my career, relationships, and my reputation. I had reached an all-time low in which I was financially broke, friendless, jobless, homeless, and without a vision for the future. I had nothing left to my name other than my clothes and a rucksack. If you can relate to any part of this story, you might be accustomed to the feelings of helplessness, hopelessness, and despair that accompany knowing how severely one has "messed" one's life up. Prior to hitting this low, I had connected with a man called Pete. Pete was a respected builder and businessman in the town where I lived at the time. I had previously offered Pete business support in designing a basic business growth plan for him. Up to that point in my life, I'd never had a mature male role model who taught me basic life skills such as how to act with integrity or conduct myself respectfully in public. Please respect that my prior career had been in the military for almost a decade, where I worked very hard and played even harder. My relationships during that time were poor, and this fed my harmful lifestyle of drinking, gambling, and doing drugs. The issue was that I had no money left and had lost my job due to reasons that involved my lack of personal character..

I was a mentally and emotionally crushed man without a plan or any money. To say that I'd been humbled during this season of my life would be an understatement. Out of the blue one day, Pete invited me for coffee, and I knew he wanted to talk about my recent string of bad luck. He asked how I was "doing" before giving me a chance to answer honestly—which I did. The next half hour was filled with me pouring my heart out to Pete as I explained the mess I got myself into. He listened quietly without judgment. Once I'd finished talking, Pete looked at me and said, "Well, I can relate to your circumstances, so why don't I create room in our home for you to stay until I can help you get your life back on track?" I promptly accepted his offer.

Pete invited me into his home to live with him and his family for the nine months that followed. Pete became a role model for me in a short period of time. He was a devoted husband and father of three who worked hard to ensure that his family had a good standard of living. Soon a yearning stirred within me to change my circumstances. I went for a walk on my thirtieth birthday, furious with myself and how I had nothing to show for three decades of existence. That day, I made the decision to change everything about how I was living my life. Pete set me an example of a lifestyle that was worth working hard to earn. During the time I lived with Pete and his family, he became my friend, mentor, coach, and teacher. He showed me what it was like to be part of a functional family. Even though I had led a destructive lifestyle in the past, he never once judged me for it. On the few occasions when I slipped up and went back to my old ways, Pete never scolded me but instead helped me to pick myself up and get back on track.

For those nine months, I experienced Pete's patience, unconditional acceptance, empathy, and realness. In a nutshell, Pete taught me more about what it meant to live life in a responsible, genuine, integral, and consistent way than any theory I've received throughout all of my studies and practice in the Life Coaching industry. Pete's unconditional acceptance gave me the motivation to turn my life around. He was a role model through one of the most challenging years of my life, and I solely attribute his positive influence as being what's set me on the path I am on now. Without me having had a Pete, you would not now be reading this handbook.

Bill Gates once said, "Everyone needs a coach. It doesn't matter whether you're a business person, a tennis player, a movie star, or a bridge player." Whether or not you decide to pursue being a Life Coach, you will be a coach of some kind to someone in your life. Pete was my coach at a crucial time in my life, and I only hope that everything I have shared is enough for you to help another person through a difficult time in theirs. Even though a Life Coaching relationship must come with healthy boundaries, the intimacy that you go on to experience with your coachees need be no less valuable than what Pete's relationship was for me. The trajectory my life has taken was indirectly set in motion by one man, and as a result, Pete, like the honey bee, has had an indirect hand in the lives of hundreds of thousands of people.

In turn, it is now your opportunity to become a Life Coach who can positively influence others in a way that many more thousands of people can be positively influenced. Just become a role model and source of unconditional acceptance. You might even be the only form of healthy connection that some people have ever had. And this is what inspires me to summarize this handbook with Operation Pete: Life Coaching Initiative.

It is my great hope that the material shared in this handbook has been of use to you and that you have found value in the frameworks for accountability that have been shared. As we bring this handbook to a close, I would like to offer one last framework for coaching accountability, which is a seven-step journey that all people can go through who are intent on taking responsibility for creating positive changes within any area of their lives.

### STEP 1: MAKE A DECISION TO CHANGE

Tomorrow's results are determined by today's decisions. All people must choose when the "right" time to change is for themselves. It can be frustrating to watch people make reckless decisions that undermine themselves and hinder their progression. Most people resist change until their desire to change becomes greater than their longing to stay the same. Some people change after losing a job, getting divorced, or going bankrupt. Others never make that decision. Even if you really want to help people, they will only change once they are ready and devoted to doing so. This can be tough to accept, but everyone has their own timeline for change. Regardless of how expert a coach you become, you cannot help someone change until they're so fed up with their circumstances that making a life improvement is their only valid option. All people have the same choices to make: to accept life's conditions as they currently are, or take responsibility for changing them. Taking responsibility for producing the life outcomes you want to see more of is the source that your future fulfillment and self-respect will spring from.

> **In a Coaching Conversation.** Listen to your coachee during this conversation and pay close attention to what they want, don't want, what their priorities are, and understand what long-term objectives they want to achieve. There is no point in allowing your coachee to complain about their problems unless they are willing to set goals and take decisive, intentional action steps toward fulfilling them. Without setting compelling future goals, your coachee has no valid reason for working hard to create the positive lifestyle changes they want.

**STEP 2: TAKE DECISIVE, INTENTIONAL ACTION**

The secret of getting ahead in life is simply getting started. There is no shortage of people in the world with a desire to see change happen in their lives. The law of inertia states that an object will remain unchanged unless it's acted on by an outside force. This means that change will not happen in a person's life until they take action in a direction that will get them closer to achieving what they want. Marketers often promote quick-fix solutions directed toward the innate desire many people have to get something in exchange for nothing. There is no such thing as a quick "long-term" fix. Action-taking is the only way to make change happen because thinking doesn't create new circumstances, it only mulls over existing ones. Some people get so focused on what they're thinking that they forget to take any action at all. But intentional action-taking, even if just one small step, is the only option through which progress gets made. It took me years to realize that major achievements come from consistently taking lots of small steps in the right direction. It's impossible to take a second step until a first has been taken.

> **In a Coaching Conversation.** Focus on establishing the potential next steps your coachee could take to improve their circumstances or progress toward a longer-term goal. The sooner your coachee starts taking action the better, as this is what distinguishes Life Coaching from talking therapy—i.e., taking practical action steps rather than just talking about problems. Before the end of each coaching session, agree on what action steps your coachee will take before the next coaching session. This gives you a basis for coaching accountability.

### STEP 3: COMMIT TO A FUTURE DIRECTION

There is no such thing as a stagnant existence. All people are moving forwards, backward, or just moving sideways at any given moment. The decisions we make shape the direction of our progress. If you went on a long walk into the forest and got lost, does this mean you no longer want to return home? Of course not. Having a sense of where you ideally want to end up in life will provide you with the motivation you need to reorient yourself if you do find yourself lost or whenever necessary. If you want to get married, you cannot stay single forever. If you want to own your own business, you'll have to give up the security of employment. If you want to build a reputation as a great and credible Life Coach, you must first get your own life in order. Some people waste years of their life on busy schedules and overbearing to-do lists without ever stopping to consider if they're making progress in a direction that's right for them. While it's good to have plans and items on a to-do list, it's generally better to weigh these things up in light of a direction that you want to take your life in. This way, you can ensure that all of your short-term action steps are headed in the direction of your longer-term priorities.

> **In a Coaching Conversation.** Focus on establishing the highest purpose that each of your coachee's goals serves. If they want to build a business, why? What will this give them? If they want to build a marriage or start a family, again, why? What will this give them? What is the greatest vision your coachee has for the future? Once this vision is clear, all goal-setting, action-taking and decision-making becomes significantly easier to facilitate. If a goal doesn't allow for progress to be made toward a vision, it shouldn't have any time wasted on it.

### STEP 4: TAKE STOCK, ADAPT AND ADJUST

It is impossible to value the effectiveness of a life apart from in relation to a goal. You cannot know if a ten-year-old boy will become a famous footballer, or whether a thirty-five-year-old woman will ever commit to a man and settle down in marriage. As with all future outcomes, only time will tell what they may be. Making mistakes is an inevitable part of life. We sometimes take two steps in the wrong direction, make an unwise decision or misplace our priorities and put work before people, or profits before delivering value. Mistakes are rarely permanent; most of them can be fixed with less drama than most people imagine. And there's certainly nothing shameful about making mistakes—but only so long as they are reflected upon and learned from. There is something sad and limiting about the angst that many people have about making them.

Fear of making mistakes can stop people from taking risks, learning valuable life lessons, entering new relationships, or pursuing opportunities that might enrich their lives. Taking stock involves identifying which of our attitudes and actions may be hindering progress. Adapting and adjusting involves accepting mistakes as an opportunity for growth and changing in light of them to ensure that they never get in the way of further progression being made in the future.

> **In a Coaching Conversation.** Focus on establishing what barriers or obstacles might be getting in the way of your coachee "feeling" like they are getting closer to their long-term goals or vision. By asking your coachee to describe the main sources of their frustration, you will discover the obstacles (tangible or mental) that they will likely be unaware of. Once you know what these blocks are, you can set new goals to surpass them as efficiently as possible.

## STAGE 5: DITCH UNHELPFUL HABITS AND ATTITUDES

Making a positive change in any area of life usually involves giving up an unhelpful habit or attitude. Imagine that you want to break an unhelpful habit like stress eating or spending too much time scrolling on social media. What if, instead of just succumbing to the habit of eating potato chips or Facebook scrolling, you substituted curiosity about the craving itself as a new behavior? What might you learn about yourself? Why would any rationally minded person waste their time doing anything that might potentially cost them their long-term priorities?

Without a clear sense of what they want to achieve, many people find it difficult to change their habits and attitudes, making it hard for them to let go of old ways of thinking or behaving. The self-improvement industry is known for superhero gurus who falsely claim to have life-changing solutions. The only effective approach to alter harmful habits or attitudes, in my experience, is to accept full personal responsibility and apply effortful discipline toward learning new strategies and modifying them. There are no magical pills, deep breathing exercises, special diets, or gurus with techniques that can cure life's problems. Unhelpful habits and attitudes will forever remain until they have owners who are mature and disciplined enough to adapt, adjust and overcome them. This is how character is developed and where inner strength comes from.

> **In a Coaching Conversation.** As your conversations with a coachee evolve, rapport will be developed and trust will inevitably grow. The more trust that a coachee has in you, the more readily they will accept your provocations and challenges. It is not uncommon for a coachee to want to discuss their problems within a Life Coaching session, which naturally creates a great opportunity for you to ask them exactly how they plan to overcome and surpass them.

**STEP 6: CULTIVATE A CONTRIBUTORS MINDSET**

If you ever speak with someone who is upset, anxious, or sad, try to see if you can find a self-centered attitude at the root of their problem. Social contribution is the cure for most types of mental health issues. When individuals focus less on themselves and more on the endless number of ways they might improve society, woe and sadness are replaced with passion and enthusiasm. Some mental health experts would disagree with this statement, but only because their income depends on people believing that their emotions are unmanageable illnesses. As stated multiple times in this handbook, individuals who discover a life purpose that extends beyond themselves typically find the most fulfillment and leave behind the greatest legacies. As you develop a contributors mindset, rather than asking how you might achieve more goals for your own appeasement, you may become more focused on looking out for innovative and entrepreneurial ways that you might use your knowledge, understanding, and talents to serve a larger body of people within your hometown, city, organization, community, or nation. Those who achieve their goals can find short-lived satisfaction, but those who find ways to make a positive impact in the world are those who get acquainted with long-term fulfillment.

**In the Coaching Conversation.** You cannot coach another person beyond a stage of maturity or mental development that you haven't already reached for yourself. If you have control over your mind and emotions, it will come naturally to coach others through achieving the same level of self-control. If you have been successful in building an international enterprise, your past experiences will educate you in coaching others through the process of doing the same. If you already have a contributor mindset, your questioning will naturally provoke your coachees to compare the goals they bring to you to a higher or more socially serving purpose.

## STEP 7: BECOME A PETE FOR SOMEONE TODAY

As I mentioned at the beginning of this closing chapter, Pete was my first ever Life Coach, while also simultaneously serving me as a father figure role model. I must impress that in 2023, Life Coaching is an unregulated industry, it always has been, and I hope it remains this way. I say this because it's not accredited Life Coaches who will make the greatest impact in this world—life isn't something that can be taught in a classroom (neither is wisdom). Instead, it's the passionate individuals who have a fire burning inside of themselves to help others live better lives that will enter the history books. So if you're reading this and can identify with this fire burning inside, the world needs more people like you, right now. Life's greatest lessons come from our mistakes and experiences—not from textbooks. Sometimes these lessons are learned the hard way, but they are nonetheless essential for personal growth. In order to learn from our experiences, we must be ready to reflect on them and identify the lessons they have to offer. This can be a difficult process, but it's worth the effort. Peter Hope wasn't an accredited Life Coach, and his companionship through the lowest point of my life was more valuable than any information that I've taken from any textbook or training resource since. Pete helped me to see a more responsible way of living life and provoked me to become a better man in the process. And this is the last idea I want to share with you. Go forth and become a Pete for someone.

You only have the life experiences that you have. You only have the wisdom you have. You only have the people skills you have. Some people spend the best years of their life overcome by the notion that they are in some way "not good enough," "not knowledgeable enough," or "not skilled enough," and thinking these thoughts is a habitual pattern of thinking that must be broken. You get to do this by becoming a Pete. You get to do this by including someone in your life. You get to do this by being honest with someone. You get to do this by being honest with yourself. You get to do this by becoming less self-oriented and more socially focused. As Mahatma Gandhi once said, "Become the change that you wish to see in the world." Some other wise man said, "You eat an elephant by taking one bite at a time." In the same way, if you have any inclination toward leaving the world in a better state than what it was when you first entered into it, you can get started on laying your future legacy today. You can show someone unconditional acceptance to help them out of their circumstance; you can be the influence that sets them on the right path. Maybe you feel you aren't qualified because you haven't figured everything out yet, but you have figured something out. Help those who haven't figured that thing out. At least one person in the world can benefit from the current wisdom you have—so go, don't think about it, and just become a Pete for that person today.

**PRINCIPLES INTO PRACTICE EXERCISE:**

If you feel that you might benefit from receiving coaching in one or more areas of your life, become a member of the Academy of Modern Applied Psychology and benefit from the input of one or more of our Achologists in training who want someone to practice on pro-bono.

Alternatively, identify someone you know who might benefit from a listening ear, a wise perspective, and some positive input in their life—and become a Pete for that person today.

# SUMMARY AND CONCLUSION

*"I am not as good as I ought to be. I am not as good as I want to be. I am not as good as I'm going to be. But I am thankful that I am better than I used to be."*

—COACH JOHN WOODEN

John Wooden was an American basketball coach at UCLA. He led the UCLA Bruins to eighty-eight consecutive wins and seven national championships. No other coach in basketball history has been as successful as Wooden; his impressive coaching ability has inspired many in and out of sports. When speaking of what makes a good coach, Wooden said, "The best coaches really care about people. They have a sincere interest in people. Coaching is a profession of passion. You can't coach people unless you genuinely care about them." Life Coaching is no different. The best Life Coaches care about human beings and are motivated to make a positive difference in other people's lives before everything else. Being a Life Coach is not about giving people inspirational wisdom or platitudes. It's not about writing a prescription for every situation.

While many of the principles I have shared are universal, the Life Coaching process will be unique to every person. There is no prescriptive "one size fits all" approach you can take. As we draw this Life Coaching handbook to a close, I hope that you have enjoyed the learning journey, gained some valuable insights along the way, and will continue to revisit these ideas, principles, and processes into the future. It has been my great honor and privilege to be your guide on this journey and I sincerely thank you for entrusting me with your time and attention.

Please feel welcome to visit the Academy of Modern Applied Psychology (www.Achology.com). The website hosts an international community of learners, who just like you, want to master their Life Coaching skills in view of making their mark on the world. You can receive coaching, practice on others (in a peer-learning environment and confidential space), and benefit from an extensive knowledge base of articles and tutorial videos. Learning these principles will increase your skill set and enable you to provide a far richer Life Coaching experience for your coachees. We have covered much ground, exploring what Life Coaching is, how it can benefit your life, and the general assumptions that effective Life Coaches embody. We have also looked at some of the key principles and practices, including active listening, people skills, goal setting, and action planning. I trust that you now have a fair understanding of what it takes to be an effective Life Coach and are well on your way to making positive improvements in your own life and also in the lives of others. We began this handbook by talking about the concept of vision. I hope you have caught a greater glimpse of what your own future life vision might now entail.

Now is the time to put these principles into practice and turn that vision into a reality. My Life Coaching experiences so far give testament to the power of the principles I have shared. As you apply them to your life and do the necessary work on yourself, may you become able to make impactful changes in your own life and also in the lives of countless others. The road ahead is open to you. The only question remains: will you take that next step to realize the future that you are more than capable of achieving?

I hope your answer is yes. People are waiting for you.

—KAIN RAMSAY

Made in United States
Orlando, FL
10 March 2025